RESILIENT BUSINESSES FOR SUSTAINABILITY

ADVANCED SERIES IN MANAGEMENT

Series Editors: Miguel R. Olivas-Luján and Tanya Bondarouk

Previous Volumes

Social Media in Human Resources Management
Eds. Tanya Bondarouk and Miguel R. Olivas-Luján

Social Media in Strategic Management
Eds. Miguel R. Olivas-Luján and Tanya Bondarouk

(Dis)honesty in Management: Manifestations and Consequences
Eds. Tiia Vissak and Maaja Vadi

Commercial Diplomacy and International Business: A Conceptual and Empirical Exploration
Ed. H. Ruël

Electronic HRM in Theory and Practice
Eds. T. Bondarouk, H. Ruël and J. C. Looise

Relational Practices, Participative Organizing
Eds. Chris Steyaert and Bart Van Looy

Autopoiesis in Organization Theory and Practice
Eds. Rodrigo Magalhaes and Ron Sanchez

Organizations as Learning Systems "Living Composition" as an Enabling Infrastructure
Ed. Marjatta Maula

Complex Systems and Evolutionary Perspectives on Organizations: The Application of Complexity Theory to Organizations
Ed. Eve Mitleton-Kelly

Managing Imaginary Organizations: A New Perspective on Business
Eds. Bo Hedberg, Philippe Baumard and A. Yakhlef

Systems Perspectives on Resources, Capabilities and Management Processes
Eds. John Morecroft, Ron Sanchez and Aimé Heene

Tracks and Frames: The Economy of Symbolic Forms in Organizations
Ed. K. Skoldberg

Human Resource Management, Social Innovation and Technology
Eds. Tanya Bondarouk and Miguel R. Olivas-Luján

Dead Firms: Causes and Effects of Cross-Border Corporate Insolvency
Eds. Miguel M. Torres, Virginia Cathro and Maria Alejandra Gonzalez Perez

New Ways of Working Practices: Antecedents and Outcomes
Ed. Jan de Leede

Age Diversity in the Workplace
Eds. Silvia Profili, Alessia Sammarra and Laura Innocenti

International Business Diplomacy: How Can Multinational Corporations Deal With Global Challenges?
Ed. Huub Ruel

Organisational Roadmap Towards Teal Organisations
Eds. Tanya Bondarouk, Anna Bos-Nehles, Maarten Renkema, Jeroen Meijerink and Jan de Leede

Indigenous Management Practices in Africa: A Guide for Educators and Practitioners
Eds. Uchenna Uzo and Abel Kinoti Meru

Diversity Within Diversity Management: Country-Based Perspectives
Eds. Andri Georgiadou, Maria Alejandra Gonzalez-Perez and Miguel R Olivas-Lujan

Diversity Within Diversity Management: Types of Diversity in Organizations
Eds. Andri Georgiadou, Maria Alejandra Gonzalez-Perez and Miguel R. Olivas-Luján

HRM 4.0 for Human-Centered Organizations
Eds. Rita Bissola and Barbara Imperatori

Sustainable Hospitality Management: Designing Meaningful Encounters With Talent and Technology
Eds. Huub Ruël, Angelique Lombarts and Jeoren A. Oskam

Agri-Food 4.0: Innovations, Challenges and Strategies
Eds. Rahul S. Mor, Dinesh Kumar and Anupama Singh

Smart Industry – Better Management
Eds. Tanya Bondarouk and Miguel R. Olivas-Luján

Management and Information Technology in the Digital Era: Challenges and Perspectives
Eds. Chemma Nawal, Mohammed El Amine Abdelli, Anjali Awasthi and Emmanuel Mogaji

Sustainable Management in COVID-19 Times
Eds. Aldo Alvarez-Risco, Marc A. Rosen and Shyla Del-Agulia-Arcentales

Technology, Management and Business: Evolving Perspectives
Eds. Rajnish Kumar Misra, Archana Shrivastava and Charu Sijoria

Smart Cities for Sustainability: Approaches and Solutions
Eds. Mohammed El Amine Abdelli, Asma Sghaier, Atilla Akbaba, Samia Chehbi Gamoura and Hamid Doost Mohammadian

Development of International Entrepreneurship Based on Corporate Accounting and Reporting According to IFRS: Part A
Eds. Mansur P. Eshov, Gulnora K. Abdurakhmanova, Aktam U. Burkhanov, Nodira B. Abdusalomova and Shakhlo T. Ergasheva

Development of International Entrepreneurship Based on Corporate Accounting and Reporting According to IFRS: Part B
Eds. Mansur P. Eshov, Gulnora K. Abdurakhmanova, Aktam U. Burkhanov, Nodira B. Abdusalomova and Shakhlo T. Ergasheva

Resilient Businesses for Sustainability: Artificial Intelligence, Technology, Supply Chain Management and Society, Part A
Eds. Rajnish Kumar Misra, Shriram A. Purankar, Divya Goel, Shivani Kapoor and Ridhima B. Sharma

ADVANCED SERIES IN MANAGEMENT VOLUME 34B

RESILIENT BUSINESSES FOR SUSTAINABILITY: ADVANCES IN HUMAN RESOURCE MANAGEMENT AND MARKETING, PART B

EDITED BY

RAJNISH KUMAR MISRA
Jaypee Institute of Information Technology, India

SHRIRAM A. PURANKAR
Jaypee Institute of Information Technology, India

DIVYA GOEL
Jaypee Institute of Information Technology, India

SHIVANI KAPOOR
Jaypee Institute of Information Technology, India

AND

RIDHIMA B. SHARMA
Jaypee Institute of Information Technology, India

emerald PUBLISHING

United Kingdom – North America – Japan – India – Malaysia – China

Emerald Publishing Limited
Emerald Publishing, Floor 5, Northspring, 21-23 Wellington Street, Leeds LS1 4DL

First edition 2024

British Library Cataloguing in Publication Data
A catalogue record for this book is available from the British Library

ISBN: 978-1-83608-129-6 (Print)
ISBN: 978-1-83608-128-9 (Online)
ISBN: 978-1-83608-130-2 (Epub)

ISSN: 1877-6361 (Series)

Printed and bound by CPI Group (UK) Ltd, Croydon, CR0 4YY

CONTENTS

SECTION 2: MARKETING FOR BUILDING RESILIENT BUSINESSES

RESILIENT BUSINESSES FOR SUSTAINABILITY: ADVANCES IN HUMAN RESOURCE MANAGEMENT AND MARKETING: AN OVERVIEW

Rajnish Kumar Misra, Shriram A. Purankar, Divya Goel, Shivani Kapoor and Ridhima B. Sharma

Jaypee Institute of Information Technology, India

In the rapidly changing global business landscape, the ability of organizations to adapt and thrive amid challenges has become crucial for long-term success. Resilient businesses not only weather uncertainties effectively but also contribute to sustainability by ensuring continuity, growth and positive social impact. Two key functions that play pivotal roles in building resilience are Human Resource Management (HRM) and Marketing. This essay explores how these functions are interconnected and contribute to the resilience and sustainability of businesses.

HRM is a strategic function that goes beyond traditional personnel management. In the context of building resilient businesses, HRM plays a crucial role in developing a workforce that can navigate uncertainties, adapt to change and contribute to organizational sustainability.

1. TALENT ACQUISITION AND DEVELOPMENT

Effective HRM begins with acquiring and developing the right talent. Resilient businesses prioritize hiring individuals with not only the required skills but also the ability to adapt and innovate. HRM practices such as continuous training, mentorship programs and leadership development contribute to creating a workforce capable of overcoming challenges (Dessler, 2019).

Resilient Businesses for Sustainability
Advanced Series in Management, Volume 34B, 1–6

Published under exclusive licence by Emerald Publishing Limited
ISSN: 1877-6361/doi:10.1108/S1877-636120240000034B001

2. EMPLOYEE WELL-BEING AND ENGAGEMENT

A resilient workforce is one that is motivated, engaged and feels supported. HRM practices focusing on employee well-being, work–life balance and open communication channels foster a positive organizational culture. Engaged employees are more likely to proactively contribute to overcoming challenges and supporting the company's sustainability efforts (Harter et al., 2020).

3. CHANGE MANAGEMENT

In a dynamic business environment, change is inevitable. HRM is responsible for leading effective change management initiatives. Whether it's technological advancements, market shifts or organizational restructuring, HR professionals play a vital role in helping employees adapt to change. A well-managed change process enhances organizational resilience (Cameron & Green, 2015).

4. MARKETING FOR RESILIENCE

Marketing is not just about selling products or services; it's about creating value for customers and building strong, lasting relationships. In the context of resilience and sustainability, marketing is instrumental in developing a brand that can withstand challenges and contribute positively to society.

5. CUSTOMER-CENTRICITY

Resilient businesses are customer-centric, understanding and meeting the evolving needs of their target audience. Marketing strategies that prioritize customer satisfaction, feedback loops and personalized experiences contribute to building a loyal customer base that supports the business during tough times (Kotler et al., 2021).

6. INNOVATION AND ADAPTATION

Marketing is at the forefront of innovation and adaptation. Resilient businesses continuously evolve their products, services and marketing strategies to stay relevant in the market. Marketing research and analysis contribute valuable insights, enabling businesses to anticipate changes in consumer behaviour and market trends (Lambin, 2018).

7. BRAND MANAGEMENT AND REPUTATION

The reputation of a business is a valuable asset, especially during challenging times. Marketing professionals are responsible for managing and enhancing the brand image. A strong and positive brand reputation not only attracts customers but also instills confidence in stakeholders, contributing to the overall resilience of the business (Keller, 2013).

8. INTERCONNECTED ROLES: HRM AND MARKETING COLLABORATION

While HRM and Marketing are distinct functions, their collaboration is essential for building resilient businesses. The alignment of HR and Marketing strategies ensures that internal and external aspects of the organization work cohesively to achieve sustainability.

9. EMPLOYER BRANDING

The intersection of HRM and Marketing is evident in employer branding. A resilient business needs to attract and retain top talent. Marketing strategies are employed to create an appealing employer brand, showcasing the organization as a great place to work. HRM then ensures that the internal organizational culture aligns with the external brand image, creating a cohesive and attractive workplace (Backhaus et al., 2017).

10. INTERNAL COMMUNICATION

Effective communication is key to resilience. HRM and Marketing collaborate to ensure that internal communication is clear, transparent and align with the organization's values and goals. This collaboration enhances employee engagement and ensures that employees understand their roles in achieving marketing and organizational objectives (Argenti, 2018).

11. CRISIS MANAGEMENT

During times of crisis, the collaboration between HRM and Marketing is crucial. HR professionals are responsible for managing internal crises, such as workforce challenges, while Marketing professionals address external crises affecting the brand image. A coordinated effort ensures that the organization presents a united front to both internal and external stakeholders (Coombs, 2014).

In conclusion, the role of Human Resource Management and Marketing in building resilient businesses for sustainability is intertwined and essential for the long-term success of organizations. HRM ensures that the workforce is equipped with the skills, mindset and support needed to navigate uncertainties, while Marketing focuses on creating value for customers, adapting to change and managing the brand's reputation. The collaboration between HRM and Marketing creates a holistic approach to resilience, aligning internal and external strategies for organizational success. As businesses continue to face unprecedented challenges, the integration of HRM and Marketing practices becomes even more critical. The symbiotic relationship between these functions strengthens the organizational fabric, fostering adaptability, innovation and a positive impact on society. In the pursuit of sustainability, businesses must recognize the interconnectedness of HRM and Marketing, leveraging their combined strengths to build resilient and enduring enterprises.

The book is divided into two sections namely the following with suitable chapter included to elucidate the section:

(1) Section 1: *Role of Human Resource for sustainability*
(2) Section 2: *Marketing for Building Resilient Businesses*

12 Section 1: Role of Human Resource for Sustainability

Organizational sustainability and its integration with human resource function has been the focus of researchers for two decades now with the pioneering work done by Boudreau and Ramstad (2005). Existing literature suggests numerous challenges for human resource professionals for creation of a sustainable organization that caters to all the three pillars of sustainability, i.e. economic, social and environmental aspects.

In order to accomplish the goal of organizational sustainability, human resource policies should focus on a long-term and systematic approach that can lead to the achievement of economic, social and environmental sustainability (Yong et al., 2020). In the given context, this section of the book presents different perspectives highlighting the role of women labour workforce, industrial relation and humanizing practices in achieving the goal of sustainability.

Labour welfare as a part of industrial relations plays an important role in the context of industrial growth. In line with this, Chapter 2 delineates the industrial relations in Kerala newspaper industry. This chapter highlights that leaders were not at all satisfied with any of the facilities except for safety practices for the employees and the grievance handling process. The authors emphasize that the welfare measures such as housing schemes, medical facilities, educational facilities, recreational facilities and counselling facilities need to be implemented as statutory measures.

Business organizations experienced numerous challenges during COVID-19 for which the leaders prepared contingency plans for maintaining business operations. In line with this, Chapter 3 presents the insights on the personal and professional problems experienced by remote working employees of a Non-Financial Banking company along with the strategies used by human resource professionals of the company to handle the challenge by initiating responsive humanistic management practices.

In the same context, Chapter 4 presents a bibliometric review of employee happiness at the workplace. Authors emphasize that workplace happiness is an important dimension for retention of employees and to promote resilience at the workplace. This chapter also highlights that there is a rise in publication after 2018, and most of the studies were done in India, the United States and Malaysia. Authors also suggest that employee's happiness at the workplace can be boosted by using strategies like care and respect for employees; providing proper work–life balance; maintaining transparency, honesty and credibility; recognizing and rewarding employees; encouraging open communication; and most importantly creating a culture that is congenial and trustworthy.

Learning organizational culture plays an important role in achieving organizational resilience and sustainability. Chapter 5 focuses on this aspect and analyzes the significance of human capital in fostering company resilience through the process of learning. This chapter suggests that a learning organization has the capacity to promptly and effectively respond to unexpected events, crises and challenging conditions. The implementation of ongoing learning initiatives fosters employee engagement and enhances the overall resilience of the organization.

Labour force participation has an important role in achieving the organizational goals of sustainability. Women workforce participation has always been an area of concern. In this context, Chapter 6 highlights the role of female labour force participation in building resilient businesses. This chapter examines top performing firms and sectors that survived the pandemic, key characteristics of business resilience and characteristics of women's labour and their role in building business resilience. A framework is also presented to discuss how female labour force participation can contribute to different sectors in order to build resilient businesses.

The challenges of the volatile business world and competitive advantage can only be dealt with highly engaged employees. Chapter 7 highlights the linkage between employee perception of the Corporate Social Responsibility (CSR) dimensions and dimensions of employee engagement. The study suggests that the organizations should consider CSR as a strategic investment for the organization instead of a mode of corporate philanthropy since all the three dimensions of CSR, i.e. philanthropic activities, ethical and environmental aspects of the organization do lead to intellectual, social and affective engagement among employees.

13 Section 2: Marketing for Building Resilient Businesses

Marketing for sustainability may initially seem like a paradox, but it gains significance when businesses undergo transformation through innovation and technology (Lim, 2016; McDonagh & Prothero, 2014). These tools are enablers to understand and address sustainability needs effectively, ensuring that aspirations are not only acknowledged but also met, hence creating resilient business practices (Dermody et al., 2015).

Marketing approach initially targeted sectors facing evident environmental risks and concentrated solely on environmental concerns in the context of sustainability which has evolved over time; this section of the book thus explores different concepts from Green Marketing to Consumer's Sustainability Consciousness to address the complexity of the issues involved from marketer's perspective (Lim, 2017).

Chapter 8 delves into Higher Education Institutes and University's promotional strategies, specifically through social media, to foster enduring connections. This chapter explores the impact of social media promotions on students' choices of educational institutions. The findings highlight the importance of gaining new followers, showcasing prominent content and engaging with stakeholders to establish lasting connections within the educational environment. These insights provide a foundation for crafting resilient social media marketing strategies for higher education institutions.

Chapter 9 scrutinizes the role of sustainable purchase intention and post-purchase dissonance in connecting consumers' sustainability consciousness to consumer evangelism. Given the pervasive influence of social media, trusted recommendations from reliable sources become crucial in co-creating products. In this chapter, the author intricately investigates consumer behaviour, accentuating the equilibrium between economic growth and socio-environmental well-being. It contributes valuable insights for marketers seeking successful strategies in catering to sustainability-conscious consumers.

Chapter 10 addresses the escalating significance of mobile fitness applications. Recognizing user retention and engagement as pivotal to commercial success, the research comprehensively explores the impact of digital innovations, gamification, artificial intelligence (AI) and machine learning (ML) on user interactions. It underscores the interplay between gamification, AI/ML and technology adoption in influencing user engagement and intent to use.

Chapter 11 investigates the transformative influence of digital marketing practices on the performance of manufacturing enterprises in Delhi-NCR. By scrutinizing the perceived benefits and challenges of digital marketing, the study identifies a crucial correlation between the strategic utilization of digital marketing and enhanced business performance. The findings underscore the role of digital marketing in not only increasing awareness among consumers and industries but also in facilitating its implementation across diverse businesses.

Chapter 12 is all about the profound impact of the COVID-19 pandemic on consumer behaviour, prompting a significant shift towards e-commerce. It examines the transformative effects of the pandemic on customer buying behaviour and contributes insights essential for businesses looking to adapt and thrive in the changed economic landscape.

Chapter 13 employs a bibliometric analysis to assess the landscape of luxury marketing research in the emerging economy of India over a span of 21 years. With the surge of the upper-middle class in India, the study highlights a notable dearth of scholarly research in these domains. This chapter spotlights a substantial scope for future research within the realm of Indian-grown luxury brands, aligning with the theme of building resilience in the dynamic luxury marketing landscape.

While we recognize the wealth of literature on sustainable, green, environmental and ethical marketing, our effort here is to distill a complex and multifaceted topic. Further research on the perspectives and opinions of consumers regarding sustainability marketing, as well as its implementation by marketing professionals, demands continued attention within the overarching theme of building resilience in marketing practices.

REFERENCES

Argenti, P. A. (2018). *Corporate communication*. McGraw-Hill Education.

Backhaus, K., Tikoo, S., & Su, C. (2017). The effects of business-unit strategy and corporate culture on the integration of corporate-level cooperative strategies. *Journal of Product Innovation Management*, *34*(1), 22–42.

Boudreau, J. W., & Ramstad, P. M. (2005). Talentship, talent segmentation, and sustainability: A new HR decision science paradigm for a new strategy definition. *Human Resource Management: Published in Cooperation with the School of Business Administration, The University of Michigan and in Alliance with the Society of Human Resources Management*, *44*(2), 129–136.

Cameron, E., & Green, M. (2015). *Making sense of change management: A complete guide to the models, tools, and techniques of organizational change*. Kogan Page Publishers.

Coombs, W. T. (2014). *Ongoing crisis communication: Planning, managing, and responding*. Sage Publications.

Dermody, J., Hanmer-Lloyd, S., Koenig-Lewis, N., & Zhao, A. L. (2015). Advancing sustainable consumption in the UK and China: The mediating effect of pro-environmental self-identity. *Journal of Marketing Management*, *31*(13–14), 1472–1502.

Dessler, G. (2019). *Human resource management*. Pearson.

Harter, J. K., Schmidt, F. L., & Hayes, T. L. (2020). Business-unit-level relationship between employee satisfaction, employee engagement, and business outcomes: A meta-analysis. *Journal of Applied Psychology*, *105*(8), 966.

Keller, K. L. (2013). *Strategic brand management: Building, measuring, and managing brand equity*. Pearson.

Kotler, P., Keller, K. L., Brady, M., Goodman, M., & Hansen, T. (2021). *Marketing management*. Pearson.

Lambin, J. J. (2018). *Marketing strategy, values and sustainable development*. Palgrave Macmillan.

Lim, W. M. (2016). A blueprint for sustainability marketing: Defining its conceptual boundaries for progress. *Marketing Theory*, *16*(2), 232–249.

Lim, W. M. (2017). Inside the sustainable consumption theoretical toolbox: Critical concepts for sustainability, consumption, and marketing. *Journal of Business Research*, *78*, 69–80.

McDonagh, P., & Prothero, A. (2014). Sustainability marketing research: Past, present and future. *Journal of Marketing Management*, *30*(11–12), 1186–1219.

Yong, J. Y., Yusliza, M. Y., Ramayah, T., Chiappetta Jabbour, C. J., Sehnem, S., & Mani, V. (2020). Pathways towards sustainability in manufacturing organizations: Empirical evidence on the role of green human resource management. *Business Strategy and the Environment*, *29*(1), 212–228.

SECTION 1

ROLE OF HUMAN RESOURCE FOR SUSTAINABILITY

INDUSTRIAL RELATIONS: TOWARDS RESILIENT BUSINESS IN THE PRINT INDUSTRY – A STUDY WITH RESPECT TO KERALA TRADE UNIONS FROM A LEADER'S PERSPECTIVE

K. S. Chandrasekar

University of Kerala, India

ABSTRACT

Kerala, being the most literate state in India, has at least one newspaper being subscribed to every household and thus the Print industry in Kerala is doing a commendable job. Labour welfare as a part of industrial relation is assuming greater significance with the growth of industrialization. An industry today is a co-operative undertaking with both the capital and the labour as equal partners. The workers in the modern context are not simply a marketable commodity to be purchased by the owners, but human beings with their own needs, emotions and aspirations who invest their labour in making the industry a success. It is normally believed that the model employer maintains harmonious relation with the employees. Considering the conflicts are usually natural, the employer always tries to minimize the disputes by offering the right mix of labour welfare measures and ensure the loss of man days and the loss of production to the lowest possible extent. This article delineates the industrial relations in Kerala newspaper industry. The data were analyzed related to age, occupation, region of working, education and experience on the leaders' attitude on various factors related to labour welfare. The primary data collected from the trade union leaders were analyzed using the statistical computer package SPSS. Appropriate tests were used for analysis. It can be seen that the leaders were not at all satisfied with any of the facilities except for safety practices for the employees and the grievance handling process since they were directly involved.

Resilient Businesses for Sustainability
Advanced Series in Management, Volume 34B, 9–19

ISSN: 1877-6361/doi:10.1108/S1877-63612024000034B002

Keywords: Labour relations; trade unions; leaders; print; Kerala; India

1. INTRODUCTION

Labour welfare may be viewed in three concepts. These are total concept, social concept and relative concept. This in turn is considered as a desirable state of existence including the physical, mental, moral and emotional well-being. These four elements are considered to be the structure of labour welfare and on which its totality is dependent. The role of the Print media as a major instrument of bringing the change was critical in bringing people together since freedom struggle. This was a role which is equivalent of creating awareness and educating the public. The findings were a rich bunch of periodicals both newspapers and magazines sponsored by individuals in some cases, and by movements and organizations. Kerala being highly literate state has a major role in ensuring the awareness among the common public. The impact of the press during the last three decades since independence has proved its maturity beyond doubt. The press, which acts as a mirror of public opinion held up to the authorities so they can see how they are perceived by the populace and adjust their actions and policies accordingly, is actually the fourth estate. It is regarded as crucial and required that the press be given every convenience and freedom to access news sources while carrying out this duty. The system of press correspondents receiving government accreditation is one of the many tactics used to provide and guarantee this accessibility to real news, its investigation and its interpretation. Similarly, the correspondent has a moral duty that boosts the correspondent's sense of moral and social responsibility.

According to Trade union Amendment Act, 1947, the employer could recognize any trade union voluntarily. Nagaraju (1981) mentioned that if a trade union is not recognized voluntarily, it is entitled to recognition by order of a Labour Court, provided it fulfils certain conditions. One of the basic criteria is that the Union must be a representative of all the workmen employed by the employer. The court, after being satisfied, will give recognition to the Union and that Union will be entitled to have all rights of a recognized Union. In the Indian context, industrial relations can be used to refer to any subject that brings up interactions between employees and employers. Employees could be unionized or non-unionized.

According to Dunlop (1958), as they relate to industrial peace or conflict, union–management relations should not be the sole focus of industrial relations. It should be viewed as one that deals with the more general issue of an industrial relations system that defines the role, status and behaviour of different groups of people who collaborate for productive purposes in an economy that is distinct in its specific and peculiar social and economic conditions that prevail under given technological, market and power orientation, giving rise to the creation of a body of rules to regulate the interactions of the various groups. It may be noted that as the journalists are often found to move from one to another and the attrition rates are high, they were classified along with the non-journalists. It also indicates the reasons of the success and failure of newspaper companies in order to understand the labour welfare issues.

This study also reveals the importance of workers and leaders towards the labour welfare activities in Kerala. Since the advent of COVID-19, there are many issues plaguing the labour welfare across the world with many companies opting for work from home, layoff, etc. In this context, the study becomes significant and addresses the resilient measures in the wake of the changed scenario especially in the media industry with particular focus on newspaper sector.

2. LITERATURE REVIEW

Arya (1989) studied the culture and environment of labour–management relations in the general public sector. According to the study, common human resources practices, such as appropriate training after hiring, a just wage structure, welfare benefits, employee involvement in decision-making and a clearly defined promotion policy, all have a positive impact on labour–management relations.

Putnam (2019), while discussing the results of Hawthorne Studies, observed that the relationship between the first line supervisor and the individual worker was of importance in determining the attitude of the employees.

According to Jacoby (1997), the majority of industrialized nations provide for the welfare of their people through state-sponsored systems that ensure their citizens' health and safety while also shielding them from the negative effects of economic fluctuations. Contrarily, in the United States welfare capitalism system emerged as employers assumed a greater responsibility for ensuring the health and welfare of employees and their families than did the government.

Williams and MacDermid (1994) offered two dimensions. One dimension related to benefit level, reflecting the value of various benefit plans. The new variable measured employee perceptions of the system use to deliver these benefits and was related to benefit system satisfaction. The system dimension reflected the employee's perceptions of how these benefits were administered, while the benefit level dimension concentrated on the details of the benefit plans.

According to Dencker et al.'s (2007), individual differences in benefit preferences result from the specific employment relationships with those who have the most experience. Actuarial and perceived benefit levels have different effects on ensuring benefit satisfaction, according to research. For example, Williams (1995) experimented a model of labour benefit satisfaction. She discovered that benefit satisfaction was more strongly related to an employee's perceived level of benefits than to the level of benefits that were 'true' to their actuarial value. The perceived level and actuarial value may be positively correlated in the benefit–satisfaction paradox, but she was unable to find any evidence to support this. According to Pepke (1995), employer-sponsored pension plans (ESOP) play a crucial role for both employers and employees. Because they may be beneficial to both employers and employees thanks to government tax breaks, employer-sponsored pre-tax savings plans are very common. Employers profit from the ability to deduct any contributions made to the retirement plan at the time of the contributions with the backing of the overall administration. Even though employers may match employee contributions up to a certain amount, they only do so for those employees who actually make contributions.

As Nossiter (1982) has observed, 'By Indian standards Kerala has a significant trade union movement. In 1961–62 reported union membership in India was 2 percent of the total workforce but in Kerala 5 percent. Actual membership may have been double. In the same year 7 percent of reported union membership in India was from Kerala. Unions in Kerala are also comparatively militant, industrial disputes in the state accounting for 8, 17, and 9 percent of all disputes in 1961, 1966, and 1969 respectively'.

Srivastava (1966) conducted research on the specific conciliation and arbitration practices in the state of Uttar Pradesh and discovered that the conciliation machinery had not improved industrial relations by reducing the frequency and severity of strikes or by providing a suitable mechanism for dispute resolution.

Lallan Prasad (1968) covered a wide range of subjects in his study, including organizational structure and relationships, hiring and training of personnel, paying the hired staff, employee morale, labour relations and labour involvement in management initiatives in the steel industries. Additionally, it was discovered that labour disputes not only negatively affected the community as a whole but also caused losses to employers and employees.

By highlighting Kerala's fascinating history of industrial relations development, Ramchandran Nair (1973) attempted to analyze Kerala's labour relations. He also learnt that much of the talk surrounding the state's industrial unrest situation had been focused on the history of labour–management relations and practices. Contrary to popular belief, the study found that the industrial environment was not as unfavourable as anticipated for investment.

Gangadhara Rao (1970) conducted an evaluation of the state of industrial relations within the company in an effort to pinpoint the factors that contributed to the union management and employees of the Indian Railways having positive and productive working relationships.

Debraj Ray and Subramaniam (2020) indicated clearly how each sector is improving from the lockdown and newspaper sector has shown tremendous growth as the case of health industry and the labour force had no problems in their livelihood.

Blundell et al. (2020) found that workers with lower incomes and less education are more likely to work in industries that have been negatively impacted by the pandemic in a study on leadership and employment disparities. The specific sectors include domestic services, retail, passenger transportation, arts and entertainment, child care and food and lodging.

The published works on the subject are confined to brochures and pamphlets issued by certain trade unions and political parties. Some isolated studies have been undertaken to study trade unionism in Kerala. The work of Prakasam (1979), on the growth of trade union in Kerala is one among them. Another attempt was made by Jayadevadas (1983) to study the working class politics in Kerala. Raveendran (1989) in the study on the societal background of trade unions in Kerala among the unorganized sector analyses the impact of union movement in the socioeconomic development of the coir workers in Kerala.

3. DISCUSSION

The primary data collected from 50 trade union leaders were analyzed using the statistical computer package SPSS. Appropriate tests such as ANOVA, *T*-test, Standard Deviation, Mean, Ranking, Goodman and Kruskal tau, Kruskal Wallis Equality Test, Duncan's Post hoc test, Friedman Test for dependent sample and Correlation were used for analysis. The computer generated analysis result was tabulated and further analyzed. The result of the study was interpreted; hypotheses were verified and discussed in further topic of this Chapter. The analysis of various research problems were analyzed on the various factors like age, occupation, region of working, education, experience, trade union affiliation, etc.

56.0% of the respondents were in the 36–40 age groups. 29.0% were belonging to above 40 groups. 10.0% from 26–30 group and 5.0% from 31–35 group. 68.0% of the respondents were having HSS as educational qualification. 24.0% were having Degree and 8.0% SSLC. All the respondents were married, as it is evident that all the leaders are in a higher age group. Even those belonging to the 26–30 age group was also married and those belonging to this are internal leaders and hence there was a strong career ahead of this group that made them marry. Normal cases, the age group of leaders who marry are in the 30–35 age groups only. It is found that 55% of the leaders belong to the rural areas and the rest from the urban areas. There is a predominance of leaders coming from rural areas as specific as that of the newspaper industry.

It can be seen that 52.5% are from the southern region of Kerala, 27.5% from the central Region of Kerala. Only 20% are from the Northern region. The leaders were belonging to various political parties. Those from the northern region are primarily belonging to the Left parties specifically to the CPI (M).

In the newspaper industry, 60% belong to the internal leaders who are actually working with the journalists, non-journalists and executives. This indicates the fact that these leaders will be aware of the developmental and welfare needs of the employees. However those from the external leaders were amply supported by the internal team of task masters. The external leaders were found to have more negotiating powers and their leadership traits are something which the internal leaders often lack. The above table indicates the fact that 36% are having leadership experience of 1–3 years and those belonging to less than a year and 3–5 years are equal in number. However, only two leaders were having more than 5 years. These are the people who are internal leaders from the newspaper companies. It can be seen that 35% of the leaders took 1–3 years for reaching this position and 30% have taken 3–5 years while four leaders took more than 5 years to reach the leadership position. All the respondents were having political party memberships. Out of them, 50% were CPI (M) members, 30.0% INC members, 12.0% were CPI members and the rest BJP members. 60.0% of the respondents were in the area-level leadership, 25.0% were just members and the rest in the district level.

55.0% of the total leader respondents were strongly agreeing to the statement that 'effective political back up is required for trade union growth'. 40.0% of the total respondents were agreeing to the statement that 'effective political back up is required for trade union growth'. 5.0% of the total leader respondents were having no clear opinion to the statement that 'effective political back up is required for trade union growth'. None of the leader respondents were disagreeing to the statement that 'effective political back up is required for trade union growth'. To test the difference in opinion on the statement 'effective political back up is required for trade union growth' ANOVA test was conducted. The 'F' value obtained was 0.651 (Sig. 0.526) which is not significant at 5% level of significance. So the test indicated that there is no significant difference in opinion among leaders with different educational backgrounds on the statement 'Effective political backup is needed for the TU growth'.

To test the difference of opinion among the leaders having different political party affiliations on the statement 'effective political back up is required for trade union growth', ANOVA Test was conducted. The 'F' value obtained was 24.667 (Sign. 0.000) which is significant at 1% level of significance. There is a significant difference in opinion among leaders with different party affiliations about the statement 'Effective political backup is needed for the TU growth' (Sig.0.000).

The test shows that the union leaders have opinion that can be classified into three subsets. Unions with affiliation to CPI(M) and CPI (mean scores 1.00 and 1.27, respectively) belong to the first sub set and are having the strongest opinion that 'effective political back up is required for trade union growth'. The unions affiliated to INC have a mean score of 2.40 and can be classified in the second subset. The unions affiliated to the BJP falls in the third subset with mean score of 3.00. The test clearly shows that the opinion of the left parties, INC and BJP were significantly different.

To test the difference of opinion among the leaders in different positions on the statement 'effective political back up is required for trade union growth', ANOVA Test was conducted. The 'F' value obtained was 0.590 (Sign. 0.559) which is not significant at

5% level of significance. There is no significant difference in opinion among leaders in different positions on the statement 'Effective political backup is needed for the TU growth' (Sig.0.559). There is no significant difference in opinion among leaders in different positions held on the statement 'Effective political backup is needed for the TU growth' (Sig.0.559). The results of the same are depicted in the Table 1.

The mean values of the internal and external leaders on the statement 'effective political back up is required for trade union growth' are 1.67 and 1.50, respectively. The opinion is positive in the two categories. To test the difference of opinion among the leaders having different political party affiliations on the statement 'effective political back up is required for trade union growth', Student's *t* Test was conducted. The 't' value obtained was 0.711 (Sign. 0.481) which is not significant at 5% level of significance. There is no significant difference in opinion among internal and external leaders on the statement 'Effective political backup is needed for the TU growth'. ANOVA test as in Table 2 corroborates the same.

All the leaders were asked to rate on the importance scale what the welfare facilities that are needed to be in a newspaper company. The responses revealed the following:

- 25% strongly agreed to the satisfaction level with respect to bonus and the number is 70% in the case of those opposing the same. The above analysis is backed by the population of agreement at 0.79 which indicates that there is a strong agreement among the respondents on the issue. It can be clearly seen that the satisfaction towards the disbursements of bonus is not agreed upon by the leaders as such.
- 25% strongly agreed to the satisfaction level with respect to canteen and the number is 57.5% in the case of those opposing the same. The above analysis is backed by the population of agreement at 0.74 which indicates that there is a strong agreement among the respondents on the issue. Here again the facilities offered in the canteen with subsidized food, cleanliness, availability as per menu, the quality of the food, etc., were being questioned by the leaders and they remarked for the change in the current pattern of canteen operation and those affiliated to the Centre of Indian Trade Unions (CITU) informed that Kudumbasree could be given the lease for conducting the canteen facilities at various companies. 37.5% agreed to the satisfaction level with respect to medical facilities and the number is 57.5% in the case of those opposing the same. The above analysis is backed by the population of agreement at 0.85 which indicates that there is a strong agreement among the respondents on the issue. The leaders have asked for the inclusion of all the employees under the health insurance schemes particularly those having symptoms of cardiac and other diseases which is costly for the employee's capability.
- 30.0% strongly agreed to the satisfaction level with respect to recreational facilities at the premises and those offered by the organization at large and the number is 50% in the case of those opposing the same. In fact 10% has agreed to the satisfaction level also. This can be seen that there is not much of agreement in terms of the responses.

Table 1. Analysis on Effective Political Backup for Trade Union (TU) Growth.

Source	Sum of Squares	Df.	Mean Square	F	Sig.
Between groups	0.863	2	0.431	0.651	0.526
Within groups	31.137	37	0.662		
Total	32.000	39			

Source: Primary data.

Table 2. ANOVA for Effective Political Backup.

Source	Sum of Squares	Df.	Mean Square	F	Sig.
Between groups	0.863	2	0.431	0.651	0.526
Within groups	31.137	37	0.662		
Total	32.000	39			

Source: Primary data.

The above analysis is backed by the population of agreement at 0.32 which indicates that there is no agreement among the respondents on the issue.

- 25.0% strongly agreed to the satisfaction level with respect to rest/lunch room facility along with the fact that 25.0% are also agreeing to the satisfaction level and the number is same in the case of those opposing the same. The above analysis is backed by the population of agreement at 0.64 which indicates that there is a strong agreement among the respondents on the issue. However, 50% are disagreeing to the facilities being offered with respect to rest/lunch room facilities. This can be seen from the responses received from the employees and that the rest/lunch room facilities require more facelift.
- 25% strongly agreed to the satisfaction level with respect to shift allowance and the number is very high as 75% in the case of those opposing the same. The above analysis is backed by the population of agreement at 0.72 which indicates that there is a strong agreement among the respondents on the issue. This is a strong indication that the current shift allowance is low and is given based on the earlier rates. This needs a revision as per the leaders' opinion on the issue.
- 37.5% strongly agreed to the satisfaction level with respect to drinking water facilities and the number is very low in the case of those opposing the same. The above analysis is backed by the population of agreement at 0.78 which indicates that there is a strong agreement among the respondents on the issue.
- 37.5% strongly agreed to the satisfaction level along with 40.0% agreeing with respect to first aid facilities and the number is very low in the case of those opposing the same. The above analysis is backed by the population of agreement at 0.74 which indicates that there is a strong agreement among the respondents on the issue.
- 45.0% strongly agreed to the satisfaction level with respect to safety along with 40.0% agreeing and the number is very low in the case of those opposing the same. The above analysis is backed by the population of agreement at 0.66 which indicates that there is a strong agreement among the respondents on the issue.
- 32.5% strongly agreed to the satisfaction level with respect to cooperative society along with 32.5% agreeing to it and the number is very low in the case of those opposing the same. The above analysis is backed by the population of agreement at 0.73 which indicates that there is a strong agreement among the respondents on the issue.
- 32.5% strongly disagreed to the satisfaction level with respect to latrine and urinal facilities along with 67.5% disagreeing to it and the number is very low in the case of those opposing the same. The above analysis is backed by the population of agreement at 0.70 which indicates that there is a strong agreement among the respondents on the issue.
- 15% strongly disagreed to the satisfaction level with respect to provision for advance along with 85% disagreeing to it and the number is very low in the case of those opposing the same. The above analysis is backed by the population of agreement at 0.69 which indicates that there is a strong agreement among the respondents on the issue.

This indicates that the leaders were asking in their charter of demands to increase the provision for advance for the non-journalists. However, this has become one of the important issues among the leaders.

- 25.0% strongly disagreed to the satisfaction level with respect to retirement benefits along with 70% disagreeing to it and the number is very low in the case of those opposing the same. The above analysis is backed by the population of agreement at 0.71 which indicates that there is a strong agreement among the respondents on the issue. The area of contention is retirement benefits. There are cases where the benefits are being deferred beyond a particular time and hence this issue became important for the leaders.
- 45% strongly agreed to the satisfaction level with respect to spittoons along with 5% agreeing to it and the number is very low in the case of those opposing the same. The above analysis is backed by the population of agreement at 0.76 which indicates that there is a strong agreement among the respondents on the issue.
- 40.0% strongly agreed to the satisfaction level with respect to work surroundings along with 35.0% agreeing to it and the number is very low in the case of those opposing the same. The above analysis is backed by the population of agreement at 0.70 which indicates that there is a strong agreement among the respondents on the issue. 53.5% of the respondents were of the opinion that 'time honoured grievances' would considerably reduce industrial unrest. 37.5% of the respondents were of the opinion that 'wages according to the price level' would considerably reduce industrial unrest. 10.0% of them opined that 'training on industrial relations' would considerably reduce industrial unrest. Out of the responses, 36.0% is wage-related and the balance 64.0% is HRM-related.

The opinion of trade union leaders on the factors that would develop labour management relations, their satisfaction towards union activities and hindrances to union activities was analyzed. 65.0% of the respondents were of the opinion that 'Creation of mutual trust and confidence between workers and management' is the best way of developing labour management relations. 15.0% of the respondents were of the opinion that 'giving recognition of the works of the workers' is the best way of developing labour management relations. 10.0% each opinioned that 'To give priority on organizational goals over political differences' and 'Awareness about the labour laws' is the ways of developing labour–management relations. The necessity of man management was made out by the responses received. The give and take policy in disguise was predominant. By implementing mutual trust itself we can improve the industrial climate to a greater extent.

62.5% of the respondents were pointing their fingers towards lack of government policies as hindrance to union performance. 25.0% opinioned that inter union rivalry was the hindrance on union performance. 7.5% opinioned that union inefficiency is the hindrance on union performance. So by framing the employee friendly policies by the government, the unrest can be minimized to a greater extent.

There were number of aspects which determine the satisfaction level of leaders on the additional benefits that are being provided by the companies. The satisfaction level statements were created on a five point scale.

The statements were:

- Recreation of employees.
- Appreciation and recognition offered to employees for their excellence.
- Educational assistance given to children's education.
- Organization's policy for ensuring death in harness.

- Post death formalities of employees and relatives assistance.
- Career advancement for the workers.
- Ensuring work place safety for the workers.
- Benefits upon super annuation.
- Staff Benevolent Fund.
- Training programs conducted.
- Counselling process.
- The grievance handling procedure.
- Work shift timings.

These statements clearly delineate the welfare activities undertaken by the newspaper companies and the response to these statements were obtained from the leaders. It can be seen that the leaders were not at all satisfied with any of the facilities except for safety practices for the employees and the grievance handling process since they were directly involved.

To a certain extent, there is clear understanding of the welfare activities undertaken by the newspaper companies and hence these statements were put to a *t*-test analysis of the data for the statement rate the welfare activities is shown in Table 3. The analysis shows that the welfare activities are not proper as for as the leaders are concerned in contrast to the employees and there are no existing facilities which are being used effectively by journalists, non-journalists and the executives alike. The mean scores is less than 3 at 1% level of significance. Generally, the leaders were of a bad opinion on the welfare activities of the newspaper companies in Kerala. Only safety practices for the welfare of its employees was significant and all others were not significant and that indicates the resentment among the leaders on this issue.

Table 3. *T* Test Analysis for Welfare Measures.

Sl.No	Statement	Test Value = 3			
		t	df	Sig.	Mean Difference
1	Recreation of employees	1.414	39	0.000	0.54
2	Appreciation and recognition given to employees for their excellence	2.247	39	0.000	0.68
3	Educational assistance provided for children's education	2.449	39	0.000	0.78
4	Organization's policy for death in harness	−1.530	39	0.000	−0.18
5	Assistance for post death formalities of employees and relatives	−4.467	39	0.000	−0.54
6	The procedure adopted for career growth of workers	1.513	39	0.000	0.60
7	Safety practices for the welfare of its workers	2.994	39	0.000	0.66
8	Retirement benefits	1.221	39	0.000	0.81
9	Staff benevolent fund	1.199	39	0.000	0.72
10	Training programs conducted	1.178	39	0.000	0.83
11	Counselling process	1.449	39	0.000	0.33
12	The grievance handling procedure	1.123	39	0.000	0.41
13	Work shift timings	0.134	39	0.000	0.04

Source: Primary data.

4. CONCLUSION

About 40 trade union leaders were also included in the analysis and based on the study and with the interaction among the experts in the area; it was suggested to follow the suggestions.

To make sure that the workers are relieved from the mundane industrial fatigue and help them improve on the intellectual, cultural and monetary conditions of better standards of living by ensuring an all-inclusive welfare programmes aimed at them. In order to do the same, there is a need to have separate human resource department catering to employee welfare measures. There needs to be an organizational chart under the leadership of a Manager with at least 10 years of industrial relations and labour welfare experience who possess either an MBA or MSW.

The welfare measures should be able to create in the mind of the individual that they belong to an organization which cares and also make them committed to increasing the productivity.

Organization needs to understand that there are many welfare measures which are above the normal measures that need to be given as statutory like housing schemes, medical, educational facilities, recreational facilities and counselling facilities.

The newspaper companies can offer flexi time for non-journalists and executives even though in this industry, journalists are already given the flexi time facilities. This can be extended to the non-journalists and executives. This will ensure that the productivity is also at a higher end in the wake of COVID-19. Currently there are no harassment clinics. This can be implemented in all the newspaper companies. Labour referral schemes can be implemented to give importance to the employees when they refer his/her relative or friend for a posting in a suitable position by internal notices. Allowing women employees to work from home during the times when they are expecting till say 8th or 9th month. This will enable the companies to utilize the talented women employees' service even when they are not able to attend office. One of the most common complaints raised by the employees is that post retirement the companies need to monitor and when somebody dies or takes ill, the company Employee relations team needs to arrive and console or provide the necessary medical attention.

REFERENCES

Arya, P. P. (1989). *Labour management relations in public sector undertakings*. Deep and Deep Publications.

Blundell, R., Costa Dias, M., Joyce, R., & Xu, X. (2020). COVID-19 and inequalities. *Fiscal Studies*, *41*(2), 291–319.

Dencker, J. C., Joshi, A., & Martocchio, J. J. (2007). Employee benefits as context for intergenerational conflict. *Human Resource Management Review*, *17*, 208–220.

Dunlop, J. T. (1958). *Industrial relations systems* (p. 3). Henry Holt and Co.

Gangadhara Rao, M. (1970). *Industrial relations in Indian Railways – A study of the personnel and union management relations with special reference to the post independence period*. Ph.D. Thesis, Andhra University.

Jacoby, S. (1997). *Modern manors: Welfare capitalism since the new deal*. Princeton University Press.

Jayadevadas, D. (1983). *Working class politics in Kerala*. Unpublished Ph.D. Thesis, University of Kerala.

Nagaraju, S. (1981). *Industrial relations systems in India (1981)* (p. 1). Chugh Publications.

Nossiter, T. J. (1982). *Communism in Kerala: A study in political adaptation* (p. 59). Oxford University Press.

Papke, E. L. (1995). Participating in and contributions to 401(k) pension plans, evidence from plan data. *The Journal of Human Resources*, *30*(1995), 311–325.

Prakasam, R. (1979). *Keralathile trade union Prasthanathinte Charithram (Malayalam)*. Prabhat Book House.

Prasad, L. (1968). *Personnel management and industrial relations in the public sector with special reference to the Hindustan Steel Ltd*. Ph.D. Thesis, Punjab University.

Putnam, M. L. (2019). Improving employee relation. *Personnel*, *8*, 325.

Ramchandran Nair, K. (1973). *Industrial relations in Kerala* (p. 29). Sterling Publishers.

Raveendran, N. (1989, January). *Social background of trade union movement*. Ph.D. Thesis, Department of Sociology, University of Kerala.

Ray, D., & Subramaniam, S. (2020). India's lock down: An interim report. *Indian Economic Review*, *55*(Suppl.), 31–79.

Srivastava, P. K. (1966). *Conciliation and arbitration in Uttar Pradesh*. Ph.D. Thesis, Agra University.

Williams, M. L. (1995). Antecedents of employee benefit satisfaction: A test of a model. *Journal of Management*, *21*, 1097–1128.

Williams, M. L., & MacDermid, S. M. (1994). Linkages between employee benefits and attitudinal and behavioral outcomes: A research review and agenda. *Human Resource Management Review*, *4*, 131–160.

HUMANIZING PRACTICES FOR PEOPLE MANAGEMENT: A CASE STUDY FROM COVID-19

Asiya Nasreen and Sarika Tomar

Jamia Millia Islamia, India

ABSTRACT

Regardless of where the business stood at the beginning of 2020, COVID-19 afflicted the corporate world as well as most of the workforce worked remotely due to government-mandated isolation. The range of personal and professional problems experienced due to remote working by employees was explored at one of the Non-Financial Banking companies and how the company responded to their well-being by interviewing 124 employees and a senior HR personnel. Remote work induced by COVID-19 was not a cakewalk as 56.5% of employees desired physical connectivity with colleagues, for 50.8% work done from home was not interesting and more than 50% of the respondents agreed to work more hours than usual. The outcome was anxiety for some of them. The imbalance between personal and professional life was dissipated with the support of the management as 94.4% of them got sufficient support from their respective managers and colleagues, as they were able to communicate and collaborate with them. The managerial side validated the responses in a way that a flexible and target-oriented approach was adopted for employees. They organized stress management activities and ensured connections through regular employee connect and communication by Learning and Development department. Additionally, COVID-19 advisories and guidelines were followed while engaging with employees. The work–life balance shaken due to remote work was managed with responsive humanistic management practices that had the enduring effect of garnering employee engagement levels with the organization.

Resilient Businesses for Sustainability
Advanced Series in Management, Volume 34B, 21–35

ISSN: 1877-6361/doi:10.1108/S1877-63612024000034B003

Keywords: COVID-19; remote work; purposeful business; well-being; human resources

1. INTRODUCTION

The world in 2019 witnessed a never-before-experienced public health crisis known as COVID-19. It was a respiratory infectious disease that has been highly communicable and serious in nature caused by (SARS-COV-2). The symptoms include fever, shortness of breath, sore throat, muscle pain, reduced sense of taste and smell, chills, respiratory failure and pneumonia. The large-scale casualties were caused by COVID-19, to the extent that World Health Organization (WHO), 2021, confirmed 93 million cases of infection and 2 million deaths till January 2021 while Cascella et al. (2023) reported that 6 million people lost their life. Perhaps, the massive stroke caused to human lives, led WHO, 2020, to declare it a 'Public Health Emergency of International Concern'. To thwart the speed of the virus strong containment measures were imposed all over the world in line with the guidance from the WHO. In India, the nationwide lockdown paused almost everything. According to the International Labour Organization (ILO), which works for the social justice and rights of labour stated in 2021, in countries with COVID-19-related restrictions, more than 90% of the workers experienced some or other form of workplace closure measures and for some sectors, it had become a norm to close the workspaces. The impact was felt on businesses as they were closed down as well as on people's psyche who led a forced isolated life.

During COVID-19, as businesses also experienced some form of lockdown, employers prepared for adjustment and created contingency plans for maintaining business operations. An alternative option for work considered by companies was working from home or remote working. Remote work, simply, is an operating model that allows the workforce to fulfil its tasks away from the typical work environment. It is based on a common understanding that staff does not have to be available in an office to perform their duties but a forced form of remote work creates threats to the employee well-being. Working from one's bedroom or even the kitchen table was quite normal, balancing virtual school or meeting job deadlines was a regular challenge that impacted the mental health of employees. The incidences of depression and blurring of professional and personal lines were noted (Economic Times, 2021). Business organizations around the world responded to the challenge, and those that responded in humanizing manner managed the exhaustion of the staff, their family members and made it easy to manage the pressure of performance. While carving out strategies to recover during uncertain times, the role of HR professionals has been commendable (Aitken-Fox et al., 2022; Al-Jubari et al., 2022; Jain & Aggarwal, 2021; Saxena et al., 2022) by carving indigenous solutions. However, except for few research studies of secondary nature, any official comprehensive data regarding people's management is not yet available. With this backdrop, this chapter has explored the humanizing practices initiated by human resource professionals to manage people during COVID-19in one of the Non-Financial Banking Organizations (NBFC).

2. LITERATURE REVIEW

Remote work and well-being: A lot of psychological versatility was caused due to remote working as was reflected in the unfavourable mental health impacts and symptoms such as anxiety, depression and stress (Economic Times, 2021). The level of psychological effects increased due to the sudden shift to remote working or temporary layoffs, the threat of catching the virus that exacerbated anxiety for key workers and brought new stresses to cope with. For many people, remote working was a challenge to their work–life harmony although earlier it was used as a technique to attract, manage and retain talent, strengthen the psychological relation between employees and organization and was perceived as a support for employee well-being (Shirmohammadi et al, 2022). Earlier remote work provided employees an opportunity for a better fit between themselves and their jobs and hence was possible to perform multiple roles of their life. It is none but a work–life balance because by doing so 'an individual remains equally engaged in and equally satisfied with his or her work role and family role' (Greenhaus et al., 2003). Evidence supports that working from home's office has not been a highly popular type of remote working because of the blurring between personal and professional boundaries.

During the pandemic, the consequences of remote work had been extreme for the work–life balance of employees because it was involuntary, both from the side of the employer and for the employee and was generally applicable for all types of employees and for all roles whether they could be performed remotely or not. To this effect, many people experienced distress because they were not prepared to work in isolation, worked intensely 24 × 7 without time periods when work was not done as timelines and targets were to be met and were being done in the presence of other members of the household who were also staying-at-home (Sandoval-Reyes et al., 2021). An article by Forbes (Tsipursky, 2022) confirmed that well-being was hurt by remote work and reported that two-thirds of the employees who worked from home had difficulty in getting away from work at the end of the day. Lonska et al., 2021; Xiong et al., 2020 (as cited in Ruffolo et al., 2021) emphasized that due to remote working during the COVID-19 crisis, work–life imbalance was experienced by employees, there were changes in work schedules that affected the sense of well-being and caused anxiety. Jain and Aggrawal (2021) outlined the psychological and behavioural changes caused by COVID-19 related anxiety which included depression, psychological distress, worry, anxiety about being infected, subjective well-being and reduced quality of life. Al-Jubari et al. (2022) reinforced that work from home was necessitated due to successive lockdowns and perceived employee stress was inversely related to employee well-being. Prolonged periods of working from home in full-time mode caused more stress, and achieving work–life balance was a challenge. Harju et al., 2021 also confirmed that there was suffering for some of the employees yet others were able to cope and manage with lockdown-induced stress. Economic Times, 2021; Forbes, 2022; Lonska et al., 2021; Sandoval-Reyes et al., 2021; Shirmohammadi et al., 2022; Xiong et al., 2020 (as cited in Al-Jubari et al., 2022; Ruffolo et al., 2021).

To counter the unparalleled human problems, parallel humanitarian response was prompted by industrial and business organizations. Many organizations purposefully and intentionally created a culture where employee productivity was enmeshed with employee well-being (Baumgartner, 2020; Knowles et al., 2022). Researchers (Jain & Aggarwal, 2021) mentioned that because of the psychological changes, the effectiveness of the workforce was reduced which eventually affected the overall productivity of the organizations. The authors referred of responsible HR initiatives to manage employee concerns by companies like Coca-Cola, Axis Bank, Pay Pal and Microsoft from across the globe that represented various sectors. The firms that responded with effective communication and managerial support directly impacted the well-being of employees (Harju et al., 2021) and working under stressful conditions made it difficult to spend time with family members, merged work and personal life or pursue their own pursuits (Adams, 2019). So, to manage the state of employee well-being, it has been suggested that employers should initiate various strategies in this direction.

Studies also reinforce that employee's expectations are more than merely receiving fat paychecks, in lieu of a poor workplace environment (LinkedIn survey as cited by Baumgartner, 2020). It has further been established that employees like to work with the employers who care for them and as employers create an impact on the society. People are interested to know that they add value to their companies. Work cultures are unique to every organization, and the enabling work culture is reflected when employees feel engaged, valued and believe that they are heard. The feeling of dignity and respect at the workplace is therefore valued and a determining factor in employee engagement and retention (Nasreen et al., 2019).

People's management amidst COVID-19: It has been observed by Hamouche (2021) that to meet organizational goals key functions and roles of HR department had undergone transformation during COVID-19 pandemic. Saxena et al. (2022) and Al-Jubari et al. (2022) explored engagement practices of some selected organizations during COVID-19 pandemic. Due to increase in remote work, work–life balance was affected and that employee well-being could be maintained through flexibility and communication. The spurt in psychological problems led to creation of psychological response centre within the organizations that were responsible for providing mental health support and developing strategies for coping (Verma, 2022). Aitkin-Fox et al. (2020) mentioned that recruitment and selection, onboarding and training and performance management were done through virtual tools. The supportive role for employee well-being was played by HR but required interventions need to be customised according to size, location, culture and type of industry.

Gaps in research: The combing of the researches indicated that COVID-19 hit the well-being of employees and human resource professionals rendered a helping hand in various organizations. The perspective of well-being and stress has been explored but empirical investigation is required to understand how the work–life imbalance was minimized and well-being of employees was facilitated due to the adoption of remote work. In situations where people have not worked remotely, they had to figure out how employees can work from remote locations and explore strategies to support their mental and physical health for the functioning of their organizations. The benchmark data from employee's perspective has remained scanty and exploration is required from this perspective.

Research methodology: A descriptive research design was used with a mixed-method approach. The objectives were as follows:

- To understand personal and professional problems experienced by employees due to remote working.
- To explore HR interventions for ensuring the emotional well-being of employees working remotely.
- To suggest measures for the well-being of the employees working remotely.

The industry type was Non-Financial Banking Company wherein all its employees working in the Northern region were considered as a sample population. The primary data were collected using a simple random sampling technique. In all, 124 employees from various levels responded to the questionnaire. This aside, the HR personnel of the company were also interviewed. A structured questionnaire was administered with the employees. The second tool used was a structured interview schedule to collect qualitative information from senior HR personnel of the company. This tool helped in understanding the approaches used by the HR department during the lockdown which made all the difference. The data were analyzed by carrying out Chi-square test in order to establish the relationship between variables.

3. HYPOTHESIS

$H\mu_{01}$. There was no impact of remote working on the working hours of employees.
$H\mu_{02}$. There was no impact of remote working on the work performed by employees.
$H\mu_{03}$. There was no impact of remote working on the speed of the work performed by the employees.
$H\mu_{04}$. There was no impact of remote working on mental health of employees.

4. FINDINGS

The selected company is one of the pioneers in providing innovative financing solutions for equipment purchasers all through the equipment life cycle. The company has a broad spectrum of customers ranging from those requiring finance followed by maintaining continuous liaison and engagement with them from the stage of procurement to exit stages. Therefore, most of the employees are in sales, collection and support for financing equipment for local and industrial customers Pan-India.

5. DEMOGRAPHIC PROFILE

Age: Out of 124 respondents, 18 respondents, i.e. 14.5% were in the 25–35 years of age group, followed by 29% in the 36–45 years age group and the majority of them 56.5% (70 respondents) fall in the age bracket of 45 years and above. This is detailed in Table 1.

The prominence was of the male respondents (N-117), i.e. 94.4% and the remaining seven respondents, i.e. 5.6% were females.

Experience, role performed and region: The length of stay of an employee determines their adjustment and adaptation to the culture of the organization and also impacts the engagement and retention of the employee.

Table 1. Age and Gender of Employees.

Age Groups	Frequency	Percent
25–35 years	18	14.5
36–45 years	36	29
46 and above	70	56.5
Total	124	100
Gender	*Frequency*	*Percent*
Male	117	94.4
Female	7	5.6
Total	124	100

Table 2. Length of Experience, Roles and Region of Employees.

Overall Years of Experience	Frequency	Percent
2–5 years	8	6.5
5–10 years	30	24.2
10–20 years	70	56.5
20 years and above	16	12.9
Total	124	100
Role	*Frequency*	*Percent*
Sales	29	23.4
Collection	69	55.6
Support	26	21
Total	124	100
Region	*Frequency*	*Percent*
Delhi-NCR	44	35.5
Punjab-Himachal Pradesh-Haryana	28	22.6
Rajasthan	27	21.8
Uttar Pradesh-Uttrakhand	25	20.2
Total	124	100.0

As shown in Table 2, it was informed that nearly 3/4th of the employees had been working for more than 10 years, followed by those who had been with the organization for more than 5 years (nearly 1/4th). There were very few employees who either had experience of more than 20 years or less than 5 years with the organization. Being the NBFC, the majority of the employees 55.6%, i.e. 69 of them were involved in a collection role in a sense that their major task was field-based that included loan recovery from the clients, 21% (26 respondents) were performing a support role which means support to the clients after the sanction of the loans and in its recovery while and 29 respondents, i.e. 23.4% were doing the sales role which included maintaining contact and professional relationship with the potential customers through different electronic mediums.

Region wise classification indicated that 35.5% of respondents, made up the majority, were from the Delhi-NCR region. 22.6% of the respondents were from Punjab-Himachal Pradesh-Haryana region. Remaining 42% were from Rajasthan and Uttar Pradesh-Uttrakhand region.

6. REMOTE WORKING AND WELL-BEING

6.1 Region and Working More Hours Than Normal

The above-mentioned Table 3 shows myriad responses of employees with regard to work from home with the majority of them agreeing to working more than in normal circumstances. 38.6 % from the same region were also found to be giving similar feedback. However, employees from Rajasthan, Punjab, Himachal Pradesh and Haryana did not agree strongly to it and almost 50% of employees from these states disagreed.

Table 3. Employees Working More Hours Than Normal.

Region	Employees Working More Hours Than Normal (In Percent)					
	Strongly Agree	Disagree	Neutral	Agree	Strongly Agree	Total
Delhi-NCR	4.5	2.3	20.5	38.6	34.1	100
Punjab, HP and Haryana	14.3	25	32.1	25	3.6	100
Rajasthan	3.7	22.2	29.6	33.3	11.1	100
Uttar Pradesh-Uttrakhand	–	12	20	48	20	100
Total	5.6	13.7	25	36.3	19.4	100

Chi-Square Test: Employees Working More Hours Than Normal

	Value	df	Asymp. Sig. (2-Sided)
Pearson Chi-Square	26.641[a]	12	0.009
Likelihood Ratio	29.625	12	0.003
Linear-by-linear association	0.892	1	0.345
No of valid cases	124		

8 cells (40%) have expected count less than 5. The minimum expected count is 1.41

Since significant value (0.009) is less than alpha value (0.01), there is an association between 'Region' and 'Working more hours than normal'. The Pearson Chi-Square value is 26.642 with 12 degrees of freedom. This result suggests that there is a significant association between the variables being analyzed. A statistically significant relationship has been found between both variables. The results reveal that employees working in various locations in the northern region were found to be working more than the usual hours. As organizations provided flexibility to its employees, the employees were able to complete their tasks within the stipulated time. This finding rejects the null hypothesis.

Anova

Model	Sum of Squares	df	Mean Square	F	Sig.
Regression	1.123	1	1.123	0.891	0.347[b]
Residual	153.977	122	1.261		
Total	155	123			

a. Dependent Variable: Region

b. Predictors: (Constant), Work is more demanding than usual

The regression significant value (0.347) is more than alpha value (0.01), the association between 'Region' and 'Working more hours than normal' is a weak association.

6.2 Region and Work as More Demanding

Table 4 indicates that 45.5% of employees from Delhi-NCR agreed that work during the lockdown became more demanding than usual. 51.9% of employees from Rajasthan also

Table 4. Employees to Consider Work More Demanding.

Region	Employees to Consider Work More Demanding Than Usual (in Percent)					
	Strongly Agree	Disagree	Neutral	Agree	Strongly Agree	Total
Delhi-NCR	4.5	2.3	20.5	45.5	22.7	100
Punjab, HP and Haryana	10.7	10.7	46.4	28	3.6	100
Rajasthan	7.4	22.2	7.4	51.9	11.1	100
Uttar Pradesh-Uttrakhand	–	4	20	48	28	100
Total	5.6	8.9	25	43.5	16.9	100

agreed that work became more demanding than usual. In total, 43.5% employees from all the regions found work to be more demanding and challenging during the lockdown.

Chi-Square Test: Employees to Consider Work More Demanding

	Value	df	Asymp. Sig. (2-Sided)
Pearson Chi-Square	28.217[a]	12	0.005
Likelihood Ratio	30.372	12	0.002
Linear-by-linear association	0.207	1	0.649
No of valid cases	124		

11 cells (55%) have an expected count of less than 5. The minimum expected count is 1.41

Since significant value (0.005) is less than alpha value (0.01), there is an association between 'Region' and 'Working is more demanding than usual'. The Pearson Chi-Square statistics is 28.217 with 12 degrees of freedom. This result is very similar to the previous analysis, and the low p-value (0.005) suggests a significant association between the variables. Based on the results it can be concluded that employees across most regional offices of the North region admitted that work became more demanding than usual. The relationship which is found to be significant here rejects the null hypothesis.

Anova

Model	Sum of Squares	df	Mean Square	F	Sig.
Regression	0.273	1	0.273	0.206	0.651[b]
Residual	161.944	122	1.327		
Total	162.218	123			

a. Dependent Variable: Region

b. Predictors: (Constant), Work is more demanding than usual

The regression significant value (0.651) is more than alpha value (0.01), the association between 'Region' and 'Working is more demanding than usual' is a weak association.

6.3 Region and Slow Pace of Work as Compared to Usual Pace

Table 5 details that in the Delhi-NCR region, 36.4% of the respondents do not really agree that work has been at a slow pace compared to the usual pace. 44.4% of the respondents

Table 5. Employees Considered Work to Be at a Slow Pace.

	Employees Considered Work to Be at a Slow pace (In Percent)					
Region	Very Much	Somewhat	Undecided	Not Really	Not at All	Total
Delhi-NCR	13.6	20.5	6.8	36.4	22.7	100
Punjab, HP and Haryana	14.3	46.4	21.4	10.7	7.1	100
Rajasthan	44.4	25.9	3.7	18.5	7.4	100
Uttar Pradesh-Uttrakhand	32	24	4	16	24	100
Total	24.2	28.2	8.9	22.6	16.1	100

from Rajasthan and 32% of the respondents of Uttar Pradesh-Uttrakhand region strongly agreed that the pace of the work became slow during remote working. It can be said that 24.2% of the respondents felt that the pace of the work was affected due to remote working.

Chi-Square Test: Employees to Consider Work to Be at the Slow Pace			
	Value	Df	Asymp. Sig. (2-Sided)
Pearson Chi-Square	30.422[a]	12	0.002
Likelihood Ratio	28.939	12	0.004
Linear-by-linear association	5.156	1	0.023
No of valid cases	124		

a. 7 cells (35%) have expected count less than 5. The minimum expected count is 2.22

Since significant value (0.002) is less than alpha value (0.01), there is an association between 'Region' and 'Slow pace of work as compared to usual pace'. The Pearson Chi-Square is 30.422 with 12 degrees of freedom. As the p-value is 0.002 which is low and suggests a significant association between the categorical variables. Although, the employees found the work to be more demanding during the pandemic but they admitted that the pace of the work also slowed down. The null hypothesis is rejected here.

Anova					
Model	Sum of Squares	df	Mean Square	F	Sig.
Regression	10.778	1	10.778	5.338	0.023[b]
Residual	246.343	122	2.019		
Total	257.121	123			

a. Dependent Variable: Slow pace of work as compared to usual pace

b. Predictors: (Constant), Region

The regression significant value (0.023) is more than alpha value (0.01), and the association between 'Region' and 'Slow pace of work as compared to usual pace' is a weak association.

7. REMOTE WORKING AND MENTAL HEALTH

7.1 Overall Years of Experience and Anxiety

A prominent finding that has figured is that in spite of the lockdown and employees working remotely from their homes, almost 37.5% of the respondents having 5–10 years of experience did not report any anxiety. Similarly, 30% of the respondents having 10–20 years of experience also did not report any anxiety during remote working. Table 6 shows that only respondents having more than 20 years of experience showed some signs of anxiety when they were working remotely.

Chi-Square: Years of Experience and Percentage of Employees to Experience Anxiety

	Value	df	Asymp. Sig. (2-Sided)
Pearson Chi-Square	28.535[a]	12	0.005
Likelihood Ratio	32.057	12	0.001
Linear-by-linear association	0.000	1	0.999
No of valid cases	124		

12 cells (60.0%) have expected count of less than 5. The minimum expected count is 1.03

Since the significant value (0.005) is less than the alpha value (0.01), there is an association between 'Overall Years of experience' and 'Anxiety'. The Pearson Chi-Square test indicates a strong association between both variables and thus rejects the null hypothesis.

Anova

Model	Sum of Squares	df	Mean of Square	*F*	Sig.
Regression	0	1	0	0	0.999[b]
Residual	236.218	122	1.936		
Total	236.218	123			

a. Dependent Variable: Anxiety and uncontrolled worry
b. Predictors: (Constant), Overall years of experience

The regression significant value (0.999) is greater than the alpha value (0.05), and the association between 'Overall Years of experience' and 'Anxiety' is a weak association. Organizations confronted with many complex issues during lockdown. As per various studies, if there were some difficulties it brought along some benefits to the employees. In

Table 6. Years of Experience and Percentage of Employees to Experience Anxiety.

	Employees to Experience Anxiety (in Percent)					
Years of Experience	Very Much	Somewhat	Undecided	Not Really	Not at All	Total
2–5 years	25	12.5	25	–	37.5	100
5–10 years	23.3	23.3	13.3	10	30	100
10–20 years	5.7	20	12.9	44.3	17.1	100
20 years and above	25	37.5	6.2	6.2	25	100
Total	13.7	22.6	12.9	28.2	22.6	100

this case, the greatest work-related advantage of moving away from traditional offices was lowering the risk of spreading COVID-19 as per 80.6% of respondents and saving normal transportation time to the workplace according to 49.2% of respondents, 58.1%, i.e. 72 respondents believed that remote working gave them time to inculcate new practices like spirituality and pursuing the hobbies with a change in the lifestyle. New practices help in coping with stress and improving mental health.

Remote work and anxiety: On the contrary, the main disadvantage of moving away from traditional offices which was faced by 56.5% of employees was lack of physical connectivity with colleagues, 50.8%, i.e. 63 respondents out of 124 confirmed that the work done from home was not as interesting as the work done at the workplace and could therefore predispose them towards anxiety. Age-wise, most of them are in middle adulthood and have been working for the last 10 years and above. These variables determine the physical and mental maturity and the way professional life is handled. The length of stay of the employees was cross-tabulated with the level of anxiety on a 5-point scale.

Table 7 shows that regardless of the number of years, 22.6% of the respondents did not report to have anxiety at all followed by 28.2 % of the respondents had also not faced anxiety, 22.6 % of them experienced little bit of it and only 13.7 % experienced it intensely. Those who had been affected by anxiety or uncontrolled worry due to remote working, informed that they felt restless and irritated, have trouble in sleeping and felt loneliness. Work wise, their productivity regressed owing to slow pace of work as compared to usual pace, felt tired and exhausted and did not feel happy in doing office chores. The reasons cited for poor work-related productivity were no contact with colleagues, trouble in focusing, concentrating or remembering things.

Employees working more hours than normal: Next, it was asked 'Do they feel like working more hours than normal?' To this, more than 50% of the respondents agreed that they worked more hours and it was more demanding than usual during remote working.

Overall, the negative effects of remote work on mental health and productivity of work had been minimal. But still, it was not a cakewalk for all the employees and the desire was expressed to resume full-time office after the pandemic is over. The reason for not so much anxiety was explored which according to the employees was

- The respective managers provided sufficient support (94.4%) to them. The management shared relevant information and services as well as opportunities for engagement with peers by organizing online activities.
- 80.6% were able to communicate and collaborate with their colleagues while working remotely. In case of help, they could reach to the concerned person telephonically.

Table 7. Percentage of Employees Having Anxiety.

	Employees Having Anxiety (in Percent)					
Years of Experience	Very Much	Somewhat	Undecided	Not Really	Not at All	Total
2–5 years	25	12.5	25	–	37.5	100
5–10 years	23.3	23.3	13.3	10	30	100
10–20 years	5.7	20	12.9	44.3	17.1	100
20 years and above	25	37.5	6.2	6.2	25	100
Total	13.7	22.6	12.9	28.2	22.6	100

8. HR PRACTICES FOR THE WELL-BEING

In order to substantiate the management perspective about initiating enabling management practices for employees during COVID-19, a senior HR manager was interviewed telephonically. Due to a busy schedule and considerations for social distancing, face-to-face interview was not possible. The selected manager had been working with the organization for the last 5 years and had been handling and managing all HR core functions like Recruitment, Training and Development and PMS.

Experience of remote work: In the first lockdown that lasted for 3 months, the entire workforce was at home. Most of the work related to marketing and sales collection was not done. In the second lockdown, which was for 2 months, people were allowed to work with all COVID-19 advisories like social distancing and double masks. In the first instance, it was a bit difficult but somehow struggled to maintain business. It was intense pressuring and gradually, things were learnt and managed.

Strategies followed to manage employee's productivity during WFH: The organization followed flexibility and avoided keeping roasters to make employees feel better during remote working. Flexibility was provided to even profiles of sales and marketing which are target-driven and time-bound. The employees were not burdened with output and were told that they could work according to the situation. The organization focused on strengthening interpersonal communication by ensuring that employees connect with each other more than ever. As poor communication during remote working could have had a detrimental effect on the well-being of employees, the organization paid attention to developing empathetic communication between superiors and subordinates which involved engaged and reflective thinking. Gradually this led to the building of trust amongst them and employees became supportive and appreciative of each other. The organization also encouraged independent diligence and helped employees to prioritize their work as per their situation. Although the environment was not conducive still remote work provided leaders and managers of the organization to understand and engage with their staff. Other strategies included:

- Had organized stress management activities for internal staff members by calling experts. These sessions were mostly online and tips for coping and managing stress were shared.
- The HR department ensured to connect with employees by regularly connecting with the employees and free flow of communication was initiated by Learning and Development department. Almost every week, employees were contacted to know their physical and mental health and were assured to reach the organization in case of any requirements.
- During office hours, after lifting the lockdown, followed COVID-19 Advisories and guidelines for employees.

The practices had been great for the company that allowed the employees to remain delightful as far as possible while working under changed circumstances. The support of managers and empathetic communication facilitated the workforce to adapt to the sudden call of changed work patterns and behave responsively.

9. DISCUSSION

The contemporary business world is dynamic, agile and complex. The year 2019, brought with itself watershed changes in all spheres of life including the way business is operated. Vulnerability created due to the pandemic and imposition of successive lockdowns in 2020 led many business organizations to respond to embrace a new way of operating and assisting the workers that had not been foreseen by even the most drastic business continuity plans (Forbes, 2022; Jain & Aggrawal, 2021). The findings confirmed earlier researchers (Economic Times, 2021; Forbes, 2022; Lonska et al., 2021; Sandoval-Reyes et al., 2021; Shirmohammadi et al., 2022; Xiong et al., 2020 as cited in Al-Jubari et al., 2022; Ruffolo et al., 2021) that due to remote work, employees experienced a higher level of stress. Statistically also it has been validated that employees felt working more than usual hours, perceived work to be more demanding despite the slower pace of work. Findings corroborated Reyes et al., 2021; Lonska et al, 2021 that during the pandemic, remote work was a compulsion that disturbed, the balance of work and life.

At the helm of affairs human resource professionals worked at the cutting edge and considered their people (Adam, 2019; Harju et al., 2021; Jain & Aggarwal, 2021) and the same has been established through the present case study. HR professionals supported the business and helped the employees to navigate from the fear of catching illness. HR professionals, therefore, contributed to improving organizational effectiveness by treating people in a humane manner. These can also be considered as purposeful or humanizing business decisions rooted in employee-centric organizational culture (Knowles et al., 2022). Purposeful business affects the organization in different ways and has been re-established and strengthened. While relating this argument with the selected NBFC, it is reinforced that the organization follows employee-centric work culture and there is an appreciation for HR and the organization as a good corporate citizen. Such purposeful decisions create inroads for the sustainability of the organization.

10. MANAGERIAL IMPLICATIONS AND SUGGESTIONS

The research aims to provide an understanding of personal and professional problems experienced by employees due to remote working and its impact on well-being of employees. It also helps in understanding the changing role of HR professionals from merely devising practices for enhancing people's productivity to supporting them. During crises like COVID-19, when people management practices became more humane and flexible, the employees faced fewer issues of anxiety. Proactive management could promote work–life balance and encourage employees to develop a mindset of learning that would promote a learning culture which would help the employees and organizations to maintain productivity.

The research had limitations as the data could be collected only from 124 employees of the organization although the number working in the organization was very high. Another limitation is that only one perspective of employee well-being has been considered for the study. Further research is required to know the success of HR interventions used to facilitate employees during remote working. Qualitative research can also be carried out to have an in-depth understanding of the personal challenges faced by employees during COVID-19 and the impact of the humane approach followed by the organization on their performance. Finally, further research can be conducted to understand the variations in the perceptions of male and female employees toward HR interventions used by the organization.

11. CONCLUSION

Remote work was an automated offshoot of lockdowns to limit the spread of COVID-19. Employee well-being was impacted but was well managed by many organizations that had been following purposeful business practices woven into their culture. Employees also keenly look forward to workplaces where there is the intertwining of their own beliefs with that of the organization and the two stakeholders work in tandem with a common idea of purpose and success. Certainly, that could be one of the prerequisites for the sustainability of business operations.

REFERENCES

Adams, J. M. (2019). The value of worker well-being. *Public Health Reports, 134*(6), 583–586. https://doi.org/10.1177/003335491987843

Aitken-Fox, E., Coffey, J., Dayaram, K., Fitzgerald, S., Gupta, C., McKenna, S., & Wei Tian, A. (2020). *The impact of Covid-19 on human resource management: Avoiding generalisations.* LSE Business Review.

Al-Jubari, I., Mosbah, A., & Salem, S. F. (2022). Employee well-being during COVID-19 pandemic: The role of adaptability, work-family conflict, and organizational response. *Sage Open, 12*(3). https://doi.org/10.1177/21582440221096142

Baumgartner, N. (2020). Build a culture that aligns with people's values. *Harvard Business Review*, 3–18. https://hbr.org/2020/04/build-a-culture-that-aligns-with-peoples-values

Cascella, M., Rajnik, M., Aleem, A., Dulebohn, S. C., & Di Napoli, R. (2023). *Features, evaluation, and treatment of coronavirus (COVID-19)*. Statpearls [internet].

Greenhaus, J. H., Collins, K. M., & Shaw, J. D. (2003). The relation between work-family and quality of life. *Journal of Vocational Behavior, 63*, 510–531.

Hamouche, S. (2021). Human resource management and the COVID-19 crisis: Implications, challenges, opportunities, and future organizational directions. *Journal of Management and Organization*, 1–16. https://doi.org/10.1017/jmo.2021.15

Harju, L. K., Rokka, J., Lopes, M. M., Airoldi, M., & Raïes, K. (2021). Employee well-being profiles during COVID-19 lockdown: A latent profile analysis of French and UK employees. *Frontiers in psychology, 12*, 645300. https://doi.org/10.3389/fpsyg.2021.645300

https://www.ngs-global.com/index.php/perspectives/articles/8-perspectives/articles/746-covid-hr-impact-survey. Accessed on January 23, 2023.

Jain, N., & Aggarwal, S. (2021). Wellbeing of employees during COVID-19 pandemic: A study of innovative HR practices of organisations. *Indian Journal of Public Administration, 67*(4), 573–586. https://doi.org/10.1177/00195561211057383

Knowles, J., Hunsaker, B. T., Grove, H., & James, A. (2022). What is the purpose of your purpose? Your why may not be what you think it is. *Harvard Business Review, 100*(3–4), 36–43.

Lonska, J., Mietule, I., Litavniece, L., Arbidane, I., Vanadzins, I., Matisane, L., & Paegle, L. (2021). Work–life balance of the employed population during the emergency situation of COVID-19 in Latvia. *Frontiers in Psychology, 12*, 682459. https://doi.org/10.3389/fpsyg.2021.682459

Nasreen, A., Varshney, P., & Waseem, C. (2019, September). *Organizational climate in NBFC: Implications on employee engagement* (Vol. 9). Amity Global HRM Review.

https://blogs.lse.ac.uk/businessreview/2020/05/22/the-impact-of-covid-19-on-human-resource-management-avoiding-generalisations

Ruffolo, M., Price, D., Schoultz, M., Leung, J., Bonsaksen, T., Thygesen, H., & Geirdal, A. Ø. (2021). Employment uncertainty and mental health during the COVID-19 pandemic initial social distancing implementation: A cross-national study. *Global Social Welfare: Research, Policy & Practice*, 1–10. https://doi.org/10.1007/s40609-020-00201-4

Sandoval-Reyes, J., Idrovo-Carlier, S., & Duque-Oliva, E. J. (2021, July 2). Remote work, work stress, and work-life during pandemic times: A Latin America situation. *International Journal of Environmental Research and Public Health, 18*(13), 7069. https://doi.org/10.3390/ijerph18137069

Saxena, P., Kovid, R., & Nasreen, A. (2022). Revisiting employee engagement in the new normal: A study of a few select organizations. In *Cases on emerging market responses to the COVID-19 pandemic* (pp. 191–215). IGI Global. https://doi.org/10.4018/978-1-6684-3504-5.ch010

Shirmohammadi, M., Au, W. C., & Beigi, M. (2022). Remote work and work-life balance: Lessons learned from the Covid-19 pandemic and suggestions for HRD practitioners. *Human Resource Development International*, *25*(2), 163–181. https://doi.org/10.1080/13678868.2022.2047380

The Economics Time. (2021). *Pandemic impact: Companies start looking at workers' well-being more closely*. https://economictimes.indiatimes.com/small-biz/sme-sector/pandemic-impact-companies-start-looking-at-workers-well-being-more-closely/articleshow/87270354.cms?utm_source=contentofinterest&utm_medium=text&utm_campaign=cppst. Accessed on October 26, 2021.

Tsipursky, G. (2022). *Does remote work hurt wellbeing and work-life balance?* Forbes. https://www.forbes.com/sites/glebtsipursky/2022/11/01/does-remote-work-hurt-wellbeing-and-work-life-balance/

Verma, R. (2022). Responding to COVID-19: A case of psychological response centers. In *Cases on emerging market responses to the COVID-19 pandemic* (pp. 216–241). IGI Global. https://doi.org/10.4018/978-1-6684-3504-5.ch011

HAPPINESS DYNAMICS OF EMPLOYEES AT THE WORKPLACE: A BIBLIOMETRIC REVIEW

Kajal Sitlani[a], Abhineet Saxena[b], Deepti Sharma[a] and Garima Pancholi[b]

[a]*IIHMR University Jaipur, India*
[b]*Amity University, India*

ABSTRACT

Organizations' culture and environment create a remarkable influence on the minds of the employees. Employees spend a lot of time at the workplace; hence, it is essential to take care of their happiness. Stressful workplace environment reduces the job satisfaction of employees which eventually leads to mental health issues. The study focuses on mapping the publication trends on happiness of employees at their workplace over the years. The mapping was done with the help of Scopus and VOSviewer. The study takes into consideration the research publication on workplace happiness since 2013 from Scopus database using 'Employee Happiness at Workplace' which showed around 104 publications related to happiness till Sept 2022. The database was refined and further analyzed by VOSviewer version 1.6.16. Though much research has been done on employee happiness and lot many scales are developed on the happiness index, but bibliometric analysis is yet to be carried out on workplace happiness, it's development, forms and factors. This analysis will bridge the gap of researchers and provide them directions to carry on the research for future.

Keywords: Happiness; workplace happiness; productivity; organizational culture; well-being; happy

1. INTRODUCTION

This era is an era of change in all vivid areas, and one of the major areas is employees at the workplace. The workplace is an important not to be neglected part of one's life. A person spends on average 8–9 hours of his life at the workplace. The attitude or emotion which an employee has at workplace determines their behaviour at home too. The two

Resilient Businesses for Sustainability
Advanced Series in Management, Volume 34B, 37–50

Published under exclusive licence by Emerald Publishing Limited
ISSN: 1877-6361/doi:10.1108/S1877-63612024000034B004

aspects are almost intervened with each other. Professional front will have an impact on personal front and vice versa. Happiness at workplace impacts the productivity, relationship, working environment and of course the employee's emotions not only the employee's productivity but their personal life. Hence, it is very important to keep himself happy at the workplace.

In today's competitive and stressful era, happiness at the workplace is essential to foster a healthy organizational culture. The organizational culture affects the employee's well-being and thus contributes to enhanced productivity at the workplace. The literature shows that a lot of studies are being done in the field of workplace happiness and broader aspects like well-being and job satisfaction. Happiness is considered valuable by a country like Bhutan. They have devised Gross National Happiness (GNH) which is an indicator of happiness and will also drive economy. According to Thinley (1998, 2004), 'Gross National Happiness is more important than Gross National Product'. He also focuses on the fact that every human being desires to be happy and a driver for aspiration and behaviour. When a country focuses on the happiness of its citizens, then the culture is also woven with the thread of happiness at all fronts of life.

Happiness at the workplace is a feeling of being satisfied with the systems, procedures and culture. If the organization expects employees to be efficient and effective, this in turn is possible when they are happy. Happiness at the workplace leads to a sustainable workforce. Fisher (2010) defines workplace happiness as a feeling of being happy with respect to the job, its attributes and the workplace itself. Fisher (2010) emphasized that every individual has a goal for seeking happiness. People can really contribute well when they are happy. Their creativity and innovation are also at peak when they are imbibing emotions of happiness. The belief that monetary benefits motivate employees and makes them happy stands no longer true. The desire of people has shifted from money to more concrete desires, a place which gives happiness not just money.

Problems like low productivity, more stress, lower motivation level and lower job satisfaction are very common among employees, which the management find difficult to deal with. These problems and challenges can be resolved by a more strategic move. One of the best possible solutions could be to emphasize creating happiness at the workplace for the workforce. One such research survey found by Gallup (Gupta, 2012) identified that happy employees can deal better with organizational relationships, stress and change. Jyung et al. (2021) in their study analyzed how happiness plays a significant role in selecting the jobs either based on enjoyment associated with doing the job and the perceived competence required to the job. The result revealed that happier people prefer enjoyment criteria over competence. These people stay longer with the organizations and can retain their jobs as they enjoy their work.

Much research is conducted in developing countries on happiness. One such research was conducted in employees of small and medium-sized enterprises in Thailand by Chaiprasit and Santidhiraku (2011). The research suggested that happiness of employees is affected by factors like leadership, relationship and quality of work life. Leaders play an important role in creating an organizational culture which is conducive for employees. They are a source of inspiration and motivation for employees. The quality of the work life on the other hand helps in improving the physical as well as mental health of the employees and making the employees more productive. They provide directions to employees and help in integration of individual goals to organizational goals. Better relationships at the workplace among employees as well as employer and employee create a conducive work environment and foster team spirit within the organization.

A study conducted by Atan et al. (2021) explored the impact of workplace happiness on workforce sustainability. It was being analyzed that the organizations can motivate the employees by taking care of the needs and demands of the employees. Employee motivation brings happiness to the workplace. Workplace happiness can be brought by providing employees with better career opportunities, monetary and non-monetary rewards and recognition as well as improving interpersonal communication at the workplace. Gadanecz and Kun (2022) analyzed the workplace happiness as well as well-being and the relationship of these variables with psychological capital. Hope and optimism dimension showed a strong correlation with well-being and workplace happiness for teachers in Hungary. Hope dimension helps in realistic goal setting, and that will lead to better well-being. Whereas optimism dimension results in expectations, which when fulfilled lead to happiness.

A study by Singh and Aggarwal (2018) identified four factors affecting workplace happiness. Work experiences, repulsive feelings for work, motivation as well as flow affect happiness of employees at workplace. Supportive or unsupportive experiences at the workplace have a strong effect on the employee's happiness at the workplace. The relationship between the boss and the employees causes work repulsive behaviour as the bosses are holding more power in any work setting. This creates a feeling of unhappiness among the employees, and it is one of the major reasons for employee turnover. Employees that are more inclined and engaged with work are happier. The flow of work helps to keep the employees motivated and inspired, and these employees feel satisfied and happy.

Unanue et al. (2021) identified a link between happiness and organizational citizenship behaviour. Behaviour considering aspects like kindness, generosity, etc. helps in making the employees happy at the workplace. The result of the study revealed that if the employees are happy, they will feel good, and that will help them to contribute more to the organization. Hence, happiness leads to positivity, and employees demonstrate organization citizenship behaviour.

2. METHODOLOGY

The methodology used for this research consists of framing the research objective as well as the extraction of data from the relevant source. Bibliometric analysis is being done using a structured procedure.

- The research starts with framing the research questions and designing/identifying probable solutions for these questions.
- Database is identified, and the search query string is recognized which could represent the subject area thoroughly.
- The database then shows all the research papers that contain the keywords in their title and abstract.
- The resultant research papers are further refined according to publication stage, languages, subject area, countries, etc.
- The further refined research papers are exported through CSV file into excel.
- With the extracted data, bibliometric analysis is performed.
- Data visualization and network analysis is done using VOSviewer.
- Then the interpretation of the findings is done.

3. OBJECTIVES

The study was based on the following research objectives:

- Quantitative assessment of happiness publication to determine the future trend in the field of happiness.
- Predicting the probable area of research in the field of happiness, its type and factors affecting it.
- Determining the journals focusing on the study related to happiness, to publish the work in those journals.
- Finding the keywords related to happiness to have future directions for the research.

3.1 Data Extraction

With the help of VOSviewer software, four clusters were identified.

4. RESULTS AND DISCUSSIONS

4.1 Publication Trends

4.1.1 Publication by Year

From the Scopus database, it shows that 104 documents were retrieved from the search string of TITLE-ABS-KEY 'Employee Happiness at Workplace'. Table 1 represents publications from the past 10 years. The analysis reveals that in 2013, the publication shows two papers and the number increased to 14 in 2021. The data till September 2022 reveal that 12 papers are already published. The figure shows an increase in the number of publications since 2019. A sample of 86 articles was taken for the study. The increase in number of research on the area of happiness suggests the concern of people for a better life.

Fig. 1 shows progressive increase in the publications related to 'Happiness' till 2020 with 20, but in 2021, decline in publication is clearly seen with only 14 publications in comparison to 2020.

The concept of 'Happiness' is an indispensable part of our lives which requires sheer perseverance to enhance the quality of life.

Table 1. Documents Published in Past 10 years.

Year	Documents	Percentage
2022	16	17.40
2021	15	16.30
2020	20	21.75
2019	14	15.21
2018	7	7.60
2017	8	8.70
2016	3	3.26
2015	3	3.26
2014	3	3.26
2013	3	3.26

Source: Data from Scopus.

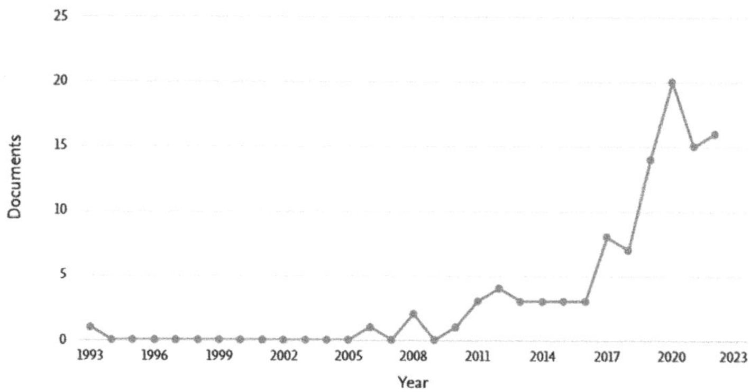

Fig. 1. Documents Published by Year Through Scopus Database. *Source:* Data from Scopus; graph created by authors.

Table 1 represents that the term 'Employee Happiness at Workplace' has gained momentum in research from 2017, but the researchers should continue the research work as it will not only enhance the quality of life of the individual, but it will also help the organizations to make workplace a great place to work.

4.2 Articles Published by Subject Area

Under different subject areas, various articles got published on the topic 'Employee Happiness at Workplace'. Out of different fields, Fig. 2 and Table 2 represents that the Business Management and Accounting domain has the highest publications with 44 documents which makes up 25.9% of total publications.

Then Social Science has 27 documents published which 16.3% followed by Medicine with 17 documents publications which is 10%.

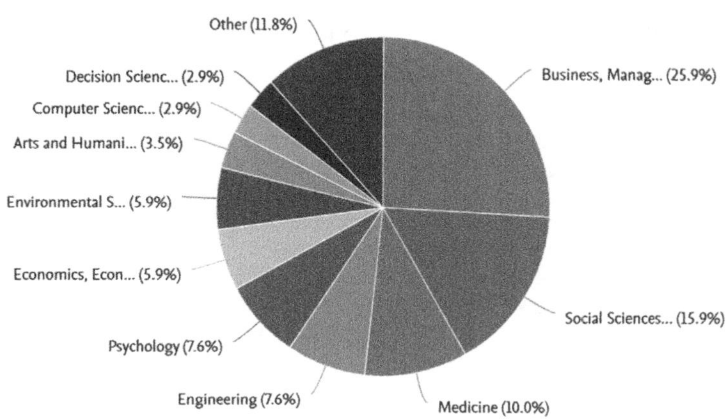

Fig. 2. Documents Published by Subject Area Through Scopus Database. *Source:* Data from Scopus; graph created by authors.

Table 2. Documents Published by Subject Area.

Subject Area	Documents	Percentage
Business Management and Accounting	44	25.99
Social Sciences	27	15.99
Medicine	17	10
Engineering	13	7.6
Psychology	13	7.6
Economics, Econometrics and Finance	10	5.9
Environmental Science	10	5.9
Arts and Humanities	6	3.5
Computer Science	5	2.9
Decision Sciences	5	2.9
Other	19	11.8

Source: Data from Scopus; table created by authors.

The engineering and psychology streams almost have same publication which is about 7.6%. The least publication is from the fields of Decision Science and Computer Science with 2.9% only.

4.3 Top Principal Author of the Last Decade

Many proficient authors are working in the subject area of Happiness at the Workplace. Fig. 3 and Table 3 represent top 10 authors who have worked maximum in the subject area. Dahiya, R. and Isa, K. has the highest publications with three documents each on the topic among all the authors. The authors named Akmal, S., Hati, L., Jandu, K., Panda, M., Peiro, J, M., Soriano, A., Pradhan, R. K., Tenah, S, S. have published two articles on the topic individually.

4.4 Country-Wise Publication

Fig. 4 and Table 4 represent that out of total 104 publications, 73 documents have been published from top 10 countries on the topic of 'Employee Happiness at Workplace'. India has got the maximum number of 21 documents published on the subject area followed by

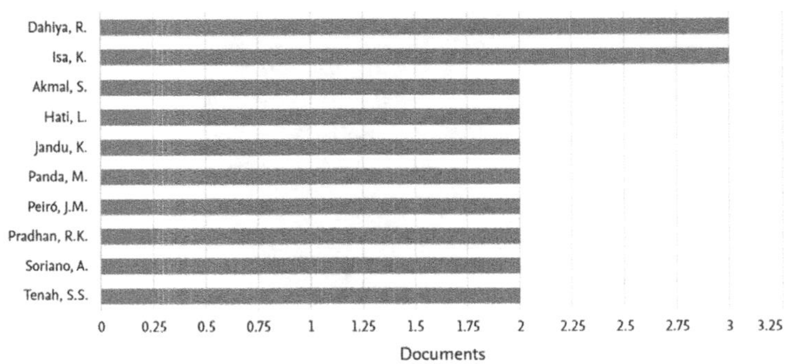

Fig. 3. Documents Published by Authors Through Scopus Database. *Source:* Data from Scopus; graph created by authors.

Table 3. Top 10 Documents Published by Authors.

Author	Documents	Percentage
Dahiya, R.	3	13.64
Isa, K.	3	13.64
Akmal, S.	2	9.09
Hati, L.	2	9.09
Jandu, K.	2	9.09
Panda, M.	2	9.09
Peiro, J. M.	2	9.09
Pradhan, R. K.	2	9.09
Soriano, A.	2	9.09
Tenah, S. S.	2	9.09

Source: Data from Scopus; table created by authors.

the United States with 17 published documents. The third country in the list is Malaysia with 14 published documents. The rest of the countries have low publications of documents on subject areas. The list includes Australia, Netherlands, Spain, UK, China, Germany and Hungry.

India has the highest number of publications that suggests that in India there is high concern for employee happiness. The above-mentioned countries are trying to gaze at the depth of the topic for further enhancement and elimination of the hindrance in the way.

4.5 Highest Cited Documents

Table 5 shows the top 10 documents which have the highest citations. The research paper published by Song, Y and Gao, J with the title 'Does telework stress out workers? A study on working at Home and subjective well-being for wages/salary workers' published in 2020 has 68 citations, which is highest. The 'Workplace based organizational interventions promoting mental health and happiness among healthcare workers: A realistic review' research paper was cited second highest citations with 51 citations, and it was authored by Gray, P., Senabe, S., Naicker, N., Kgalamano, S., Yassi, A., Spiegel, J. M. followed by 'Tossing and Turning – insomnia in relation to occupational stress, rumination, fatigue

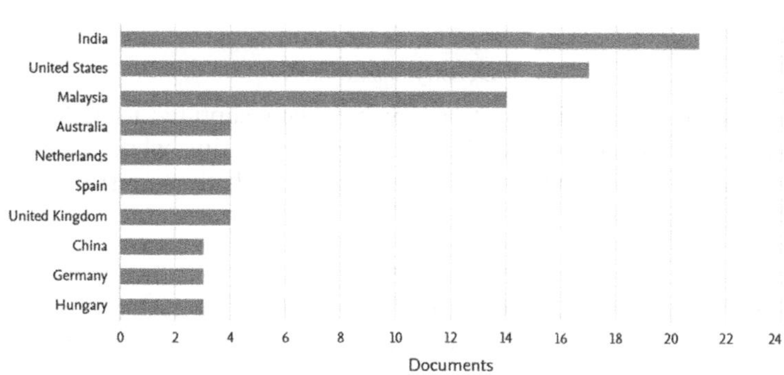

Fig. 4. Documents Published by Country Through Scopus Database. *Source:* Data from Scopus; graph created by authors.

Table 4. Top 10 Documents Published by Country.

Country	Documents	Percentage
India	21	27.27
United States	17	22.07
Malaysia	14	18.18
Australia	4	5.19
Netherlands	4	5.19
Spain	4	5.19
United Kingdom	4	5.19
China	3	3.89
Germany	3	3.89
Hungary	3	3.89

Source: Data from Scopus; table created by authors.

and well-being' (2019) research paper which was authored by Kompier et al. (2012), and it has 50 citations.

Among these top 10 highest cited documents, the research paper titled 'Psychological capital and career commitment: the mediating effect of subjective well-being' whose authors are Singhal and Rastogi (2018) and it has 33 citations. This is the only Indian author research paper that has managed to come in top 10 cited documents.

4.6 Co-occurrence of Keywords

The co-occurrence of keywords refers to frequency of recurring keywords in proximity of words that are found in different research papers across different databases. Co-occurrence include keywords that are cognate to each other on same topic but they are not.

Out of total 631 keywords, 31 meet the threshold of minimum occurrences of keywords as 5. The co-occurrence of the keywords represents the crucial points in the area of employee happiness. The co-occurrence of the keywords is vital to understand the direction of research and its vitality.

Table 6 shows the occurrence of various keywords along with the total link strength. The keyword 'Workplace' is the highest occurred keyword with 30 occurrences, and the total link strength is 210 followed by the word 'Happiness' with 35 occurrences and total link strength of 180.

4.7 Density Visualization

Fig. 5 represents the density visualization which is being captured using VOSviewer. The keywords workplace and happiness show the highest density, while adult and humans show moderate density, and the word questionnaire reveals the lowest density in total.

4.8 Cluster Analysis

Table 7 and Fig. 6 represent the network analysis and different clusters of co-occurrence of keywords. Keywords co-occurrence highlights the trends in the research area of workplace happiness. Keyword analysis reveals that only 10 keywords meet the criteria of minimum of seven occurrences of keywords. The analysis identified four clusters. The four clusters are represented by different colours, Red, Green, Blue and Yellow. Eleven keywords are

Table 5. Top 10 Highest Cited Documents.

Authors	Document Title	Year	Source	Citations
Song, Y., Gao, J.	Does telework stress out workers? A study on working at home and subjective well-being for wages/salary workers	(2020)	Journal of Happiness Studies	68
Gray, P., Senabe, S., Naicker, N., Kgalamano, S., Yassi, A., Spiegel, J. M.	Workplace based organizational interventions promoting mental health and happiness among healthcare workers: A realistic review	(2019)	International Journal of Environmental Research and Public Health	51
Kompier, M. A. J., Taris, T. W., van Veldhovan, M.	Tossing and turning – Insomnia in relation to occupational stress, rumination, fatigue, and well-being	(2012)	Scandinavian Journal of Work, Environment, and Health	50
Korpela, K., De Bloom, J., Sianoja, M., Pasanen, T., Kinnunen, U.	Nature at home and at work: Naturally good? Links between window views, indoor plants, outdoor activities, and employee well-being over one year	(2017)	Landscape and Urban Planning	49
Straume, L. V., Vitterso, J.	Happiness inspiration and fully functioning person: Separating hedonic and eudaimonic well-being in the workplace	(2012)	Journal of Positive Psychology	46
Dickson-Swift, V., Fox, C., Marshall, K., Welch, N., Willis, J.	What really improves employee health and wellbeing findings from regional Australian workplaces	(2014)	International Journal of Workplace Health Management	42
Merrill, R. M., Aldana, S. G., Garrett, J., Ross, C.	Effectiveness of a workplace wellness programme for maintaining health and promoting healthy behaviours	(2011)	Journal of Occupational and Environmental Medicine	40
Golden, L., Henly, J. R., Lambert, S.	Work schedule flexibility: A contributor to happiness?	(2013)	Journal of Social Research and Policy	37
Singhal, H., Rastogi, R.	Psychological capital and career commitment: The mediating effect of subjective well-being	(2018)	Management Decisions	33

Source: Data from Scopus table created by authors.

identified in the first cluster. In the first Red cluster has the highest occurrence. This can be marked with the theme of Happiness and Productivity. The second Green cluster is represented by 10 keywords. Whereas the third Blue cluster is identified with eight keywords which can be represented Happiness and Well-being and the fourth Yellow cluster is the one with two keywords.

4.9 Discussion

RQ1. Quantitative assessment of happiness publication to determine the future trend in the field of happiness.

Table 6. Co-occurrence of Keywords.

Keyword	Occurrences	Total Link Strength
Workplace	30	210
Happiness	35	180
Human	19	180
Humans	13	141
Article	14	129
Female	11	125
Male	11	125
Adult	11	124
Employee	13	102
Questionnaire	9	97

Source: Data from Scopus; table created by authors.

The publication of papers on the topic reveals the interest of researchers. The database of Scopus tells us that in the year 2013, there were two papers published on 'Happiness'. This number increased to 14 in the year 2021. This increase took place after the year 2019. After that, there was a decline to 11 publications in the year 2022. More research needs to be done in the field so that better strategies, models and policies can be developed for happy people.

RQ2. Predicting the probable area of research in the field of happiness, its type and factors affecting it.

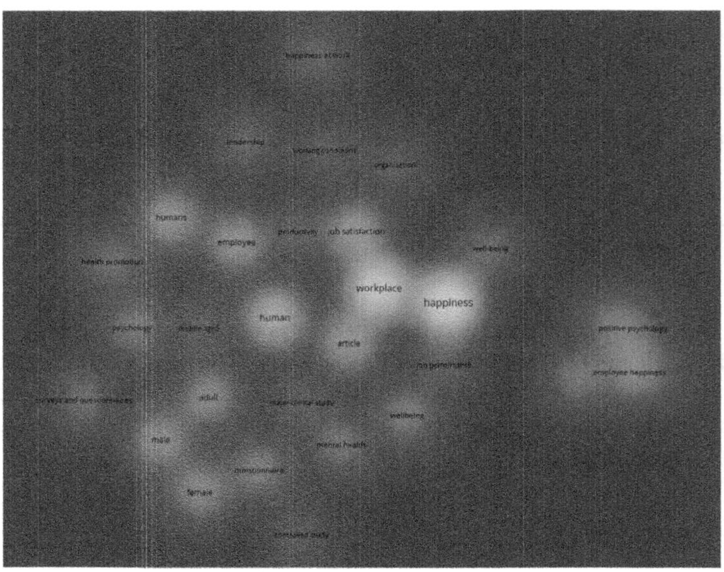

Fig. 5. Representing Density Visualization. *Source:* Data from Scopus; graph created by authors.

Table 7. Cluster Analysis of Keywords.

Cluster	Keywords	Occurrences	Total Link Strength
Red	• Article • Employee • Happiness at work • Human • Job satisfaction • Leadership • Organization • Productivity • Well-being • Working condition • Workplace	• 14 • 13 • 06 • 19 • 14 • 06 • 05 • 05 • 09 • 30 • 05	• 129 • 102 • 011 • 180 • 072 • 043 • 048 • 042 • 085 • 210 • 047
Green	• Adult • Male • Female • Questionnaire • Psychology • Surveys and questionnaire • Middle aged • Mental health • Health promotion • Humans	• 11 • 11 • 11 • 09 • 08 • 07 • 05 • 08 • 07 • 13	• 124 • 125 • 125 • 097 • 092 • 81 • 68 • 66 • 52 • 141
Blue	• Happiness • Employee well-being • Employee happiness • Job performance • Positive psychology • Psychological capital • Subjective well-being • Well-being	• 35 • 05 • 08 • 05 • 06 • 05 • 08 • 07	• 180 • 007 • 009 • 033 • 012 • 004 • 021 • 031
Yellow	• Controlled study • Major clinical study	• 05 • 05	• 047 • 046

Source: Data from Scopus; table created by authors.

The research data depict that not much work has been done in the relevant area, and it requires more research in almost all fields, may be related to 'corporate working and Happiness', 'Technological changes and managing Happiness in fast moving era'.

Also, more work needs to be done in 'Personal Happiness Enhancement'. The factors that need to be identified for happiness and those factors which vary due to circumstances and environment are also the probable areas of future research.

RQ3. Help in determining the journals focusing on the study related to happiness, to publish the work in those journals.

The research data reveal the journals where one can find the article related to happiness. It also suggests the areas or categories of these journals.

RQ4. Finding the keywords related to happiness to have future directions for the research.

The various keywords that can be taken for future research can be happiness, job performance, well-being, employee happiness, psychological capital, employee well-being,

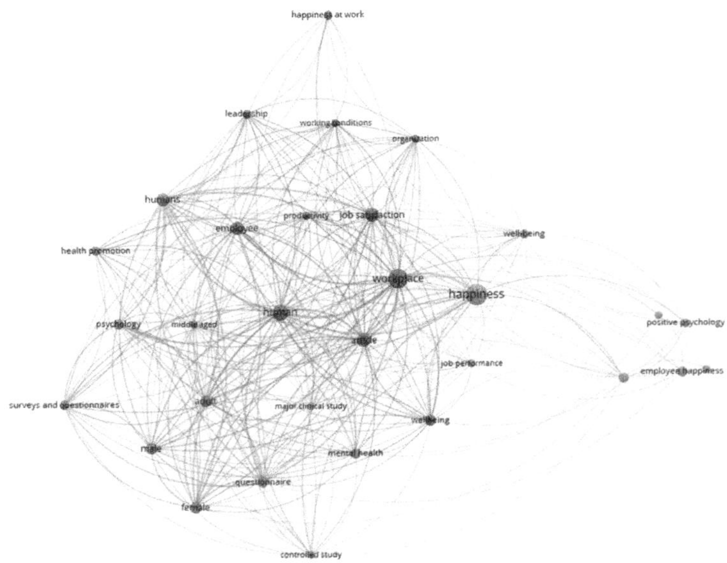

Fig. 6. Network and Cluster Analysis With VOSViewer. *Source:* Data from Scopus; graph created by authors.

positive psychology and subjective well-being. These words have more occurrences (32 in total) in the research and can be taken forward for research.

4.10 Suggestions and Implications

The bibliometric analysis revealed that the employee's happiness at the workplace can be boosted by following strategies:

- *Care and Respect for Employees:* First and foremost, the important thing for an organization is to keep employees happy by providing care and respect for the employees. It provides the employees with a feeling of warmth, a feeling of being associated with and leading to happiness in the workplace. Companies like Netflix give 1 year of paid leave to the employees who became new parents. This is one way of showing that the organization cares for its employees.
- *Work–Life Balance:* The work–life balance is the most crucial thing for the employees. The policy of the organization needs to be designed in such a manner that proper work–life balance can be managed. If employees are happy in their personal life, then they are more productive at the workplace.
- *Transparency, Honesty and Credibility:* Employees expect that the organization provides transparency and honesty in various aspects of the organization. It may be related to the benefits, career progression, etc. These provide a sense of satisfaction which results in happiness in the employees.
- *Recognize and Reward Employees:* Motivation always makes employees dedicated to the work. This motivation comes from the recognition and rewards given to the employees. These rewards and recognition make employees happy, which in turn motivates them to perform better in the organization. The policy of the organization can be made that focuses on extrinsic and intrinsic compensation for the employees. It also creates a

healthy environment which is a win-win situation for the organization and for the employees.

- *Encourage Open Communication:* Communication is very crucial in all aspects of life whether personal or professional. When people communicate, they share their experiences, their feelings, their expectations and work-related topics. This communication resolves many issues, provides solutions to many things; also this helps to develop better understanding among employees which results in happiness.
- *Organization Culture:* The top leaders play a significant role in creating a culture that is congenial, inducive and trustworthy. Feeling of openness, collaboration and proactiveness will be reciprocated by the employees in such an authentic culture.

4.11 Limitations and Future Scope of the Study

The publication revels that not much work has been done on 'Employee Happiness at Workplace' as only 104 research papers were retrieved through Scopus database. The research needs to be done on 'Employee Happiness at Workplace' considering various demographic factors and geographical locations. The researchers need to take this topic as vital one for overall growth and satisfaction of people. This can be the future of study in organizational culture and environment. There can be development of approaches, and models of happiness can be created. Further based on findings of present research, some policy can be devised to enhance happiness at organization level as well as at national level.

4.12 Conclusion

Workplace happiness is an important dimension for retention of employees and to promote resilience at the workplace. A happy employee is a satisfied employee. The study will help the organizations to understand the need to keep the employees happy at their workplace. In the study, publications were analyzed using VOSviewer. The study explored the regions where mostly the research related to happiness was carried out. There was a rise in publication after 2018, and most of the studies were done in India, United States and Malaysia. The co-occurrence of the keyword suggests 'workplace' and 'happiness' are the most crucial keywords.

A structured and systematic analysis was carried out through this study with the help of which clusters of research were identified. The two clusters on which further research can be carried on are happiness and productivity and the other is happiness and well-being. The study will help future researchers to understand areas where there are research gaps. One of the major limitations was that the research was based on Scopus database, and there will be variations when the research would be done on other databases. Secondly, future studies can be carried out on broader samples of articles.

REFERENCES

Atan, A., Özgit, H., & Silman, F. (2021). Happiness at Work and Motivation for a Sustainable Workforce: Evidence from Female Hotel Employees. *Sustainability*, *13*, 7778. https://doi.org/10.3390/su13147778

Chaiprasit, K., & Santidhiraku, O. (2011). Happiness at work of employees in small and medium-sized enterprises, Thailand. *Procedia – Social and Behavioral Sciences*, *25*, 189–200.

Dickson-Swift, V., Fox, C., Marshall, K., Welch, N., & Willis, J. (2014). What really improves employee health and wellbeing findings from regional Australian workplaces. *International Journal of Workplace Health Management*, *7*(3). https://doi.org/10.1108/IJWHM-10-2012-0026

Fisher, C. (2010). Happiness at work. *International Journal of Management Reviews, 12*, 384–412. https://doi.org/10.1111/j.1468-2370.2009.00270.x

Gadanecz, P., & Kun, A. (2022). Work place happiness, well-being and their relationship with psychological capital: A study of Hungarian teachers. *Current Psychology*, 185–199. https://doi.org/10.1007/s12144-019-00550-0

Golden, L. H., Henly, J. R., & Lambert, S. (2013). Work schedule flexibility: A contributor to happiness? *Journal of Social Research and Policy, 4*(2). https://doi.org/10.2139/ssrn.2129520

Gray, P., Senabe, S., Naicker, N., Kgalamano, S., Yassi, A., & Spiegel, J. M. (2019, November). Workplace based organizational interventions promoting mental health and happiness among healthcare workers: A realistic review. *International Journal of Environmental Research and Public Health, 16*(22), 4396. https://doi.org/10.3390/ijerph16224396

Gupta, V. (2012). Importance of being happy at work. *International Journal of Research and Development, 1*(1), 9–14.

Jyung, M., Choi, I., & Shim, Y. (2021). Enjoyment versus competence trade-off: Happy people value enjoyment over competence more than unhappy people. *Journal of Happiness Studies, 22*(8), 3679–3701. https://doi.org/10.1007/s10902-021-00374-5

Kompier, M. A. J., Taris, T. W., & van Veldhovan, M. (2012, May). Tossing and turning – Insomnia in relation to occupational stress, rumination, fatigue and well-being. *Scandinavian Journal of Work, Environment & Health, 38*(3), 238–246. https://doi.org/10.5271/sjweh.3263

Korpela, K., De Bloom, J., Sianoja, M., Pasanen, T., & Kinnunen, U. (2017). Nature at home and at work: Naturally good? Links between window views, indoor plants, outdoor activities and employee well-being over one year. *Landscape and Urban Planning, 160*, 38–47. https://doi.org/10.1016/j.landurbplan.2016.12.005

Merrill, R. M., Aldana, S. G., Garrett, J., & Ross, C. (2011, July). Effectiveness of a workplace wellness program for maintaining health and promoting healthy behaviors. *Journal of Occupational and Environmental Medicine, 53*(7), 782–787. https://doi.org/10.1097/JOM.0b013e318220c2f4

Singh, S., & Aggarwal, Y. (2018). Happiness at work scale: Construction and psychometric validation of a measure using mixed method approach. *Journal of Happiness Studies, 19*(5), 1439–1465. https://doi.org/10.1007/s10902-017-9882-x

Singhal, H., & Rastogi, R. (2018). Psychological capital and career commitment: The mediating effect of subjective well-being. *Management Decision, 56*(2), 458–473. https://doi.org/10.1108/MD-06-2017-0579

Song, Y., & Gao, J. (2020). Does telework stress employees out? A study on working at home and subjective well-being for wage/salary workers. *Journal of Happiness Studies, 21*(3). https://doi.org/10.1007/s10902-019-00196-6

Straume, L. V., & Vitterso, J. (2012). Happiness inspiration and fully functioning person: Separating hedonic and eudaimonic well-being in the workplace. *The Journal of Positive Psychology, 7*(5), 387–398. https://doi.org/10.1080/17439760.2012.711348

Thinley, L. J. (1998, 2004). Values and development: Gross national happiness, happy life years: A measure of gross national happiness. In *Indigeneity and universality in social science: A south Asian response (2004)*. https://www.uwosh.edu/sirt/wp-content/uploads/sites/86/2020/04/4.Re-thinkingdev.pdf

Unanue, W., Barros, E., & Gómez, M. (2021). The longitudinal link between organizational citizenship behaviors and three different models of happiness. *International Journal of Environmental Research and Public Health, 18*(12).

LEARNING ORGANIZATION AND ORGANIZATIONAL RESILIENCE: A LITERATURE REVIEW

Sreeja K.[a] and Hemalatha K. G.[b]

[a]*NSB Academy, India*
[b]*Dayananda Sagar College of Engineering, India*

ABSTRACT

The primary goal of the present chapter is to analyze and evaluate the importance and significance of human capital in fostering company resilience through the process of learning. In addition to the inherent interconnectedness between organizational resilience and learning organizations, there appears to be less understanding regarding the impact of learning organizations on organizational resilience. To present a succinct overview of the findings, a thorough analysis of empirical studies on organizational resilience and the notion of a learning organization was conducted. The outcomes of the research reveal a learning organization ensures its effective response to unexpected events, crises and challenging conditions. The implementation of ongoing learning initiatives fosters employee engagement and enhances the overall resilience of the organization. To enhance resilience, confront difficulties directly, endure and prosper, organizations must actively acquire knowledge and skills to adapt. Learning organizations cultivate a skilled workforce, which afterwards serves as a robust defence against unfavourable circumstances. The primary objective of this study is to investigate and provide answers to the following research inquiries by conducting an analysis of empirical research on learning organization and organizational resilience: (1) What are the fundamental themes identified in the literature on these concepts? (2) How are learning organization and organizational resilience interconnected? Firstly, defining the concept of resilient enterprises is crucial. Secondly, understanding the concept of learning organizations holds significant importance and the significance of fostering a learning organizational culture to enhance organizational resilience.

Resilient Businesses for Sustainability
Advanced Series in Management, Volume 34B, 51–59

ISSN: 1877-6361/doi:10.1108/S1877-63612024000034B005

Keywords: Organizational resilience; literature review; significance; learning organization; human capital

1. INTRODUCTION

The notion of resilience has gained significant popularity within the realm of business and management research since the onset of the 21st century. According to Lengnick-Hall et al. (2011), the concept of organizational resilience can be defined as the capacity of a company to successfully absorb and adapt to unexpected disruptions, while also strategically responding and taking advantage of these disruptions in order to guarantee the ongoing viability of the organization. Before an organization can fully develop its potential for resilience, it is imperative to have individuals who possess the quality of resilience. The concept of personal resilience pertains to an individual's capacity to recover from negative emotional encounters and adapt successfully to the dynamic challenges presented by their surroundings. The notion of organizational resilience comprises the capacity to effectively absorb and withstand disruptive events, restructure internal processes, acquire new knowledge and adjust strategies accordingly. It is characterized by the key capacities of resistance, adaptation and adaptability.

A learning organization can be characterized as an entity that actively promotes and cultivates a culture of ongoing learning and consistently adjusts its strategies and practices in response to the dynamic nature of its surroundings. According to Murray and Donegan (2003), learning organizations foster a positive environment that fosters creativity, leading to improved behaviour and adaptability among individuals. The research suggests that employees who receive consistent praise for their ability to overcome obstacles and generate innovative solutions in the face of change are more likely to develop a readiness for future changes. This readiness, in turn, contributes to the development of employee resilience (Sundblad et al., 2013).

The extent and depth of learning are critical in shaping the conditions required for not just surviving in a constantly changing environment but also for effectively strategizing and executing successful actions in the long run. It can be argued that numerous modern companies display the attributes commonly associated with a learning organization. Moreover, it is imperative for any enterprise aspiring to navigate through crises or unexpected shifts to acquire the necessary knowledge and skills, namely by operating with a focused approach, comprehending the intricacies of the market and their own position within it, devising adaptable strategies, surmounting obstacles and proactively cultivating resilience.

2. PROBLEM STATEMENT

The relationship between organizational resilience and learning organizations is indeed noteworthy. However, it appears that our understanding of the impact of learning organizations on organizational resilience is limited.

3. RESEARCH GAP

The existence of a research gap is a crucial aspect to consider in any scholarly investigation. While the existing body of literature offers numerous studies on the impact of organizational learning process and organizational resilience, it is worth noting that at present, there is a notable paucity of research investigating the significance of learning organizational culture in relation to organizational resilience.

4. OBJECTIVES

The following is a list of the study's objectives:

- Acquaintance with the idea of organizational resilience.
- To comprehend the learning organization paradigm.
- To examine the significance of learning organization for organizational resilience.

5. RESEARCH METHODOLOGY

This paper presents a comprehensive analysis of the existing scholarly literature pertaining to the topics of learning organizations and organizational resilience. This is a conceptual paper written after collecting secondary data from existing journal articles in the area of research.

6. ORGANIZATIONAL RESILIENCE IN LITERATURE

Holling (1973) introduced the notion of 'resilience' as a metric for evaluating the capacity of an ecological system to withstand unexpected disruptions and later recover from them. According to Woods (2006), resilience is perceived as a broader capacity of a system to effectively manage and navigate through unexpected changes and disruptions that do not align with its established approach or framework for adaptation. Subsequently, individuals with expertise in diverse disciplines, such as management (Sheffi, 2005), positive psychology (Powley, 2009) and engineering (Hollnagel et al., 2006), proceeded to employ this particular methodology. The concept of 'resilience' in organization-related literature is still underdeveloped, despite being referenced by authors such as Mallak (1998), Tierney (2003) as well as Mousa et al. (2018). These authors have used the concept to discuss the implementation of professional education and growth opportunities by reputable organizations with the aim of managing crises and anticipating changes. However, further exploration and analysis are needed to fully understand and articulate the significance and implications of resilience in organizational contexts.

Resilience in the corporate setting is regarded as a strategic approach, as posited by Williams et al. (2017) and Duchek (2020), wherein resources are consistently aligned with desired outcomes. The concept of organizational resilience, according to the studies conducted by Cooper et al. (2014), Annarelli and Nonino (2016), Lengnick-Hall et al. (2011) and Clément and Rivera (2017), the term 'resilience' pertains to an organization's ability to endure and adequately address difficult situations as well as to adjust and thrive in the face of sudden and unfavourable transformations. The concept of resilience has been identified as one crucial determinant of organizational performance in the present-day global context. It is considered to be an essential competency that organizations must possess in order to thrive in the modern business landscape (Britt et al., 2016; Näswall et al., 2013).

The concept of organizational resilience, as discussed by Gittel et al. (2006) and Cheng (2007), involves the strategic implementation of proactive measures aimed at effectively managing a particular crisis and eventually achieve a commendable degree of operational performance. According to Duchek (2014), resilience of organizations pertains to the corporation's ability to anticipate and effectively address difficult circumstances. This includes responding to unexpected events and transforming threats into opportunities, all of which contribute to the overall development of the organization (Hamel & Vaelikangas, 2003). Duchek (2020) proposes a conceptualization of resilience that encompasses three distinct stages: anticipation, coping and adaptation. In the course of anticipation, organizations actively engage in monitoring and identifying potential risks, ensuring that they are adequately prepared to address and mitigate them. In order to effectively address an unforeseen event, organizations must first acknowledge and embrace the reality of the situation. This acceptance serves as a crucial foundation for designing and implementing appropriate solutions. One must engage in retrospective analysis of the incident and extract valuable insights from it subsequent to its occurrence. In summary, it can be argued that an organization's resilience is often determined by its ability to effectively prepare for, manage and adjust to challenging circumstances. However, it is important to note that true resilience is only proven when an organization successfully overcomes setbacks caused by adversity.

Certain businesses have made a deliberate effort to establish and maintain a culture centred on resilience, going so far as to develop their own unique models for fostering resilience. IBM, a prominent technology company, has created a resilience framework that encompasses various crucial components. These components include staff knowledge, data security, business continuity management, integrated risk management and market readiness. This framework was developed by IBM in 2004, as stated by the IBM Corporation.

7. THE LEARNING ORGANIZATION CONCEPT

In 1990, Peter M. Senge authored a book termed 'The Fifth Discipline: The Art and Practice of the Learning Organisation'. This seminal piece of literature presented the notion of the learning organization and presented a model that consisted of five essential 'learning disciplines'. These disciplines include personal mastery, mental models, the cultivation of a shared vision, systems thinking and team learning. The author proposes that individuals should abandon their preconceived notions or mental models. They should instead focus on developing personal mastery, which involves being receptive to different perspectives. Additionally, it is important for individuals to acquire a comprehensive understanding of their organization's operations through systems thinking, which emphasizes interconnectedness rather than linear cause-and-effect relationships. Furthermore, the author suggests that individuals should collaborate to establish a shared vision for the future and actively work together as a team to achieve that vision. According to Senge (1990), a learning organization can be defined as an environment in which individuals constantly improve their capacity to attain desired objectives. It is a setting that fosters the development of innovative and broad-minded thought processes (Fig. 1). In such an organization, collective aspirations are liberated, and individuals are actively participated in the educational endeavour of acquiring knowledge and skills pertaining to collaborative learning.

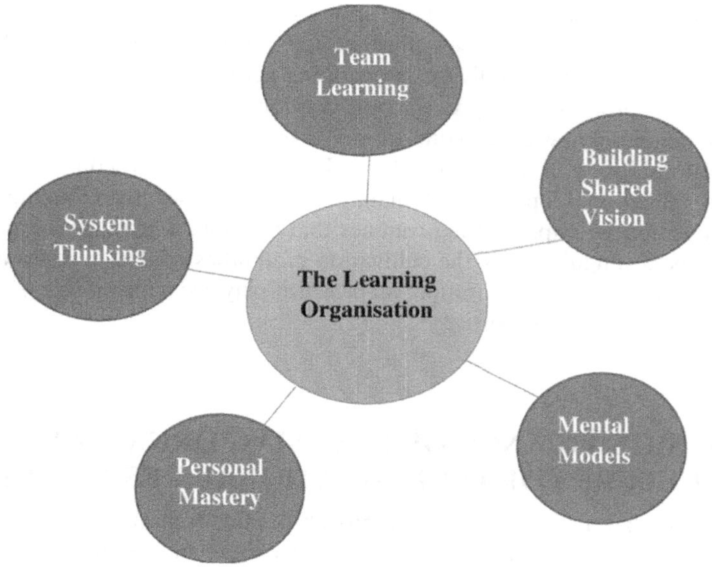

Fig. 1. The Learning Organization: Adapted From Senge, 1990.

According to N. Longworth (2018), a crucial element of a learning organization is the process of learning through activity, whereby individuals engage in reflection and strive to enhance their own practice. The adoption of this particular approach presents the potential for the exploration of novel experiences and the acquisition of knowledge. In light of the rapidly evolving practice environment, it is imperative for individuals to engage in continuous learning. This is due to the fact that learning fosters the development of novel perspectives, which in turn facilitate the necessary adaptations in practice. The distinction between the point at which learning concludes and activities commence or the point at which activities terminate and learning initiates poses a challenge in terms of differentiation (Longworth, 2018; Simonaitienė, 2003).

As stated by Ashton et al. (1999), the capability to acquire knowledge and effectively apply it holds significant importance for teams, companies and individuals, resulting in substantial benefits. The enhancement of employees' self-assurance in their abilities, as a result, contributes to the development of their psychological capabilities. Garvin et al. (2008) argue that an organization engaged in learning is characterized by an environment in which individuals excel at generating, obtaining and disseminating knowledge. In addition to the aforementioned description, according to Watkins and Marsick (1993), a learning organization is distinguished by its ongoing learning processes and transformative qualities.

Simonaitienė (2003) asserts that learning organizations have several advantages as compared to organizations that do not prioritize learning. The salient attributes of an organization that effectively engages in the process of learning from and adjusting to shifting circumstances can be succinctly encapsulated as follows: Firstly, it showcases the organization's capacity to adapt the extent of its operations and emphasize its primary business objectives. Additionally, it modifies its internal structural components in order to adapt to the evolving surroundings. Thirdly, it leverages advanced information technology to expedite the decision-making process. Additionally, the organization endeavours to harness the hitherto unutilized expertise and potential of its workforce through the exploration of novel methodologies. Furthermore, it facilitates the establishment of interpersonal linkages among individuals operating across disparate sectors of the organization, thereby promoting improved coordination and cultivating an environment conducive to ongoing knowledge acquisition. Lastly, it replaces traditional vertical, hierarchical relationships with more flexible and collaborative structures. Acevedo and Diaz-Molina (2022) had opined that managers can enhance their overall success in fostering innovation by implementing routines that promote a learning culture. This culture ought to be distinguished by the cultivation of abilities related to exploration, innovation, empowerment and collaboration, all of which play a significant role in the creation of knowledge and practical expertise.

8. THE SIGNIFICANCE OF LEARNING ORGANIZATIONAL CULTURE FOR ORGANIZATIONAL RESILIENCE

One could argue that a highly effective approach to effectively managing change within organizations is to actively promote and foster a culture of continuous learning. In a learning organization, employees are consistently striving to improve their ability to achieve desired outcomes. They actively engage in developing new cognitive frameworks, understanding the objectives of the collective and ultimately cultivating a culture characterized by ongoing learning and collaborative efforts. The notion of organizational learning is sometimes utilized to assess the degree to which a company proficiently assimilates knowledge from external occurrences and adapts its practices correspondingly.

The link between how resilient a company is and how much it learns is intrinsically interconnected; nevertheless, there is limited understanding of the mechanisms of successful learning that might bolster organizational resilience (Evenseth et al., 2022).

Organizational adaptability, according to Miri et al. (2019), is the power of an organization to change its guiding principles, goals and structure when things change in the outside world. When faced with difficult situations, it is imperative for businesses to foster a culture that promotes creativity and the ability to adapt and persevere. The learning organization's stability is enhanced by its ability to be imaginative, flexible and adaptable to change. By actively acknowledging and responding to changes, as well as generating novel ideas, the organization gains a deeper understanding of how to improve its learning processes.

In order to enhance their resilience, overcome challenges and thrive, organizations must actively engage in continuous learning to adjust to the constantly shifting surroundings (Garratt, 1987). The ability of the organization to adapt to new information and perspectives allows it to effectively generate, acquire and disseminate knowledge, while also being capable of modifying its actions and behaviours (Garvin, 1993). Sulastri et al.'s research from 2023 has effectively shown how elements like digital transformation, collaboration skills and innovation value have a substantial impact on small and medium-sized enterprises' (SMEs') resilience.

A learning organization prioritizes its ability to promptly and efficiently adapt to shifts in its environment, unexpected challenges and adverse circumstances. According to Punzienė (2002), it can be argued that this approach not only enhances organizational resilience but also fosters a workforce that is capable of actively participating in continuous learning. Pal et al. (2014) conducted a study that revealed a positive correlation between learning and resilient performance. Conversely, Nyman (2019) posited that the acquisition of knowledge and skills is an essential antecedent for the development of resilience.

The capacity of learning organizations to maintain resilience, as described by F. H. Norris et al. (2008), lies in their ability to effectively utilize their existing resources and competences, effectively address and manage the demands, challenges and changes they face and maintain a delicate equilibrium between various elements during times of crisis. Learning is an inherent process within any organization; however, the true significance of knowledge lies in its dissemination and regular updating. Because of the facilitation of learning and information sharing, learning organizations have greater production and competitiveness. This allows the company to establish new plans, address issues effectively and engage in unique activities (Brown & Duguid, 2004).

García et al. (2012) argue that learning organizations prioritize the development of knowledgeable human resources. This strategic approach is believed to create a strong defence mechanism against adverse situations.

9. FINDINGS

An organization that prioritizes learning recognizes the importance of being equipped to effectively and promptly address unexpected events, crises and challenging circumstances. According to the statement, there is a beneficial relationship with improving organizational resilience and encouraging employee participation in lifelong learning. Learning is considered a crucial prerequisite for developing resilience. In order to cultivate resilience, effectively address challenges and thrive, organizations must actively engage in a continuous learning process that allows them to adapt to and navigate through dynamic environmental changes. Resilience can be defined as a learning organization's intrinsic ability to effectively allocate their existing capabilities and resources, while adeptly navigating the complexities posed by demands, challenges and changes. Moreover, it involves the delicate task of striking a harmonious equilibrium among multiple elements amid a crisis scenario. Learning organizations have the ability to cultivate and develop highly skilled individuals, who in turn can act as a formidable safeguard against adverse situations.

10. CONCLUSION

According to research undertaken within the framework of learning organizations, an organization must be able to adapt to change and satisfy the developing demands of the social environment in order to survive unexpected situations, situations of crisis and surprises. The acquisition of knowledge essential for an organization can solely be achieved through a commitment to lifelong learning. Further investigation is warranted in order to deepen our understanding of the connection between learning organizations and organizational resilience. This conceptual study will serve as the framework for future research.

REFERENCES

Acevedo, J., & Diaz-Molina, I. (2022, August 3). Learning organizations in emerging economies: The effect of knowledge management on innovative culture in Chilean companies. *The Learning Organization*, *30*(1), 37–54. https://doi.org/10.1108/tlo-01-2021-0009

Annarelli, A., & Nonino, F. (2016). Strategic and operational management of organizational resilience: Current state of research and future directions. *Omega*, *62*, 1–8. https://doi.org/10.1016/j.omega.2015.08.004

Ashton, E. C., Hogarth, P. J., & Ormond, R. (1999). Breakdown of mangrove litter in a managed mangrove forest in Peninsular Malaysia. In R. S. Dodd (Ed.), *Diversity and function in mangrove ecosystems, hydrobiologia* (Vol. 413, pp. 77–88). Springer Netherlands.

Britt, T. W., Shen, W., Sinclair, R. R., Grossman, M. R., & Klieger, D. M. (2016). How much do we really know about employee resilience? *Industrial and Organizational Psychology*, *9*(2), 378–404.

Brown, J. S., & Duguid, P. (2004). *Socialinis informacijos gyvenimas*. Charibdė.

Cheng, P. (2007). The cultural value of resilience: The Singapore case study. *Cross Cultural Management: An International Journal*, *14*(2), 136–149.

Clément, V., & Rivera, J. (2017). From adaptation to transformation: An extended research agenda for organizational resilience to adversity in the natural environment. *Organization & Environment*, *30*(4), 1–20.

Cooper, C. L., Liu, Y., & Tarba, S. Y. (2014). Resilience, HRM practices and impact on organizational performance and employee well-being. *International Journal of Human Resource Management*, *25*(17), 2466–2471.

Duchek, S. (2014). Growth in the face of crisis: The role of organizational resilience capabilities. *Academy of Management Meeting Proceedings*, *2014*(1), 861–866.

Duchek, S. (2020). Organizational resilience: A capability-based conceptualization. *Business Research*, *13*(1), 215–246.

Evenseth, L. L., Sydnes, M., & Gausdal, A. H. (2022). Building organizational resilience through organizational learning: A systematic review. *Frontiers in Communication*, *7*, 837386. https://doi.org/10.3389/fcomm.2022.837386

García, M., Romas, M., & Sanchez, M. (2012). Technological distinctive competencies and organizational learning: Effects on organizational innovation to improve firm performance. *Journal of Engineering and Technology Management*, *29*(3), 331–357.

Garratt, B. (1987). Learning is the core of organisational survival: Action learning is the key integrating process. *The Journal of Management Development*, *6*(2), 38–44. https://doi.org/10.1108/eb051639

Garvin, D. A. (1993). Building a learning organization. *Harvard Business*, *71*, 78–91.

Garvin, D. A., Edmondson, A. C., & Gino, F. (2008). Is yours a learning organization? *Harvard Business Review*, *86*(3), 109–116.

Gittel, J., Cameron, K., & Lim, S. (2006). Relationships, layoffs, and organizational resilience: Airline industry responses to September 11. *The Journal of Applied Behavioral Science*, *42*(3), 300–329.

Hamel, G., & Vaelikangas, L. (2003). The quest for resilience. *Harvard Business Review*, *81*(9), 52–63.

Holling, C. S. (1973). Resilience and stability of ecological systems. *Annual Review of Ecology and Systematics*, *4*(1), 1–23.

Hollnagel, E., Woods, D. D., & Leveson, N. (2006). *Resilience engineering: Concepts and precepts*. Ashgate Publishing.

IBM Corporation. (2004). *Business resilience: Proactive measures for forward-looking enterprises*. www-935.ibm.com/services/us/bcrs/pdf/br_business-resilience.pdf. Accessed on October 20, 2018

Lengnick-Hall, C. A., Beck, T. E., & Lengnick-Hall, M. L. (2011). Developing a capacity for organizational resilience through strategic human resource management. *Human Resource Management Review*, *21*(3), 243–255.

Longworth, N. (2018). *Attributes of an entrepreneurial learning city region* (pp. 22–42). Springer International Publishing.

Mallak, L. A. (1998). Measuring resilience in health care provider organizations. *Health Manpower Management*, *24*(4), 148–152.

Miri, F., Shahabi, N., & Asadipour, E. (2019). Relationship between learning organization and creativity in teaching hospitals. *International Transaction Journal of Engineering, Management, & Applied Sciences & Technologies*, *10*(10).

Mousa, M., Sai, A., & Salhin, G. (2018). An exploration for the motives behind enhancing senior banker's level of organizational resilience: A holistic case study. *Journal of Intercultural Management*, *9*(4), 141–163.

Murray, P., & Donegan, K. (2003). Empirical linkages between firm competencies and organisational learning. *The Learning Organization*, *10*(1), 51–62.

Näswall, K., Kuntz, J., Hodliffe, M., & Malinen, S. (2013). *Employee resilience scale (EmpRes): Technical report*. https://core.ac.uk/reader/35471320

Norris, F. H., Susan, P., Pfefferbaum, B., Wyche, K. F., & Pfefferbaum, R. L. (2008). Community resilience as a metaphor, theory, set of capacities, and strategy for disaster readiness. *American Journal of Community Psychology*, *41*(2), 127–150.

Nyman, M. R. (2019). Collective learning in organizations: Opportunities and constraints. Case study of an avalanche blocking a railway line. *Risk, Hazards & Crisis in Public Policy*, *10*, 332–359. https://doi.org/10.1002/rhc3.12159

Pal, R., Torstensson, H., & Mattila, H. (2014). Antecedents of organizational resilience in economic crises: An empirical study of Swedish textile and clothing SMEs. *International Journal of Production Economics*, *147*, 410–428. https://doi.org/10.1016/j.ijpe.2013.02.031

Powley, E. H. (2009). Reclaiming resilience and safety: Resilience activation in the critical period of crisis. *Human Relations*, *62*(9), 1289–1326.

Punzienė, A. (2002). Profesinio mokymo institucija kaip besimokanti organizacija: problemos ir kaitos gairės. *Profesinis rengimas: tyrimai ir realijos*, *4*, 74–83.

Senge, P. M. (1990). *The fifth discipline: The art and practice of the learning organization*. Random House.

Sheffi, Y. (2005). Building a resilient supply chain. *Harvard Business Review*, *1*(8), 1–4.

Simonaitienė, B. (2003). *Mokykla – besimokanti organizacija*. Technologija.

Sulastri, S., Mulyadi, H., Disman, D., Hendrayati, H., & Hadi, P. (2023, July 1). Resilience acceleration model of small and medium enterprises through digital transformation. *Journal of Eastern European and Central Asian Research; IEECA*. https://doi.org/10.15549/jeecar.v10i4.1355

Sundblad, F., Älgevik, T., Wanther, O., & Lindmark, C. (2013). *Leading change without resistance: A case study of Infrafone* (pp. 1–14). Department of Project, Innovation and Entrepreneurship, Linköping University.

Tierney, K. (2003). *Conceptualizing and measuring organizational and community resilience: Lessons from the emergency response following the September 11, 2001 attack on the World trade center*. Preliminary Paper No. 329 (pp. 1–8). University of Delaware Disaster Research Center.

Watkins, K. E., & Marsick, V. J. (1993). *Sculpting the learning organization: Lessons in the art and science of systemic change*. Jossey-Bass Inc.

Williams, T. A., Gruber, D. A., Sutcliffe, K. M., Shepherd, D. A., & Zhao, E. Y. (2017). Organizational response to adversity: Fusing crisis management and resilience research streams. *Academy of Management Annals*, *11*(2), 733–769.

Woods, D. D. (2006). Essential characteristics of resilience for organizations. In E. Hollnagel, D. D. Woods, & N. Leveson (Eds.), *Resilience engineering: Concepts and precepts* (pp. 21–34). Ashgate.

ROLE OF FEMALE LABOUR FORCE PARTICIPATION IN BUILDING RESILIENT BUSINESSES

Bhavna Jaidwal and Kshama Sharma

K.R. Mangalam University, India

ABSTRACT

This chapter examines how more women in the workforce can contribute towards making businesses more resilient. The overall objective of the study is to assess how women's employment influences various factors related to resilience and that in turn drives business activities. The methodology used is qualitative in nature using thematic analysis as a tool. Some quantitative data have been assessed in order to understand how companies survived the pandemic and to examine the trends in female labour force participation. This chapter also builds on observational research methodology in places to arrive at certain key inferences. The analysis examines top performing firms and sectors that survived the pandemic, key characteristics of business resilience and characteristics of women's labour and their role in building business resilience. A conceptual framework has been developed to discuss how female labour force participation can contribute to different sectors in order to build resilient businesses.

Keywords: Women's employment; female labour force participation; trends in FLFPR; resilient business; business resilience

1. INTRODUCTION

It has been observed that Labour Force Participation of women in India has seen a persistent decline in the last three decades. At present, the Female Labour Force Participation Rate stands at 20.3%, while it is 18.2% for Urban India. This is a considerably low number considering that women's employability has seen a rise from 41.25 % in 2021 to 51.44% in 2022 (Business Standard, 2022). The post-pandemic economic recovery phase has shown some favourable signs that hold the potential to significantly augment female labour force participation in India. In order to do so, it seems pertinent to find out how women in the workforce can contribute to business growth, and how they can help create

Resilient Businesses for Sustainability
Advanced Series in Management, Volume 34B, 61–71

Published under exclusive licence by Emerald Publishing Limited
ISSN: 1877-6361/doi:10.1108/S1877-63612024000034B006

resilient businesses so that firms are better equipped to handle economic shocks in the future. It has been observed that while previous crises impacted male employment majorly, hence gaining the term 'mancession' as in the case of the financial crisis of 2007–2008, this pattern has been reversed by the current crisis. This time, it has been women who experienced greater employment losses. One statistic points out that in the United States, women's unemployment increased by 12.8% as opposed to 9.9% between February and April 2020 (Stemmler, 2022). The cause of this pattern can be attributed to the lockdown and the resulting closing down of businesses in the high-contact sectors like restaurants, travel and hospitality where women represent a large share of workforce. Another reason is the increased burden of at-home care of children and old-age persons triggered by the pandemic that led to the withdrawal of women from the workforce.

However, studies have shown that usually female employment varies less over the cycle and remains largely unaffected by downturns, owing mostly to insurance within the family. Whereas men's employment is seen to be more concentrated in sectors with a high cyclical exposure, women have representation in sectors that see more stable employment over the cycle, that is, healthcare and education. The economic shock led by the pandemic has shown that traditional patterns of employment are subject to change, and thus, businesses need to be resilient enough to adapt to such changes. In case of female labour force employment, business resilience has two aspects, firstly firms need to harness the untapped potential of women outside the labour force and secondly, firms need to assess how they can sustain female employment in case of such crises. To do so, it would be important to find out what the characteristics of resilient businesses are, and how female employment can contribute to it.

2. LITERATURE REVIEW

The recent pandemic that started as a health crisis turned into an economic crisis as countries went under lockdown. Different sectors were impacted differently depending on whether they were providing key or non-key services (ILO, 2022). As businesses start to recover, experts have been exploring ways of speeding up recovery and building businesses that are resilient to such shocks in the future. Many studies have pointed out the role of women in making businesses more resilient, considering the different impact that the pandemic had on men and women and the particular characteristics they possess that could be conducive to making systemic changes. It has been found that women often run up against systemic challenges and resource scarcity when it comes to entrepreneurship (WEF, 2022). To understand this analysis in the Indian context, female labour force participation has declined to 103.6 million in 2011–2012, from 126.49 million in 2004–2005 (Samantroy & Tomar, 2018). During that period, it was also seen that the proportion of self-employed was higher in females than males. This details an important indication that women can contribute significantly to building new enterprises and act as the backbone of a small and medium enterprise–led economic revival. It has also been found that there was a decrease in the female share in the labour force from 29.4% in 2004–2005 to 22.5% in 2011–2012 (Mahapatro, 2013). Different studies have found reasons such as females being undercounted in the labour force due to poor methodology being used, increasing enrolment in schools and technological changes that make it a challenge for females who have lacked educational opportunities to participate in the workforce. This was seen in a study undertaken using Periodic Labour Force Survey (PLFS) data on 31 major states and union territories that discussed how work lives of women may get disrupted owing to the adoption of new technologies by displacing jobs, as high-skill jobs takeover (Deb, 2020). Therefore, the role of skill training and capacity-building programmes is even more crucial if women are to act as a catalyst for building business resilience.

Furthermore, an International Monetary Fund study has found that increasing female labour force participation to male levels can boost GDP and has the potential to grow the economy by about 27% (IMF, 2017). In this context, it becomes important to understand the role of female labour force participation in India in building business resilience.

3. RESEARCH METHODOLOGY

The research methodology is exploratory in nature, consisting of qualitative analysis. Thematic analysis has been used as a tool to undertake this qualitative study wherein, a set of thoughts and observations were identified as different codes and then categorized into themes by looking at patterns. Some quantitative data relating to the National Sample Survey (NSS) of India and the PLFS were examined as part of literature review in order to understand how companies survived the pandemic and to examine the trends in female labour force participation. In places, the paper builds on observational research methodology to arrive at certain key inferences. Secondary research has been undertaken under three themes in order to understand how female labour force participation can help build business resilience. These broad themes are (i) Top performing firms and sectors that survived the pandemic (ii) Key characteristics of business resilience and (iii) Characteristics of women's labour and role in building business resilience. Finally, a conceptual framework has been developed to discuss how female labour force participation can build business resilience.

4. FINDINGS AND DATA ANALYSIS

4.1 Top Performing Firms and Sectors That Survived the Pandemic

The COVID-19 pandemic highlighted the importance of firms building models that would sustain them during economic hardships. Multiple challenges were faced by the private sector in terms of low demand, disruption of supply chains and decline in investment owing to volatile business expectations. Key sectors that were essential to the smooth functioning of daily activities showed positive trends, be it food supplies, certain consumer durables and gas stations. In many developing countries, the agricultural sector showed resilience, whereas in many developed countries, e-commerce witnessed a boom in lockdown restrictions.

The need for firms to adjust business models through innovation and digitizing services was particularly highlighted. Small businesses producing face masks, protective equipment and hand sanitizers saw an unprecedented demand, showing how different economic crises in fact create newer opportunities for firms who adapt to changing demand scenarios. A study of 9,602 firms done by ILO shows that more non-key firms adjusted their mode of operation as compared to key firms, especially in terms of online activities, whereas remote work was adopted by a similar share of both key and non-key firms (Stemmler, 2022).

An analysis of top performing companies during the pandemic shows how changing conditions during economic shocks can imply newer opportunities.

Fig. 1 shows the various sectors that 100 top performing companies were associated with (Financial Times, 2020). It is seen that e-commerce and online entertainment proved to be the key sectors that survived the pandemic. Pharmaceutical and medical manufacturing is a purely pandemic-specific sector that may not show such resilience in economic shocks of a different nature. However, companies that have benefited from the boom in online payment services, food delivery, food supplies, logistics, online education, communication and other services, consumer durables and e-commerce can be studied to understand how businesses become resilient by harnessing the potential of new opportunities.

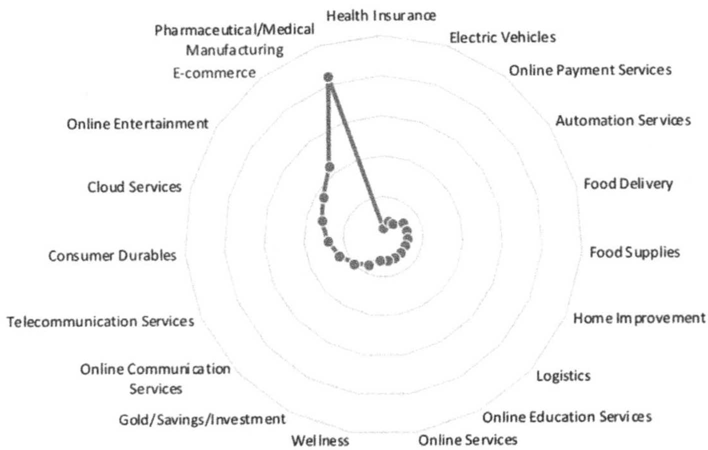

Fig. 1. Sectors of 100 Top Performing Companies During Pandemic. *Source:* Author's compilation, FT.

4.2 Key Characteristics of Business Resilience

Businesses face a number of challenges driven by the economic conditions of the country they operate in and from the impact of global headwinds. These include recessions, geopolitical tensions, volatile prices and rising interest rates to name a few. In 2020, the world witnessed a black swan-like event as the COVID-19 pandemic hit and halted the entire world. It has thus become important to build businesses that are resilient to changing conditions. To do so, it is first important to understand the basic foundation on which business resilience stands.

Forbes defines resilience as 'the ability to protect and grow value in the face of rapidly changing external conditions'. While Harvard considers resilience as 'company's capacity to absorb stress, recover critical functionality, and thrive in altered circumstances'. Different organizations have different perspectives on the characteristics important to build business resilience, which has been summarized in Table 1.

Boston Consulting Group advises firms to focus on financial resilience, operations, organizational strategy, marketing, sales and pricing and tech resilience. This includes tools such as scenario-based strategic planning, zero-based budgeting and cost-cutting or acquiring new capabilities through mergers and acquisitions, comprehensive margin management, supply chain resilience and technology innovation, cost optimization, rational pricing strategies, push for AI, tech adoption, data-driven automation, etc. Forbes, on the other hand, views resilience as a combination of financial, operational, strategic and psychological elements. According to Harvard Business Review, there are six essential principles that companies need to embrace in order to build business resilience. These are redundancy, diversity, modularity, adaptability,

Table 1. Factors and Tools for Building Organizational Resilience.

Organization	Resilience Factors	Tools and Actions
Boston Consulting Group	Financial resilience	Scenario-based strategic planning, zero-based budgeting and cost-cutting or acquiring new capabilities through mergers and acquisitions
	Operations	Resilient supply chain, managing margins and technology innovation that augments efficiency
	Organizational strategy	Dialling down costs, nimbly shifting resources
	Marketing, sales and pricing	Continuous measurement of consumer behaviour and improvement of prices
	Tech resilience	Push for artificial intelligence (AI), tech adoption, data-driven automation
Forbes	Culture	Creating deep connections for all employees for the mission, values and vision of the organization
	Leadership	Commitment to employee well-being. Empathy and awareness with respect to the impact of disruption on employees
	Change	Assessing changes that are needed in response to the shock and planning timelines for its accomplishment. For example, moving to online payments, alteration in goods delivery model, etc.
	Discipline	Focus on goals, attention to processes and resources to protect businesses from threats by undertaking risk evaluation and developing a risk-management plan
Harvard Business Review	Redundancy	Duplicating elements such that different factories have the capacity to achieve the same end
	Diversity	Inculcating multiple ways of thinking by employing people from diverse backgrounds and cognitive profiles
	Modularity	Dividing the organization into smaller units so that the whole system doesn't collapse if individual processes fail
	Adaptability	Flexible structures that have the capability to evolve through trial and error
	Prudence	Developing contingency plans and stress tests for plausible risks
	Embeddedness	Aligning goals of the company with societies, natural ecosystems, supply chains and economies
McKinsey & Company	Financial resilience	Profitability, financing, costs, liquidity and leverage, risk management
	Operational resilience	Business continuity management, production stability, third-party and supply chain management, quality standards, flexible production
	Technological resilience	IT strategy and delivery, cloud, cyber and information security, data and analytics
	Organizational resilience	Strategy and workforce planning, structure, processes, people, talent

(Continued)

Table 1. *(Continued)*

Organization	Resilience Factors	Tools and Actions
	Reputational resilience	Stakeholder management, communications, brand management
	Business model	Market structure and position, products and customer needs, business model adaptability, innovation, ecosystem, alliances

Source: Author's compilation.

prudence and embeddedness. Additionally, it suggests adopting some migration strategies like mixing portfolios across products and geographies, environmental shaping strategies in consonance with new realities and collaboration with other players. Finally, McKinsey & Company considers financial resilience, operational resilience, technological resilience, organizational resilience, reputational resilience and the business model in place as key factors to build business resilience. Based on this analysis, some key characteristics of business resilience are summarized in Fig. 2.

In order to study how more women in the workforce can contribute to these aspects of resilience for businesses, it is pertinent to understand their role during some major economic disruptions in the past.

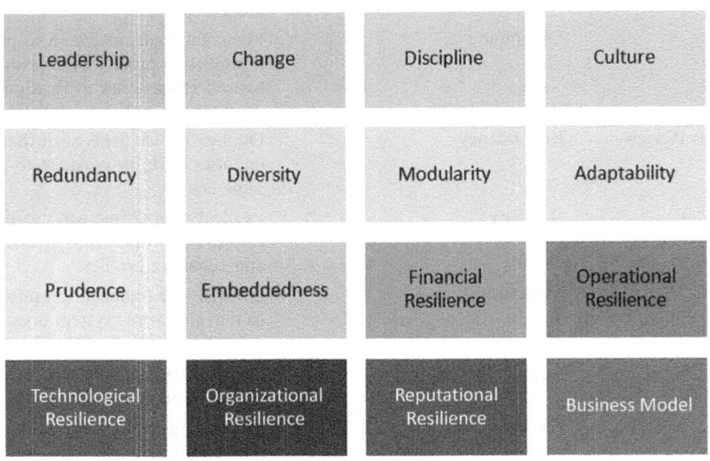

Fig. 2. Key Factors for Business Resilience. *Source:* Author's compilation.

4.3 Characteristics of Women's Labour and Role in Building Business Resilience

4.3.1 Women as Human Capital

Studies done by various multinational organizations have highlighted how women in developing countries possess unique skills that can be built into successful enterprises through vocational training and capacity-building activities. During the pandemic as well, small business owners collaborated with local craftswomen in embroidery, bangle making, basket weaving, etc. to build start-ups. Municipal corporations have been known to integrate female waste pickers into the formal waste collection system and even the government of India formalized maternity care providers under its scheme. All this shows that women's human capital provides immense potential that can be tapped on to build businesses that can survive economic shocks as these can be integrated as different business verticals to enhance modularity.

4.3.2 Role of Women in Reviving Consumption

Economic shocks bring about a vicious cycle of underspending where businesses lose profits and cut wages, thus impacting purchasing power and creating further challenges for production. Works of economists studying the Great Depression have shown that women play an important role in maintaining consumption. It has been found that women are not just buyers but, in fact, are controllers and managers of consumption as they act as key purchasing agents in family buying, a factor that is essential to revive consumption during economic downturns. And it is known that retail purchases generate enough economic demand to maintain factories and farms during such challenges. One furniture company which survived the depression credited its success to the romantic appeal of its online advertising targeted at female members of the household.

4.3.3 Relevance of Women in Supply Chains

Research has shown that women constitute around three-fourths of the workforce in the garment sector in developing countries and form a major part of the agriculture and horticulture value chain. In certain key sectors like mobile phone production and tourism, women are said to constitute more than 50% of the supply chain (ILO, n.d.). In most of these sectors, they work in low-paying jobs and face challenges in terms of job security. In the horticulture supply chain, for example, women are responsible for production and packaging, and in the tourism sector, they play a major role in providing key services like housekeeping, laundry and clerical work. Women are known to work in these sectors on short-term contracts and thus prove cost-efficient for firms. In order to build operational resilience, businesses need to ensure that women have the required safety net so that they can survive economic shocks such as the pandemic. We know that consumer demand for electronic devices increased during the lockdown and e-commerce boomed. This highlights the relevance of sectors like electronics and the garments industry where women find major employment. Similarly, small and medium enterprises benefit greatly from the availability of informal workers, daily wage earners and women workforce. International Labour Organization (ILO) reports have shown that the pandemic disrupted gender equity achieved in recent years. Additionally, 90% of the female workers who lost their job in 2020 left the labour force (ILO, n.d.). If businesses want to build long-time organizational and operational resilience, they have to figure out how to sustain women workers, especially those working in low-paying and low-skill jobs.

4.3.4 Women's Affinity for Service Provision

Studies have shown that women entrepreneurs are more likely to be found in service-based industries, be self-employed and are more likely to launch a business from unemployment. Additionally, research done of disaster relief activities has shown that women are known to function well at the grassroots level as technical assistants to one another. This has highlighted women's eagerness and effectiveness to provide support to other women. They are also known to function well as information gatherers and involve themselves in reconstruction efforts. This natural affinity of women to provide services extends to their involvement in the service sector. Firms must utilize these abilities in order to build embeddedness and sound company culture.

4.3.5 Women as Reserve Army in the 21st Century

The reserve army of labour is the relative surplus population that is not currently a part of the labour force but can be drawn in times of need. Multiple economic crises have shown that women's wages have supplemented family economies in times of need. During the Great Depression, women were seen entering the workforce through female-intensive clerical, janitorial, food services and other service sector jobs when male production workers lost their jobs. The pandemic also saw a rise in such services, with women taking up small businesses like jewellery making, baking, etc. This provided a much-needed boost for e-commerce and logistics companies. It would thus be ideal to diversify in such fields of business that could aid such work in case of future economic shocks. There also lies significant scope for rural enterprises in terms of cultivation of food items in the backyard that aid small businesses like pickle making. Companies must utilize the potential of this reserve labour to build redundancy and adaptability in their business models.

4.3.6 Potential of Women's Leadership

Research by McKinsey & Company has found a strong association between women being present on the boards of Fortune 500 companies and the performance of the corporate sector (Barsh & Yee, 2012). According to many studies, having more women in senior management leads to better financial outcomes and governance. A survey conducted of 21,980 firms across 91 countries globally showed that women leadership in the corporate sector has the potential to improve firm performance (Noland et al., 2021). In fact, one study has found that in senior management or corporate boards, replacing one man by a woman is associated with higher return on assets (ROAs) (Christiansen et al., 2016). So, even though presence of female CEO may not have a noticeable effect, creating a pipeline of female managers can help build organizational resilience by contributing to a very important factor, that is, leadership.

4.3.7 Nature of Risk-Taking by Women

Studies have shown that out of the Fortune 500 companies of 2009, more than half of them began during the recession (Stangler, 2009). Experts believe that businesses owned by women have proved crucial in leading companies out of recessions owing to their risk-taking abilities which take into account not just profits but wider social values. In fact, it has been found that during the financial recession, many women invested in themselves and undertook courses such as MBA and accounting. A study examining US firms' risk-taking after the 9/11 terrorist attacks and the 2007–2008 financial crisis has shown that the terrorist attack increased risk-taking for firms led by a female CEO, whereas the financial crisis increased risk-taking for male CEO-led firms (Kocoglu, 2022). This shows a very important difference in the nature of risk-taking by female leaders, wherein women tend to take a leap in the face of unexpected challenges. This can help in making businesses resilient by building adaptability.

4.3.8 Wider Innovation Potential

It has been observed that gender diversity positively impacts innovation, and women are credited with contributing to both technological and non-technological innovations (Table 2) (Teruel & Seggara-Blasco, 2017). This is in particular because of the unique problem-solving skills that women have with them. For example, research has shown that leaders having diverse backgrounds help companies with innovation more and improve performance. This implies larger firms can benefit greatly by investing in research and development (R&D) in order to build prudence and modularity in their business models.

Table 2. Characteristics of Women's Labour and Role in Building Business Resilience.

Benefits of Women's Labour
• Women as human capital • Role of women in reviving consumption • Relevance of women in supply chains • Women's affinity for service provision • Women as reserve army in the 21st century • Potential of women's leadership • Nature of risk-taking by women • Wider innovation potential

Source: Author's compilation.

5. DISCUSSION AND CONCLUSION

The paper began by conducting a literature review of female labour participation in India to understand the relevance of women in bringing about resilient economic recovery. It then undertook an analysis of top performing companies to examine which sectors possess the ability to absorb economic shock. Further, an overview of different characteristics of business resilience was undertaken to arrive at some key factors that firms need to accommodate in their business models in order to build business resilience. Finally, a qualitative analysis was undertaken to assess what characteristics of women's labour can help in times of crisis. The exploratory analysis undertaken has highlighted the fact that there are certain key characteristics of women in the workforce and outside it, that can prove useful for making businesses resilient in different ways. For example, if the potential of women as human capital can be realized, this can make businesses more modular, diverse and accustomed to change. Sectors like e-commerce and logistics can greatly benefit from the resultant product diversity available in the market. Certain key sectors related to the service industry could revive post-pandemic if companies can enhance their leadership and risk-taking abilities. Female labour force participation can play a key role in this. A conceptual framework has been shown in Table 3 wherein, different characteristics of women's labour have been associated with various characteristics of business resilience to show how sectors can benefit from their interaction.

Table 3. Conceptual Framework for How Female Labour Force Participation Can Help Build Resilient Businesses in Different Sectors.

Characteristics of Women's Labour	Characteristic of Business Resilience	Sectoral Relevance
Women as human capital	Modularity, diversity, change	E-commerce, logistics
Role of women in reviving consumption	Financial resilience	Retail, manufacturing
Relevance of women in supply chains	Operational and organizational resilience	Travel and hospitality, agriculture, horticulture, SMEs
Women's affinity for service provision	Embeddedness, culture	Online services, hospitality and restaurants
Women as reserve army in the 21st century	Redundancy, adaptability	Food supplies, retail

(Continued)

Table 3. (*Continued*)

Characteristics of Women's Labour	Characteristic of Business Resilience	Sectoral Relevance
Potential of women's leadership	Leadership	Revival of key sectors impacted by the pandemic
Nature of risk-taking by women	Adaptability	Revival of key sectors impacted by the pandemic
Wider innovation potential	Prudence, modularity	Automation, consumer durables, pharma/medical manufacturing

Source: Author's compilation.

BIBLIOGRAPHY

Barsh, J., & Yee, L. (2012). *Unlocking the full potential of women at work.* McKinsey & Company.

Basuki, S., & Novitasari, D. (2020). Performance analysis of female employees in the Covid-19 pandemic period: The effects of readiness for change and effectiveness of transformational leadership. *Solid State Technology, 63*, 201–217.

Bellou, A., & Cardia, E. (2021). The great depression and the rise of female employment: A new hypothesis. *Explorations in Economic History, 80.*

Bruegel, I. (1979). Women as a reserve army of labour: A note on recent British experience. *Feminist Review, 3*(1), 12–23.

Business Standard. (2022). Budget 2022 – India likely to see a jump in women workforce participation in urban India by 10 percent. https://www.business-standard.com/content/press-releases-ani/budget-2022-india-likely-to-see-a-jump-in-women-workforce-participation-in-urban-india-by-10-percent-122020200634_1.html

Choudhry, M. T., Marelli, E., & Signorelli, M. (2012). Financial crises and female work. *European Journal of Development Research, 24*, 413–433.

Christiansen, L., Lin, H., Periera, J., Topalova, P., & Turk, R. (2016). *Gender diversity in senior positions and firm performance: Evidence from Europe.* IMF Working Paper No. WP/16/50. https://www.imf.org/external/pubs/ft/wp/2016/wp1650.pdf

Deb, S. (2020). *Women and work in India: State-level analysis. Social Change, 50*(1), 160–168.

Dwyer, S., Richard, O. C., & Chadwick, K. (2003). Gender diversity in management and firm performance: The influence of growth orientation and organizational culture. *Journal of Business Research, 56*(12), 1009–1019.

Elson, D. (2010). Gender and the global economic crisis in developing countries: A framework for analysis. *Gender and Development, 18*(2), 201–212.

Financial Times. (2020). Prospering in the pandemic: The top 100 companies. https://www.ft.com/content/844ed28c-8074-4856-bde0-20f3bf4cd8f0

Grandy, G., Cukier, W., & Gagnon, S. (2020). (In)visibility in the margins: COVID-19, women entrepreneurs and the need for inclusive recovery. *Gender in Management, 35*(7/8), 667–675.

Humphries, J., & Humphries, J. (1976). Women: Scapegoats and safety valves in the great depression. *Review of Radical Political Economics, 8*(1), 98–121.

ILO. (n.d.). *Where do women work in global supply chains?* https://gbv.itcilo.org/index.php/briefing/show_paragraph/id/40.html

IMF. (2017, November 22). *5 things you need to know about the IMF and gender.* https://www.imf.org/en/Blogs/Articles/2017/11/22/5-things-you-need-to-know-about-the-imf-and-gender

Invest in women and diverse entrepreneurs to boost post-COVID recovery. (2022, May 22). World Economic Forum. https://www.weforum.org/agenda/2022/05/investing-in-women-and-diverse-entrepreneurs-to-boost-the-post-pandemic-recovery/

Keil, J. W. (2009). Women, the recession, and the impending economic recovery. *Graziado Business Review, 12*(4).

Kim, D., & Laura, T. S. (2016). Gender diversity on corporate boards: Do women contribute unique skills? *The American Economic Review, 106*(5), 267–271.

Kocoglu, I. (2022). Do female leaders take more risks in the face of life-threatening crises? In *Academy of management proceedings* (Vol. 2022, No. 1, p. 13431). Academy of Management. https://journals.aom.org/doi/abs/10.5465/AMBPP.2022.13431abstract

Mahapatro, S. R. (2013). *Declining trends in female labour force participation in India: Evidence from NSSO.* MPRA Paper 44373, University of Munich.

McColl-Kennedy, J. R., Daus, C. S., & Sparks, B. A. (2003). The role of gender in reactions to service failure and recovery. *Journal of Service Research*, *6*(1), 66–82.

Milkman, R., & Milkman, R. (1976). Women's work and economic crisis: Some lessons of the great depression. *Review of Radical Political Economics*, *8*(1), 71–97.

Noland, M., Moran, T., & Kotschwar, B. R. (2021). *Is gender diversity profitable? Evidence from a global survey.* Peterson Institute for International Economics Working Paper No. 16-3. https://www.piie.com/publications/working-papers/gender-diversity-profitable-evidence-global-survey

Samantroy, E., & Tomar, J. S. (2018). Women entrepreneurship in India: Evidence from economic censuses. *Social Change*, *48*(2), 188–207.

Sajjad, A., & Eweje, G. (2021). The COVID-19 pandemic: Female workers' social sustainability in global supply chains. *Integrating Sustainability and Gender Equity: Emerging Trends in Business Policy, Strategy, and Practice*, *13*(22).

Stangler, D. (2009). *The economic future just happened.* Kauffman Foundation.

Stemmler, H. (2022). *The effects of COVID-19 on businesses: Key versus non-key firms.* ILO Working Paper.

Teruel, M., & Seggara-Blasco, A. (2017). *The link between gender diversity and innovation: What is the role of firm size?* University Rovira i Virgili.

Yonder, A., Akcar, S., & Gopalan, P. (2005). Women's participation in disaster relief and recovery. *SEEDS-New York Population Council, 22.*

IMPACT OF EMPLOYEE PERCEPTION OF CSR ON EMPLOYEE ENGAGEMENT PRACTICES: A STUDY OF SELECTED MANUFACTURING ORGANIZATIONS OF DELHI/NCR

Mitushi Singh, Shivani Kapoor, Divya Goel and Charu Sijoria

Jaypee Institute of Information Technology, India

ABSTRACT

Research suggests that high employee engagement (EE) leads to high performance. The old notion of considering Corporate Social Responsibility (CSR) as a mode of corporate philanthropy has now changed to use CSR as a strategic investment for the organization. Thus, the purpose of the present study was to examine how the key dimensions of CSR impact the different dimensions of EE in a sample of employees from selected manufacturing organizations of Delhi NCT region. Data were collected from a sample of 300 employees working at different levels from 15 selected manufacturing organizations of Delhi NCT region. The structural model and the measurement model developed to understand the relationship between three sub-dimensions of employee perception of CSR activities, and the dimensions of EE were examined using AMOS 21. The results supported the proposed hypothesis indicating that positive perception of the employees regarding the three dimensions of CSR, i.e. philanthropic activities, ethical and environmental aspects of the organization does lead to intellectual, social and affective engagement amongst employees. The study results suggest that the organizations should realign their processes to develop a positive perception in employees about its CSR activities to affect the dimensions of EE in a positive way. The study contributes by exploring the linkage between employee perception of the CSR dimensions and dimensions of EE. This study enriches the current literature in the area of EE by highlighting the role played by employee perception of CSR dimensions.

Resilient Businesses for Sustainability
Advanced Series in Management, Volume 34B, 73–82

Published under exclusive licence by Emerald Publishing Limited
ISSN: 1877-6361/doi:10.1108/S1877-63612024000034B007

Keywords: CSR activities; employee engagement; corporate performance; manufacturing organizations; business resilience

1. INTRODUCTION

Today's business leaders are exploring every aspect of their business procedures to rise above the noise in the market and stay ahead of their competitors. Employees are one of the most invigorating resources that an organization has, to face the challenges of the volatile business world and have a competitive advantage. As the world moves towards the new normal of work from home and moonlighting, employee engagement (EE) has become the top priority of not only human resources (HR) professionals but all management professionals. EE refers to a state where an employee willfully and enthusiastically executes their job and works for the organizational welfare and reputation. As per Kahn (1990), EE is 'the harnessing of organizational members'. Schaufeli and Bakker (2004) elaborated and described EE as an employee's disposition towards work, which is full of enthusiasm, positive energy and absorption. EE is described as psychological connect and commitment to work and organization (Baumruk, 2004; Richman, 2006).

Previous researches in the area have tried to study the linkage of EE and performance. It reduces the attrition rate and increases the employee performance (Corporate Leadership Council, 2004). Gupta and Sharma (2016) study the financial aspects and found that EE improves financial performance measured in terms of profitability. The studies conducted in the area of EE have studied individual level variables and not much work is done on organizational-level variables (Albrecht et al., 2015). The current research focuses on Corporate Social Responsibility (CSR), an organizational context variable and its relation with EE.

In India, it is binding to spend 2% of the net profit on CSR initiatives for all organizations as per section 135 of the Companies Act which has led to an increase in the CSR activities in India. As defined by Waddock (2004), CSR refers to 'the policies and practices that mainly deal with an organization's voluntary relationships with its community and societal stakeholders'. The earlier studies conducted in the area of CSR have focused on the external stakeholders like consumer perception (Öberseder et al., 2013) or sustainable development (Hou et al., 2019). Not much work has been done on internal stakeholders, that is, employees.

The organizations are investing heavily in CSR. The benefits of it need to be extensively transmitted to all the strategic stakeholders. Employees being a key stakeholder, it is important to study the linkage of sub-dimensions of CSR and EE. Employees' perception of CSR has been defined as 'degree of employees' perception about the support provided by their employer to the CSR-related activities' (Choi & Yu, 2014).

Government of India introduced several schemes to uplift the manufacturing sector of the country like the 'Make in India' in September 2014 and Aatmanirbhar Bharat in May 2020. In the year 2022, as per the IBEF, 27.3 million people were working in the manufacturing sector and 17% of the nation's GDP is coming from the sector. Thus, the role and contribution of the manufacturing sector is increasing. Earlier studies surveyed the relationship between perceived CSR and employee attitude and behaviour in other sectors but very few in the manufacturing sector context (Ahmad et al., 2021; Suganthi, 2019).

The previous concept of CSR as an act of corporate charity has now transformed into the use of CSR as a planned investment for the organization. The recent study by Silva et al. (2023) not only talks about the positive influence of CSR on employee perception and performance but also highlights the importance of communicating and making the employees aware of the CSR initiatives.

Thus, the present study is conducted with a rationale to explore the linkage of sub-dimensions of CSR and EE specifically in manufacturing organizations in the national capital region.

2. LITERATURE REVIEW

CSR has become a sensitive issue for manufacturing organizations to address, since the beginning of the new millennium. Manufacturing organizations are increasingly recognizing that achieving success goes beyond focusing solely on economic aspects such as profitability and growth. There is a growing awareness that a prosperous business extends to 'actions that appear to further some social good, beyond the interests of the firm and that which is required by law' (McWilliams et al., 2006, p. 1). Consequently, this realization has led to heightened scrutiny of companies' ethical practices, emphasizing the need to consider the impact of CSR on employees' perceptions and engagement. Misinterpretations of CSR's utility or impact could potentially yield negative consequences. Moreover, scholars like Saks (2006) and Robinson et al. (2004) contend that the existing body of academic literature on EE is insufficient.

2.1 Theoretical Development

2.1.1 Employee Perception of CSR Activities

Looking at the business perspective being a responsible good corporate citizen can give companies a fact that a company can have advantage over its competitors. Such practices can be initiated within the company because commencement of CSR emerges with stakeholder theory (Carroll, 1991). Focusing on the stakeholder theory, company durability relies on the aptitude, expertise and dedication of its employees as on its relationships with investors, customers and other stakeholders (Lee et al., 2013; Wheeler & Sillanpää, 1997). Carroll's (1991) four-part framework results in specifying organizations have four major responsibilities – economic, legal, philanthropic and ethical. Employee perception of CSR activities is considered as an extent to which employees think a company supports the activities related to a social cause (Lee et al., 2013).

CSR moves beyond the horizon and gives a wider picture. Due to this extent for greater understanding, it is essential to study employees' views on CSR. Inspite of the literature provided, the studies at niche level are missing; very little is known about how CSR has a direct influence on employees as the measures of CSR are evaluated, stating on perception of individuals who are external to the organization and not part of any internal activity.

Employee involvement and overall contentment with their organization increases if they find that their organization is appreciating their good deed, perfection, and working style. Thus, CSR perceptions are related to how an employee behaves and performs. Moreover, the understanding that an employee has with his work contributes to the accountability of the task given. Every aspect of EE is governed by the CSR activities the organizations are using to keep the happiness quotient of employees high.

2.1.2 Employee Engagement

Different studies have portrayed EE in different ways, but the most well-known and popular study by Kahn (1990) proposes that engagement signifies an employee's psychological presence during the execution of organizational tasks. EE, according to Kahn's (1990) conceptualization, involves tapping into the emotional, cognitive and physical commitment of organizational members to their roles. Thus, he suggests that EE is linked to three psychological conditions: persuasion, assurance and accessibility. This perspective is supported by studies by Schaufeli and Bakker (2004) as well as Xanthopoulou et al. (2009), indicating that engaged employees exhibit high energy levels, passion for their work and full immersion in their tasks, aiming to contribute at their maximum capacity.

Recognizing the crucial role of EE in organizational success, it is emphasized that engaged employees significantly impact the bottom line by performing tasks and influencing customers, whether in back-office or front-office roles. Harter et al. (2002) underscore the business consequences of employee satisfaction and engagement, emphasizing their relevance across various organizations. Additional research suggests that EE is a potent factor contributing to business organization quality and success, with promising effects on employee detainment, devotion and ingenuity (Andre & Sofian, 2012). Ultimately, connected at work employees are characterized as the most efficient, adaptable and highly dedicated to organizational goals (Lee et al., 2013).

Based on the extensive literature reviewed on EE, employee perception and role of CSR, the following conceptual framework (Fig. 1) has been developed.

3. METHODS

3.1 Sampling and Data Collection

The responses have been collected from April to June 2022 from a sample of 300 employees working in 15 selected manufacturing organizations of Delhi NCT region. The rationale of the study was shared with the prospective respondents, and they were assured that the collected information is only for research purpose and will not be revealed as per the ethical guidelines. A total of 450 were distributed both in online and offline mode out of which 378 responses were obtained. After considering the invalid or incomplete responses, 300 responses were used for analyzing the data.

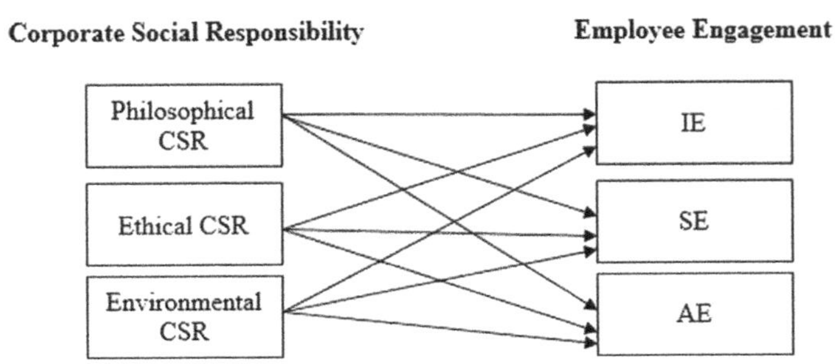

Fig. 1. Proposed Conceptual Model. *Source:* Author's own.

3.2 Measures

Data were collected through a questionnaire with three sections. The first one asked for demographic information, and the second part measured employee perception of CSR activities. The employee perception of CSR activities is operationalized to be a second-order construct involving employee perception of ethical, environmental and philanthropic activities. A 14-item scale was used for measuring CSR dimensions. The ethical dimension was measured using five items adapted from Maignan and Ferrell (2001); six items were used to measure the philanthropic dimensions which were adapted from Lichtenstein et al. (2004). The third dimension of environmental CSR activities was measured using three items modified from Montgomery and Stone (2009). The third part of the scale measured EE using Intellectual, Social, Affective Engagement Scale (ISA Engagement Scale) of Soane et al. (2012). Both employee perception of CSR and EE were measured using a seven-point Likert scale.

3.3 Analysis

First, an exhaustive literature review on CSR and EE was conducted to identify items and constructs. Second, structural equation modelling was used to identify the factor structure through confirmatory factor analysis (CFA). In order to test the relationship between dimensions of CSR and EE, path analysis was used.

4. FINDINGS AND ANALYSIS

4.1 Descriptive Statistics

The total of 300 responses is considered for analysis. Respondents were in the age group of 25–49 years with gender distribution being 76% males and 24% females. The descriptive statistics for the study variables, i.e. the three sub-dimensions of CSR viz. philanthropic CSR (measured using six items P1-P6), ethical CSR (measured using E1-E6) and environmental CSR (measured using EV1-EV3) along with three aspects of EE, i.e. Intellectual (I1-I3), Social (S1-S3) and Affective Engagement (A1-A3) is summarized in Table 1.

4.2 Reliability and Validity

CFA was used to test the reliability and validity of proposed framework (see Table 2). The model fit indices from CFA were CMIN/DF = 5.6, RMSEA = 0.901, GFI = 0.748 and CFI = 0.897. The test values denoted an acceptable model fit. The Cronbach's alpha value and the composite reliability scores are above the acceptable limit suggesting convergent validity of the model.

AVE score for each construct was higher than its correlations with other constructs (see Table 3) exemplifying an acceptable discriminant validity.

4.3 Structural Model

After ensuring reliability and validity of the model, structural model was evaluated to calculate statistics of the goodness of fit which showed indices as CMIN/DF = 5.6, RMSEA = 0.856, GFI = 0.748 and CFI = 0.897 (Table 4).

Table 1. Descriptive Statistics.

	N	Minimum	Maximum	Mean	Std. Deviation	Skewness		Kurtosis	
	Statistic	Statistic	Statistic	Statistic	Statistic	Statistic	Std. Error	Statistic	Std. Error
P1	300	1.00	5.00	3.9133	1.21273	−1.090	0.141	0.103	0.281
P2	300	1.00	5.00	3.6033	1.21280	−0.708	0.141	−0.631	0.281
P3	300	1.00	5.00	3.5933	1.04799	−0.512	0.141	−0.623	0.281
P4	300	1.00	5.00	3.5700	1.09350	−0.489	0.141	−0.731	0.281
P5	300	1.00	5.00	3.8567	0.96222	−0.866	0.141	0.255	0.281
P6	300	1.00	5.00	3.7467	0.99958	−0.830	0.141	0.129	0.281
E1	300	1.00	5.00	3.9300	0.95296	−1.143	0.141	1.251	0.281
E2	300	1.00	5.00	4.0900	0.96523	−1.372	0.141	1.795	0.281
E3	300	1.00	5.00	3.7567	1.01697	−0.899	0.141	0.270	0.281
E4	300	1.00	5.00	3.7000	1.06479	−0.934	0.141	0.237	0.281
E5	300	1.00	5.00	3.7100	1.06600	−0.751	0.141	−0.150	0.281
EV1	300	1.00	5.00	3.6700	1.04790	−0.782	0.141	−0.024	0.281
EV2	300	1.00	5.00	3.7933	1.14089	−0.934	0.141	0.106	0.281
EV3	300	1.00	5.00	3.8233	1.15899	−0.974	0.141	0.134	0.281
I1	300	1.00	5.00	3.4300	1.13552	−0.612	0.141	−0.730	0.281
I2	300	1.00	5.00	3.3733	1.12762	−0.619	0.141	−0.650	0.281
I3	300	1.00	5.00	3.3867	1.12608	−0.649	0.141	−0.665	0.281
S1	300	1.00	5.00	3.4167	1.11679	−0.645	0.141	−0.626	0.281
S2	300	1.00	5.00	3.3467	1.13318	−0.559	0.141	−0.783	0.281
S3	300	1.00	5.00	3.6400	1.16113	−0.814	0.141	−0.218	0.281
A1	300	1.00	5.00	3.2900	1.09997	−0.625	0.141	−0.716	0.281
A2	300	1.00	5.00	3.4033	1.18547	−0.629	0.141	−0.748	0.281
A3	300	1.00	5.00	3.5000	1.17527	−0.728	0.141	−0.541	0.281
Valid *N* (listwise)	300								

5. DISCUSSION AND IMPLICATIONS

The philanthropic dimension of CSR was very highly significant with all three dimensions of EE, which means that the philanthropic work done by the companies and communicated to the employees impacts all three dimensions of EE. This corresponds to the study conducted by Duthler and Dhanesh (2018), where CSR strongly impacted the social and affective dimensions of EE. Tsourvakas and Yfantidou (2018) conducted a study in two different companies, and in both companies, employees feel proud to be associated with an organization that has a caring image and is involved in philanthropical work.

The finding of the study reveals a positive relation between ethical CSR and all three dimensions of EE namely – intellectual, social and affective. This is similar to the study conducted by Mohammed et al. (2022), which revealed that philanthropic and ethical aspects of CSR had a positive direct and indirect impact on creative behaviour and affective commitment acted as a mediator between philanthropic CSR and creative behaviour, thereby positively impacting performance of employees.

Environmental CSR also showed positive significant relation with all three dimensions of EE. The findings of Tian and Robertson (2019) report that when organizations are

Table 2. Construct Reliability and Validity.

Variables	Items	Estimated (Loadings)	Cronbach Alpha	Composite Reliability	AVE
Philanthropic CSR	P1	0.614	0.926	0.841	0.500
	P2	0.737			
	P3	0.835			
	P4	0.832			
	P5	0.525			
	P6	0.646			
Ethical CSR	E1	0.695	0.931	0.83	0.503
	E2	0.694			
	E3	0.693			
	E4	0.727			
	E5	0.734			
Environmental CSR	EV1	0.762	0.924	0.848	0.651
	EV2	0.844			
	EV3	0.813			
IE	I1	0.839	0.97	0.90	0.759
	I2	0.865			
	I3	0.909			
SE	S1	0.904	0.909	0.824	0.617
	S2	0.840			
	S3	0.573			
AE	A1	0.816	0.938	0.86	0.672
	A2	0.814			
	A3	0.830			

Table 3. Discriminant Validity.

	Philan	Eth	Env	IE	SE	AE
Philan	0.707					
Eth	0.612	0.709				
Env	0.681	0.624	0.807			
IE	0.614	0.594	0.577	0.871		
SE	0.606	0.605	0.582	0.827	0.785	
AE	0.611	0.613	0.561	0.812	0.746	0.820

environmentally friendly and socially responsible, there is a high possibility of employees resonating with the organization thus increasing their engagement.

There is a substantial amount of research which was conducted in different service sectors, but there are hardly any studies in the manufacturing organizations (Ahmad et al., 2021; Suganthi, 2019). Hence, this study is very relevant especially in the current scenario as GOI is putting in a lot of effort to boost the manufacturing sector in the country. The GDP contribution and number of employees working in the manufacturing sector is growing every year.

Table 4. Hypothesis Testing and Structural Results.

			Estimate	S.E.	C.R.	*P*
IE	<—	PhilanCSR	0.482	0.069	7.028	***
SE	<—	PhilanCSR	0.408	0.068	6.006	***
AE	<—	PhilanCSR	0.375	0.064	5.818	***
IE	<—	EthCSR	0.18	0.065	2.788	0.005
SE	<—	EthCSR	0.282	0.066	4.243	***
AE	<—	EthCSR	0.305	0.063	4.819	***
IE	<—	EnvCSR	0.268	0.042	6.371	***
SE	<—	EnvCSR	0.259	0.043	6.064	***
AE	<—	EnvCSR	0.174	0.04	4.34	***

'<—' shows the direction of relationship, and '***' shows the significance level.

EE is very important in the manufacturing sector because of the mundane nature of the sector. This sector is such that it affects the morale of the employees as the physical working conditions are tough, usually, units are on the outskirts of the city with very limited social and recreational life outside the organizations.

Since this study highlights the positive linkage of CSR dimensions and EE, it shows a win-win situation for both organization and employee. Organizations by spending on CSR not only fulfil the statutory obligation of spending 2% of their profit but also convert the spending into profit by increasing the productivity and performance of employees.

Engaged employees are more productive which leads to higher satisfaction and self-motivation and a positive feeling towards the values and ethical activities of the organizations.

6. CONCLUSION

The old notion of considering CSR as a mode of corporate philanthropy has now changed to use CSR as a strategic investment for the organization. This investment in CSR initiatives has its benefits for all the key stakeholders like customers, investors, prospective hires as well as the current employees. The study highlighted a positive and significant relation between the employee perception of the three CSR dimensions and EE.

REFERENCES

Ahmad, N., Ullah, Z., Arshad, M. Z., Waqas Kamran, H., Scholz, M., & Han, H. (2021). Relationship between corporate social responsibility at the micro-level and environmental performance: The mediating role of employee pro-environmental behavior and the moderating role of gender. *Sustainable Production and Consumption*, *27*, 1138–1148.

Albrecht, S. L., Bakker, A. B., Gruman, J. A., Macey, W. H., & Saks, A. M. (2015). Employee engagement, human resource management practices and competitive advantage: An integrated approach. *Journal of Organizational Effectiveness: People and Performance*, *2*(1), 7–35.

Andrew, O. C., & Sofian, S. (2012). Individual factors and work outcomes of employee engagement. *Procedia-Social and Behavioral Sciences*, *40*, 498–508.

Baumruk, R. (2004). *The missing link: The role of employee engagement in business success* (Report of a Hewitt Associates/Michael Treacy study) Workspan.

Carroll, A. B. (1991). The pyramid of corporate social responsibility: Toward the moral management of organizational stakeholders. *Business Horizons*, *34*(4), 39–48.

Choi, Y., & Yu, Y. (2014). The influence of perceived corporate sustainability practices on employees and organizational performance. *Sustainability*, *6*(1), 348–364.

Corporate Leadership Council. (2004). *Driving performance and retention through employee engagement* (Vol. 14, pp. 1–24). Corporate Leadership Council. https://www.stcloudstate.edu/humanresources/_files/documents/supvbrown-bag/employee-engagement.pdf

Duthler, G., & Dhanesh, G. S. (2018). The role of corporate social responsibility (CSR) and internal CSR communication in predicting employee engagement: Perspectives from the United Arab Emirates (UAE). *Public Relations Review*, *44*(4), 453–462.

Gupta, N., & Sharma, V. (2016). Exploring employee engagement – A way to better business performance. *Global Business Review*, *17*(3_Suppl.), 45S–63S.

Harter, J. K., Schmidt, F. L., & Hayes, T. L. (2002). Business-unit-level relationship between employee satisfaction, employee engagement, and business outcomes: A meta-analysis. *Journal of Applied Psychology*, *87*(2), 268.

Hou, C. E., Lu, W. M., & Hung, S. W. (2019). Does CSR matter? Influence of corporate social responsibility on corporate performance in the creative industry. *Annals of Operations Research*, *278*, 255–279.

Kahn, W. A. (1990). Psychological conditions of personal engagement and disengagement at work. *Academy of Management Journal*, *33*(4), 692–724.

Lee, E. M., Park, S. Y., & Lee, H. J. (2013). Employee perception of CSR activities: Its antecedents and consequences. *Journal of Business Research*, *66*(10), 1716–1724.

Lichtenstein, D. R., Drumwright, M. E., & Braig, B. M. (2004). The effects of corporate social responsibility on customer donations to corporate-supported nonprofits. *Journal of Marketing*, *68*(4), 16–32.

Maignan, I., & Ferrell, O. C. (2001). Antecedents and benefits of corporate citizenship: An investigation of French business. *Journal of Business Research*, *51*, 37–51.

McWilliams, A., Siegel, D. S., & Wright, P. M. (2006). Corporate social responsibility: Strategic implications. *Journal of Management Studies*, *43*(1), 1–18.

Mohammed, A. A., Ferraris, A., & Troise, C. (2022). CSR practices and creativity during COVID-19 pandemic in the emerging market: Investigating the mediating effect of affective commitment. *Management Decision*, *60*(10), 2669–2693.

Montgomery, C., & Stone, G. (2009). Revisiting consumer environmental responsibility: A five nation cross-cultural analysis and comparison of consumer ecological opinions and behaviors. *International Journal of Management and Marketing Research*, *2*(1), 35–58.

Öberseder, M., Schlegelmilch, B. B., & Murphy, P. E. (2013). CSR practices and consumer perceptions. *Journal of Business Research*, *66*(10), 1839–1851.

Richman, A. (2006). Everyone wants an engaged workforce: How can you create it? *Workspan*, *49*, 36–39.

Robinson, D., Perryman, S., & Hayday, S. (2004). *The drivers of employee engagement*. Brighton, Institute for Employment Studies.

Saks, A. M. (2006). Antecedents and consequences of employee engagement. *Journal of Managerial Psychology*, *21*(7), 600–619.

Schaufeli, W. B., & Bakker, A. B. (2004). Job demands, job resources, and their relationship with burnout and engagement: A multi-sample study. *Journal of Organizational Behavior: The International Journal of Industrial, Occupational and Organizational Psychology and Behavior*, *25*(3), 293–315.

Silva, P., Moreira, A. C., & Mota, J. (2023). Employees' perception of corporate social responsibility and performance: The mediating roles of job satisfaction, organizational commitment and organizational trust. *Journal of Strategy and Management*, *16*(1), 92–111.

Soane, E., Truss, C., Alfes, K., Shantz, A., Rees, C., & Gatenby, M. (2012). Development and application of a new measure of employee engagement: The ISA engagement scale. *Human Resource Development International*, *15*(5), 529–547.

Suganthi, L. (2019). Examining the relationship between corporate social responsibility, performance, employees' pro-environmental behavior at work with green practices as mediator. *Journal of Cleaner Production*, *232*, 739–750.

Tian, Q., & Robertson, J. L. (2019). How and when does perceived CSR affect employees' engagement in voluntary pro-environmental behavior? *Journal of Business Ethics*, *155*, 399–412.

Tsourvakas, G., & Yfantidou, I. (2018). Corporate social responsibility influences employee engagement. *Social Responsibility Journal*, *14*(1), 123–137.

Waddock, S. (2004). Parallel universes: Companies, academics, and the progress of corporate citizenship. *Business and Society Review*, *109*(1), 5–42.

Wheeler, D., & Sillanpää, M. (1997). *The stakeholder corporation: A blueprint for maximizing stakeholder value*. Pitman Publishing.

Xanthopoulou, D., Bakker, A. B., Demerouti, E., & Schaufeli, W. B. (2009). Reciprocal relationships between job resources, personal resources, and work engagement. *Journal of Vocational behavior*, *74*(3), 235–244.

SECTION 2

MARKETING FOR BUILDING RESILIENT BUSINESSES

AN EMPIRICAL INVESTIGATION ON IMPACT OF SOCIAL MEDIA MARKETING OF HEI ON STUDENT PSYCHOLOGY

Shubhika Gaur[a], Shriram A. Purankar[a] and Namita Srivastava[b]

[a]*Jaypee Institute of Information and Technology, India*
[b]*Jaipuria Institute of Management, India*

ABSTRACT

The research goal is to summarize the insights from an investigation of the higher education institutes (HEIs) and university's educational services promotion strategy, which incorporates social media as a medium for keeping in touch with important people throughout time. The study centered on the impact of promotional efforts done by higher education Institutes (HEIs) on social media on students' decisions for their selection of HEIs and universities as well as the study focus factors that influence the students' decisions. In the third quarter of 2022, based on a carefully chosen sample, researchers used an internet questionnaire to conduct an empirical study. The assessment of the outcomes focused on identifying the significant aspects and their significance in the marketing endeavours conducted on social media platforms, which serve as predictors of student decision-making. Three important predictors Social Media Engagement, Content Contribution, and Stakeholders Review were identified and their significant impact on social media marketing by HEI are hypothesized and tested. All the study variables confirm the existence of a significant relationship with the dependent variable. The study concluded that these factors were identified as significant influences on the choice of study and higher education institution. Gaining new followers, prominence content display and stakeholders' feedback builds long-lasting linkages with the immediate environment. As a foundation for creating successful social media marketing strategies for higher education institutions, this research is useful for marketers since it elucidates the dynamics of the market and the habits of potential pupils.

Resilient Businesses for Sustainability
Advanced Series in Management, Volume 34B, 85–95

ISSN: 1877-6361/doi:10.1108/S1877-63612024000034B008

Keywords: Educational services; marketing services; social media; content contribution; institutional promotion

1. INTRODUCTION

In today's world, social media usage is practically ubiquitous. Facebook, Instagram, Twitter, YouTube, Line, LinkedIn, and other kinds of virtual interaction are paradigmatic of a mindset and set of behaviours towards all forms of social media technology (Kim et al., 2021; Alalwan et al., 2021). Case in point: Line, the texting app, Facebook, Instagram, Twitter and YouTube. Consequently, it has a wide range of potential applications in the political, social, commercial, business, academic and community life domains. There is a growing trend among consumers to utilize social media sites such as Facebook and Twitter as valuable resources for acquiring product information and ultimately determining their final purchasing choices (Klassen, 2002; Zuo et al., 2019; Yang & Che, 2020). Therefore, social media is rapidly replacing traditional methods of market research, relationship-building and crisis management (Klassen, 2002). The phrase 'social media marketing' encompasses any business activities that are initiated and concluded exclusively via the use of social media platforms (Zuo et al., 2019; Harris & Rea, 2001). Indian educational institutions have made significant advancements in enhancing its foundational education system. Furthermore, there has been a notable growth in the literacy rate, which is widely seen as a crucial determinant of economic progress. The enrolment rates in higher education have exhibited a consistent upward trend, albeit with a notable disparity when compared to other industrialized nations. The education sector in India is considered to be promising due to the country's substantial population. The government of India has demonstrated support for the cause and has increased its allocation of funds towards the domain of education. This development has made higher education accessible and of high calibre at all levels. In the pursuit of progress, the field of education has extensively employed technology to remain abreast of its contemporaries.

To make education attractive and profitable, the education sector has begun focusing one-learning and utilizing other strategies. The education industry benefits from having a presence online.

In the contemporary era, the domains of technology, business and education have become intricately interconnected. All of the components cannot be disregarded. In the digital era, social media platforms serve as valuable tools for the promotion and establishment of brand identity for educational institutions.

In addition to the United States and China, India possesses the third-largest higher education system globally.

There are currently more than 48,000 institutions serving as centres of higher education, with about 23 million students enroled.

The Indian economy has expanded beyond national boundaries and into international trade thanks to globalization, deregulation, and privatization.

The Internet transcends geographical distances, national boundaries, as well as social, economic and cultural differences. The utilization of this technology enables the customization of messages conveyed to individual recipients, transcending limitations such as temporal or spatial constraints. The field of study referred to as 'it' is characterized by constant evolution, encompassing both its operational mechanisms and the diverse array of potential applications it can be employed in (Wellman & Haythornthwaite, (2008). Primarily, possessing the requisite knowledge and skills is of utmost importance for proficiently navigating the digital realm, hence facilitating the achievement of desired outcomes through the execution of specific actions. There exist various factors that impact the operational efficiency of the internet, encompassing both environmental and personal dimensions (Ruschman & Walker, 2009; Hayes et al., 2009).

Marketing over a global network is what internet marketing is all about. The internet does not entirely replace conventional techniques of operation or create new marketing rules by rejecting the ones that were previously in use. It is a novel marketing strategy, though, so it has pros and cons. When it comes to this situation, the means and timing of communication, the simplicity, and breadth of the information available, the expansion of the recipient market to include previously unreachable customer groups, the increased flexibility of cooperation with outside partners and the potential cost savings are all particularly appealing (Sawicki, 2016; Balcerowska, & Sawicki, 2022).

In the realm of internet marketing techniques, the utilization of social networking sites is deemed vital. Social networking platforms possess significant promise in terms of facilitating the promotion of commodities, brands and individuals. The topic under consideration pertains to the enduring associations with acquaintances, alongside experiences of seclusion and the process of establishing distinct identities. During the process of establishing individualized scoring systems, some local social networking platforms have uncovered shared characteristics. User-generated content is vital to the functioning of the portal. Social networking services facilitate the establishment of social connections among users, encompassing interactions with individuals, and social service providers and the integration of such networks into the provision of substitute services.

2. HIGHER LEARNING AND SOCIAL MEDIA

The emergence of social media platforms has greatly improved the availability of information and transformed the dynamics of communication through the facilitation of instantaneous exchanges. The emergence of digital technology has had a profound impact on the methods through which universities interact with the broader public and attract potential students. Noor and Hamid (2008) assert that the internet presents organizations with significant opportunities to effectively reach their desired audience and maintain relationships with existing clients.

In 2021, the study estimates that 45% of Indians (624 million) and approximately 60% of the world's population (4.66 billion) make use of the internet. This is a growth of 7.3% worldwide and 8.2% in India by the year 2020 (Kemp, 2021).

In terms of social media, India saw a 21.2% increase, while the global increase was only 13.2%, which corresponds to around 53.6% (4.20 billion) of the world's population and about 32.30% (448 million) in India (Kemp, 2021).

Barnes (2009) study examined the admissions office's with social media.

3. MOST COMMONLY USED SOCIAL MEDIA PLAT FORM USED BY THE EDUCATION SECTOR

In order to effectively reach a wide audience in a cost-effective manner, it is imperative for businesses, regardless of their profit status, to establish a strong presence on various digital platforms and utilize social media and mobile marketing strategies (Alghizzawi, 2019). Some of the most widely used social networking platforms are Facebook, YouTube,

WhatsApp, Twitter, LinkedIn and Instagram (Kemp, 2021). One social networking site that was first created with college students in mind is Facebook. However, as time went on, the website gained popularity outside of higher education and was opened to anybody with an email address. Now, Facebook is regarded as the best platform for customer connection and self-promotion. Most involvement is promised by this platform. Thousands of users can access content for a little fee. More likes and visits can be used to improve website traffic. It guarantees minimal costs and aids in showcasing the institute's universal selling proposition (USP). The exchange of documents, movies, data, polls, etc. can happen very quickly.

Twitter is a network of information. It provides real-time feedback, posts pertinent news and provides live updates where users may send and read messages.

Instagram: Photos and videos shot on mobile devices can be uploaded to and shared on this social media website. It's a useful tool for drawing attention to campus activities. Advertise various events such as sports, conferences and seminars.

LinkedIn: It promotes alumni success stories and aids in forging connections with alumni. It serves as a platform for faculty and professional experience profiles. It aids in showcasing the worth and accomplishments of the institution.

YouTube is a website where videos can be shared. Users can upload and share videos using it. Institutions may post their lectures and videos.

Blogs: Blogs type of inline journal. On-campus activities and life are topics for student blogs. Institutes may publish their admissions policies.

4. RESEARCH OBJECTIVES

To find the social media marketing impact by higher education institute (HEI) on students' psychology as well as finding the important factors that have impact on students' decisions.

5. LITERATURE REVIEW

The meteoric rise of social media platforms has resulted in an increased amount of attention being paid to the topic of addiction to social networks. Research on addictions to social media platforms is becoming increasingly common in a variety of academic fields, including psychology, behavioural science and computer science, among others. In order to investigate how far academic research has come and how far it still has to go to fully understand the phenomena of social media addiction (SMA), the author of this study did a bibliometric analysis, which included a total of 396 papers that were published between the years 2011 and 2021. After doing a keyword cluster analysis, we were able to identify five core study areas that fall under the umbrella of the discipline of SMA. These fields encompass the investigation of the influence of negative and dark personality traits, generally known as the dark triad, on SMA. Furthermore, scholarly inquiry has been directed towards the examination of the psychological and physiological health challenges encountered by adolescents due to their apprehension regarding the possibility of being excluded or left out, commonly referred to as the fear of missing out (FOMO).The investigation of is also a topic that piques people's interests. In addition, the results of our research indicate that the collaborative networks that exist between authors and institutions working in the field of SMA studies display a high level of concentration but do not contain any major groupings. This hints that there is a significant amount of efficiency gained by coordinated effort within the sector. However, it is essential to keep in mind that this concentration may also lead to a convergence of study themes, which is something to keep in mind. The results of our study suggest that researchers have created multiple theoretical frameworks in order to clarify the fundamental factors that contribute to SMA. To promote the integration of research on Social Media Analytics (SMA) with other domains, it is recommended that future researchers undertake efforts to find other factors beyond individual characteristics. To adequately respond to the many developments in social media, it is crucial for researchers to engage in further discussions concerning user behaviours that are not exclusively influenced by social incentives (11).

By establishing digital communication channels through social media, businesses may engage with their customers and bring greater attention to the dynamic sector of marketing. The objective of this research is to look at how ride-sharing companies used social media to promote themselves during the worldwide COVID-19 pandemic. A large number of papers from reputable publishing houses are analyzed in this extensive investigation. Thirteen criteria were identified as having a significant impact on people's motivation to engage in reuse activities as a consequence of the research. Among these factors are customer behaviour, subjective standards, service quality, price, attitude and emotion, product usefulness, customer satisfaction, the reliability of information sources, reviews, trust and product evaluations. The evolution of electronic word of mouth (eWOM) as a marketing tactic within the framework of ride-hailing is examined in this chapter. A mapping model of the dimensions is provided, and the difficulties and methods used in this field are examined (Haythornthwaite & Wellman, 1998).

Customers' behaviours have been profoundly altered, and businesses' approaches to conducting business have been forced to adapt to accommodate these shifts as a result of the growth of social media platforms and the advent of the internet. Social and digital marketing present significant opportunities for businesses in the form of decreased costs, increased sales and heightened brand recognition. These benefits can be realized in tandem. However, there are significant challenges that come up in the form of unfavourable eWOM and obtrusive and annoying online brand representation. Both of these issues may be found online. This chapter compiles the collective knowledge of several leading academics working in the subject of digital and social media marketing and presents it in an accessible format. The viewpoints of experts in the field provide a thorough overview of crucial elements linked to this important subject, along with insights into more particular matters like artificial intelligence (AI), digital content management, eWOM, mobile advertising and marketing, business-to-business marketing and related ethical considerations. This work is an important and relevant addition to the academic and professional communities since it tackles challenges and possibilities simultaneously. In this work, we survey the state of the art in digital and social marketing research, point out where there is a lack of information and propose new questions and hypotheses to fill those gaps (Dwivedi et al., 2021; Hussain et al., 2018).

Despite their shared nature as online platforms for interpersonal communication, the terms 'social media' and 'social networking' are not interchangeable. There has been a meteoric rise in the usage of social media as a platform for user-generated content exchange between businesses and individuals, as well as for broadcasting, engaging and impacting large audiences (Alalwan et al., 2021; Kim et al., 2021). With the help of social media, anyone can reach a wide audience, participate in meaningful conversations and make a difference. Blogs, online communities, social networks and video sharing websites like YouTube are just a few examples of the many online resources that enable people to connect with one another and share and learn about things like hobbies, experiences and products and services (Klassen, 2002).

The term 'social network' can refer to a wide range of online resources used by groups of people who have commonalities in terms of ideology, values or personal relationships (Haythornthwaite, 2001; Kim et al., 2021). As a platform, these networks allow users to actively seek out and share information (Klassen, 2002; Barnes, 2009; Barnes & Lescault, 2011). The term 'social networking' refers to the process of fostering genuine human connections through the use of various online social media platforms to establish and maintain direct interactions with other people.

The phenomenon of eWOM has a significant influence on interpersonal communication (Knapp, 1990; Yoo et al., 2013). This is due to the fact that individuals have the ability to disseminate their favourable or unfavourable encounters with enterprises, goods and services to fellow customers through various social media platforms. This prompts researchers to direct their attention towards it, particularly the investigations on behaviour and eWOM (Kolbitsch & Maurer, 2006; Liao et al., 2023), along with the examination of eWOM and buy intention (Kolbitsch & Maurer, 2006; Ladhari & Michaud, 2015; Septiani et al., 2017). The user has provided a numerical reference without any accompanying text. The phenomenon of eWOM and its impact on repeat business has been extensively studied by researchers (Hussain et al., 2018; Knapp, 1990; Kolbitsch & Maurer, 2006; Liao et al., 2023; McAlexander & Koenig, 2001; Minhas & Jacobs, 1996; Nasution et al., 2020; Pribadi Subriadi & Baturohmah, 2022). The research conducted by the authors provides support for the notion that trust and influence play a pivotal role in the effectiveness of eWOM in both client acquisition and retention. Individuals who may potentially engage in business transactions with a firm, those who are presently engaged in such transactions or even those who have previously engaged in such transactions have the ability to express their opinions and provide feedback regarding a particular product or company on various online platforms such as e-commerce websites, blogs, online forums, review websites and social media platforms (Soyeon et al., 2018). The feedback provided can encompass both good and negative aspects. The data produced by eWOM on social media platforms are commonly perceived as a dependable, impartial and easily accessible source of information. It acts as a beneficial complement to a company's website or traditional sources of information (Shankar et al., 2020; Gandasari & Dwidienawati, 2020). Previous research has demonstrated that individuals who come across eWOM on social media platforms are required to undertake a thorough assessment of the information prior to integrating it into their purchasing choices (McAlexander & Koenig, 2001). Product or service development and endorsement can also involve prominent persons, in addition to consumer-to-consumer interactions. They have a lot of options for how to get their opinions out there, including text, photos, videos and social networking apps. In addition, people can share their thoughts by sending messages to one another.

6. RESEARCH METHODOLOGY

The research study included a combination of primary and secondary data for analysis. The collection of primary data involves the distribution of a structured questionnaire to students who are currently enroled or are in the process of applying to HEIs and universities. A sample of 300 students, representing diverse academic backgrounds such as Science, Humanities, Commerce and Technology, was randomly selected. These students are currently enroled in educational institutions and are in the process finding admission to HEIs and universities. The purpose of this survey is to find out what factors students consider most important when choosing a college or university and to see how HEIs are using social media in their marketing campaigns. The study's goals and the comprehension of the many activities conducted by HEIs and universities depend on the answers to these questions.

The Likert scale employed in this study consists of five points, ranging from 'strongly disagree' to 'strongly agree'. Participants were asked to utilize this scale to rate the various factors presented in the questionnaire. The data that were gathered were organized, categorized and presented in a tabular format in order to facilitate subsequent analysis.

The dependent variable is Social Media Marketing Impact on students' decision for deciding HEI (SMM). Based on previous literature, three independent variables were used to get the research objectives.

These are Social Media Engagement, Content Contribution and Stake holders Review.

Social Media Engagement: The phrase 'social media engagement' encompasses a broad range of activities that demonstrate and quantify the level of audience interaction with your material. The number of likes, comments and shares is a good indicator of social media engagement. Social media engagement metrics show how effectively useful and visually appealing material reaches its target demographic. Future posts or efforts to boost publicity can benefit from these data.

Content Contribution on Website: High-quality website content increases value, fosters visit or trust and establishes authority. The content draws visitors and informs the audience. Website content usually displayed by HEI and universities includes Affiliation, Vision, admission, Programs, Research, Newsletter, Students, Faculty, Events, Alumni, Blogs, Awards and Placements, etc.

Stakeholders Review: There are several factors that go into a student's decision, including reviews and feedback from a variety of stakeholders on the quality of campus life, the delivery of education, placements, personality development, exposure, industry engagement, the ability to improve, rating, etc.

7. STATISTICAL TOOLS

The appropriate statistical tools are taken to develop the variables and achieve the research objectives and test the hypothesis.

Research Hypothesis: The following research hypotheses are framed and tested.

Ho1. There is no statistically significant relationship between the impact of social media marketing on students' decision-making. The topic of discussion is social media engagement.

Ho2. There is no substantial association between the impact of social media marketing on students' decision-making process for selecting higher education institutions. Contribution of Content on a Website.

Ho3. There is no discernible correlation between the impact of social media marketing on students' decision-making process for selecting higher education institutions. A comprehensive examination of stakeholders' perspectives and interests.

8. DATA ANALYSIS AND INTERPRETATIONS

Reliability Test: Cronbach alpha is calculated to measure the internal consistency or reliability score, i.e. all items within the instrument measure the same thing or not. Researcher uses the alpha greater than 0.5 as measure of good internal consistency and acceptable.

Since the reliability score is 0.663 which is greater than 0.5, so it validates the data collected and further study can be proceeded (Table 1).

9. DEMOGRAPHIC PROFILE OF THE RESPONDENTS

The study was carried out among 298 students pursuing higher education in India through structured questionnaire method. There were about 52% male and 48% female respondents, according to region from where they belong to; there were 71.6% student belonging to urban area and 26.4% from rural areas. When a question was asked about their subject stream chosen of higher education, 30% of the students opted management, 34% opted some type of technical courses and other courses were 36%. Out of the total respondent, 45% are already pursuing higher education and 55% were seeking institution for higher education.

The participants were surveyed regarding their membership in various social networks. Facebook, being the most widely used social networking site globally, boasts a significant user base, with approximately 32% of respondents actively engaging with the website. A considerable proportion of participants, roughly 28%, mentioned the social media platform YouTube. This platform facilitates user interaction by including visual and auditory elements. In contrast, it was found that 29% of participants utilize the photo-sharing platform Instagram. LinkedIn is a communication platform that bears resemblance to Facebook, with a utilization rate of 4% among the assessed population. According to the poll, the utilization of Twitter was reported by a mere 5% of the respondents. In contrast, a total of 4% of individuals utilize multiple platforms. The participants exhibit simultaneous engagement on many social media platforms.

When the participants were surveyed regarding the average duration, they allocate to social networking sites, a significant majority of 65% reported spending between one and four hours daily.

The Table 2 presented above illustrates the outcomes of hypothesis testing. All three hypotheses are deemed invalid since their p-values exceed the threshold of 0.05, accompanied with regression estimates of 0.142, 0.010 and 0.039, respectively. According to the conclusions that were discussed earlier, the null hypothesis has been disproved, and each of

Table 1. Results of Reliability Test.

Study Variable	Cronbach's Alpha Coefficient
Social media marketing impact	0.663
Social media engagement	0.756
Content contribution on website	0.788
Stakeholders review	0.692

Table 2. Results of Testing of Hypothesis.

	Hypothesis	Estimate	S.E.	C.R.	*P* value	Assessment
Social media marketing impact<—Social media engagement	Ho1	0.142	0.121	1.175	0.240	Rejected
Social media marketing impact<—Content contribution	Ho2	0.010	0.038	0.252	0.801	Rejected
Social media marketing impact<—Stakeholder review	Ho3	0.039	0.108	0.357	0.721	Rejected

the factors that were investigated exhibited a statistically significant correlation with the variable that was being studied (the dependent variable).

10. RESULTS AND DISCUSSION

The data acquired can be further investigated as its reliability score of 0.663, beyond the threshold of 0.5, provides confirmation of its validity. Consequently, this allows for the possibility of conducting future research. The study employed the structured questionnaire approach to gathering data from a sample of 298 students who were currently enroled in higher education programmes in India. The survey results indicated that around 52% of the respondents were male, while the remaining 48% were female. Regarding the geographical origins of the students, it was observed that 71.6% of the student population hailed from metropolitan areas, while 26.4% of the students stemmed from rural areas. When questioned about the topic stream they picked to study during their time in higher education, 30% of the students selected management, 34% selected some kind of technical course and 36% selected other types of courses. Forty-five percent of all respondents are currently enroled in some kind of higher education programme, while 55% are looking at attending higher education institutions.

The participants were surveyed regarding their membership in social networks. Facebook, a well-recognized social networking site, holds the distinction of being the most popular platform of its kind globally. According to survey data, approximately 32% of the participants reported being active users of this site. Approximately, 28% of the respondents mentioned the social network YouTube. This platform facilitates user interaction by including visual and auditory elements. In contrast, it is worth noting that a significant proportion of participants, specifically 29%, utilize the popular photo-sharing platform known as Instagram. LinkedIn is a social networking platform that offers messaging functionalities, much to Facebook. According to the survey data, approximately 4% of the respondents reported utilizing LinkedIn. According to the poll, the use of Twitter was reported by a mere 5% of the respondents. In contrast, a total of 4% of individuals utilize multiple platforms. The participants exhibit simultaneous engagement on many social media platforms.

A significant proportion of participants (65%) reported dedicating a range of 1–4 hours daily to engaging with social networking platforms. The outcomes of the hypothesis test are presented in Table 2 on the right side. All three hypotheses are deemed invalid as their corresponding regression estimates surpass the 0.05 threshold. This provides evidence supporting the alternative hypothesis, which posits that there is no statistically significant association between the independent and dependent variables.

11. CONCLUSION

It's hard to conceive of a 21st-century individual who isn't connected in some way with the maintenance of social networking sites. Social networking websites, made possible by the proliferation of the internet and related technologies, have become deeply embedded in contemporary life. News on politics throughout the world, cultural happenings and product promotions are now often found on social networking sites. Businesses and service providers are using it to reach out to new clients on social media.

Students' opinions on what HEIs should and should not do in terms of social media promotion were gathered for this study. Important factors influencing students' perspectives when deciding on a major were uncovered by the study.

Social media participation, content contribution and stakeholder review were found to be important predictors of educational destination and institution of higher learning. New followers, prominent material display and input from stakeholders all contribute to stronger ties to the local community. The research findings will be used by educational institutions to guide the development of social media campaigns.

This research can help marketers of colleges and universities better understand the makeup of the market and the habits of potential students, laying the groundwork for more effective social media marketing campaigns.

REFERENCES

Alalwan, A. A., Rana, N. P., Dwivedi, Y. K., & Algharabat, R. A. (2017). Social media in marketing: A review and analysis of the existing literature. *Telematics and Informatics*, *34*, 1177–1190.

Balcerowska, J. M., & Sawicki, A. J. (2022). Which aspects of narcissism are related to social networking sites addiction? The role of self-enhancement and self-protection. *Personality and Individual Differences*, *190*, 111530.

Barnes, N. G. (2009). Reaching the wired generation: How social media is changing college admission. http://www.nacacnet.org/research/research-data/Research%20Member%20Only/SocialMediaDiscussionPaper.pdf

Barnes, N. G., & Lescault, A. M. (2011). *Social media adoption soars as higher-ed experiments and reevaluates its use of new communications tools* (pp. 5–10). *Center for Marketing Research. University of Massachusetts Dartmouth*.

Dwivedi, Y. K., Ismagilova, E., Laurie Hughes, D., Carlson, J., Filieri, R., Jacobson, J., Jain, V., Karjaluoto, H., HajerKefi, A. S. K., Kumar, V., Rahman, M. M., Raman, R., Rauschnabel, P. A., Rowley, J., Salo, J., Tran, G. A., & Wang, Y. (2021). Setting the future of digital and social media marketing research: Perspectives and research propositions. *International Journal of Information Management*, *59*, 102168. 0268-4012. https://doi.org/10.1016/j.ijinfomgt.2020.102168

Gandasari, D., & Dwidienawati, D. (2020). Content analysis of social and economic issues in Indonesia during the COVID-19 pandemic. *Heliyon*, *6*.

Harris, A., & Rea, A. (2001). Web 2.0 and virtual world technologies: A growing impact on IS education. *Journal of Information Systems Education*, *20*(2), 137–144.

Hayes, T. J., Ruschman, D., & Walker, M. M. (2009). Social networking as an admission tool: A case study in success. *Journal of Marketing for Higher Education*, *19*(2), 109–124.

Haythornthwaite, C. (2001). Exploring multiplexity: Social network structures in a computer supported distance learning class. *The Information Society*, *17*(3), 211–226.

Haythornthwaite, C., & Wellman, B. (1998). Work, friendship and media use for information exchange in a networked organization. *Journal of the American Society for Information Science*, *46*(12), 1101–1114.

Hussain, S., Wang, G., Jafar, R. M. S., Ilyas, Z., Mustafa, G., & Yang, J. (2018). Consumers' online information adoption behavior: Motives and antecedents of electronic word of mouth communications. *Computers in Human Behavior*, *80*, 22–32.

Kim, M., Lee, S. M., Choi, S., & Kim, S. Y. (2021). Impact of visual information on online consumer review behavior: Evidence from a hotel booking website. *Journal of Retailing and Consumer Services*, *60*.

Klassen, M. L. (2002). Relationship marketing on the Internet: The case of top- and lower ranked US universities and colleges. *Journal of Retailing and Consumer Services*, *9*(2), 81–85.

Knapp, T. R. (1990). Treating ordinal scales as interval scales: An attempt to resolve the controversy. *Nursing Research*, *39*(2), 121–123.

Kolbitsch, J., & Maurer, H. (2006). The transformation of the web: How emerging communities shape the information we consume. *Journal of Universal Computer Science*, *12*(2), 187–213.

Ladhari, R., & Michaud, M. (2015). eWOM effects on hotel booking intentions, attitudes, trust, and website perceptions. *International Journal of Hospitality Management*, *46*, 36–45.

Liao, C.-P., Sher, C.-Y., & Liu, Y.-H. (2023). Progress and future directions for research on social media addiction: Visualization-based bibliometric analysis. *Telematics and Informatics*, *80*, 101968. ISSN 0736-5853. https://doi.org/10.1016/j.tele.2023.101968. https://www.sciencedirect.com/science/article/pii/S0736585323000321

McAlexander, J. H., & Koenig, H. F. (2001). University experiences, the student-college relationship, and alumni support. *Journal of Marketing for Higher Education*, *10*(3), 21–43.

Minhas, R. S., & Jacobs, E. M. (1996). Benefit segmentation by factor analysis: An improved method of targeting customers for financial services. *International Journal of Bank Marketing*, *14*(3), 3–13.

Nasution, A. A., Erwina, K., & Bartuska, L. (2020). Determinant study of conventional transportation and online transportation. *Transportation Research Procedia*, *44*, 276–282.

Pribadi Subriadi, A., & Baturohmah, H. (2022). Social media in marketing of ride-hailing: A systematic literature review. *Procedia Computer Science*, *197*, 102–109. ISSN 1877-0509. https://doi.org/10.1016/j.procs.2021.12.123

Septiani, R., Handayani, P. W., & Azzahro, F. (2017). Factors that affecting behavioral intention in online transportation service: Case study of GO-JEK. *Procedia Computer Science*, *124*, 504–512.

Shankar, A., Jebarajakirthy, C., & Ashaduzzaman, Md (2020). How do electronic word of mouth practices contribute to mobile banking adoption? *Journal of Retailing and Consumer Services*, *52*.

Soyeon, K., Kandampully, J., & Bilgihan, A. (2018). The influence of eWOM communications: An application of online social network framework. *Computers in Human Behavior*, *80*, 243–254.

Yang, R., & Che, T. (2020). Do socialities matter for purchase frequency? The role of buyers' attitude towards social media marketing. *Computers in Human Behavior*, *110*.

Yoo, C. W., Lawrence Sanders, G., & Moon, J. (2013). Exploring the effect of e-WOM participation one-Loyalty in e-commerce. *Decision Support Systems*, *55*, 669–678.

Zuo, W., Zhu, W., Chena, S., & He, X. (2019). Service quality management of online car-hailing based on PCN in the sharing economy. *Electronic Commerce Research and Applications*, *34*.

IMPACT OF CONSUMERS' SUSTAINABILITY CONSCIOUSNESS ON CONSUMERS' EVANGELISM

Pooja Tripathi[a] and Sujata Kapoor[b]

[a]*Jaypee Business School, India*
[b]*Jaypee Institute of Information Technology, India*

ABSTRACT

Consumers by and large today look for economic growth and benefits without compromising on socio-environmental well-being. Having said that, it is imperative to note that consumers' consciousness may not essentially lead to sustainable purchases. This chapter aims to examine the role of both sustainable purchase intention and post-purchase dissonance in the relationship between consumers' sustainability consciousness and consumers' evangelism. With the increased role of social media pervading our lives, trusted sources' recommendations play a significant role in co-creating products. Thus, research on consumers' evangelism (especially sustainability-conscious consumers) would help marketers develop successful strategies. This study expands to the extant literature on sustainability-conscious consumers vis-a-vis consumer evangelism. We collected responses from 227 respondents to examine hypotheses, by means of structural equation modelling (SEM). The study indicates sustainable purchase intention does mediate the relationship between sustainability-conscious consumers and consumer evangelism. On the other hand, we also note that post-purchase dissonance is not a significant moderating construct between sustainability-conscious consumers and consumer evangelism.

Keywords: Sustainability-conscious consumers; sustainable purchase intention; post-purchase dissonance; consumer evangelism; sustainable consumption

1. INTRODUCTION

Global markets have been witnessing to a new turning point in human consumption (Rennollet et al., 2020). Today, consumers are more restrained in terms of 'hyper-consumerism' because they realize that no materialistic pursuit can provide them the

Resilient Businesses for Sustainability
Advanced Series in Management, Volume 34B, 97–112

Published under exclusive licence by Emerald Publishing Limited
ISSN: 1877-6361/doi:10.1108/S1877-63612024000034B009

happiness they look for; instead, such pursuits lead to pain and unhappiness. The notion of 'more is better' is diluting towards 'minimalism' (Helliwell et al., 2012; Sachayansrisakul, 2016). Consumers are turning towards more conscious consumption patterns and have begun preferring 'sustainable' products to the extent that they are even willing to spend more (Choi, 2010; Garcıa-Gallego & Georgantzıs, 2011; Kumar et al., 2018; Wang et al., 2018). In other words, they are prioritizing sustainability over their individual requirements (Pinto de Moura et al., 2012). According to an online survey conducted on environment and sustainability by Nielsen's Global in the year 2011, including 25,000 respondents across 51 countries, it was noted that consumers' concern for sustainability has enhanced significantly. Specifically, about 83% respondents wanted businesses to be sustainable, while 77% expressed their intent to purchase 'green' products (Li-Ming & Wai, 2013). IBM Institute for Business Values and National Retail Federation conducted a study in 28 countries; it was revealed that consumers are becoming conscious towards environment and other sustainability issues. They are becoming more value driven and make conscious efforts to ensure sustainability on the planet (Haller et al., 2020).

Increased sustainability awareness does bring about a change in consumers' purchase behavior (Pinto de Moura et al., 2012; Yadav et al., 2019). Due to this, marketers too have begun to shift their focus towards sustainability marketing because of 'sustainable consumption', owing to stringent environmental guidelines and increasing demand from patrons to conserve the ecosystem (Khan & Mohsin, 2017; Kumar et al., 2018; Vermeir & Verbeke, 2008). Several societal and environmental activists have blamed marketing/marketers for promoting 'unsustainable consumption'. Thus, the onus lies on marketers to showcase more commitment towards sustainability (Kahle & Gurel-Atay, 2013) and thereby encourage sustainable products to achieve sustainability goals (Paul et al., 2016). The marketers' shift to sustainable marketing has been evident from various examples like Patagonia introducing a line of clothing that is organic and sustainable, or for that matter, Walmart adding non-hazardous cookware and introducing organic provisions. However, a marketer does need to understand consumer choices and buying behaviour towards sustainable products to succeed in the market (Cherrier et al., 2011). In fact, Peattie and Charter (2003) earlier had stated customers behave differently against different attributes of sustainable products. Moreover, their behaviour patterns are often unstable, imposing thereby more significant challenges to the market (Ha & Janda, 2012; Kilbourne & Pickett, 2008). Studying consumers' sustainable purchase behaviour has therefore drawn both experts and researchers alike (Cornelissen et al., 2008). It may be pertinent to note herein that extant literature has supported the association between consumers' purchase intention and behaviours that are sustainable (Gadenne et al., 2011; Ha & Janda, 2012; Prakash & Pathak, 2017). In fact, studies advocate a similar directional correlation between consumers' sustainability consciousness and sustainable behaviour (Prakash & Pathak, 2017). Loyal buyers tend to support better positioning of a brand against their competitors (Panda et al., 2019). Consumer evangelists possibly thereby recommend communicating a brand's features to acquaintances, networks and family (Prakash & Pathak, 2017; Smilansky, 2017) making the task of marketing simpler. Nevertheless, despite such benefits, extant literature has been limited on consumer evangelism for sustainable products (Panda et al., 2019). Furthermore, it may be noted that even though conscious consumers are increasing in India, there has been a dearth of studies on sustainable product purchase behaviour in the Indian context (Kumar et al., 2017; Panda et al., 2019). Thus, Prakash et al. (2019) suggested undertaking pro-environmental consumer behaviour studies in the Indian setting.

This study investigates the role of sustainable purchase intention and post-purchase dissonance on the relationship between sustainability consciousness and consumer evangelism. It adds knowledge to a lesser researched area of sustainable consumption and consumer evangelism in the Indian context, investigating the role of sustainable purchase intention and post-purchase dissonance on the relationship between sustainability consciousness and consumer evangelism. In the process, this study's salience lies in the fact that no other study, to the best of our information, has actually addressed both consumers' pre-purchase and post-purchase behaviour, using them as mediating and moderating variables, respectively. The findings therefore would add significant value to the extant literature, highlighting essential information to marketers, so that they could develop appropriate strategies about variables understudy to shift sustainability-conscious consumers into consumer evangelists.

Remaining section of this chapter is bifurcated in five sub-parts: the part includes a literature review, based on which, we develop our hypotheses and build our theoretical model. Part 3 outlines the research methodology, while the following part 4 comprises the analysis. Finally, part 5 includes discussions, practical and theoretical suggestions, limitations and scope for further investigations.

2. LITERATURE REVIEW

2.1 Sustainability Consciousness and Consumers' Evangelism

Manchanda et al. (2023) suggested a connection between mindfulness and sustainability awareness, while materialism acting as a moderator in this relationship. Correspondingly, Nguyen et al. (2023) found a similar association, disclosing that mindfulness has an impact on altruism, subsequently influencing brand evangelism. White et al. (2019) considered consumers' consciousness towards sustainability as one of the most important psychological factors that encourage sustainable behaviours. The study also highlighted that consumers' awareness of the environment is crucial to promote both sustainable consumption and production. Panda et al. (2020) stated sustainability-conscious consumers are intended to become evangelists for sustainable makes because these makes ensure sustainability pertaining to society and environment. Kuchinka et al. (2018) indicated that sustainability-conscious consumers are more loyal to a brand if they follow sustainable practices. Their study also indicated that companies investing in sustainable actions gain more loyalty and competitive advantage. Notably, Gaspar Ferreira & Fernandes (2021) too admitted that sustainability-conscious consumers are more loyal to a sustainable brand. Panda et al. (2020) affirmed that loyal consumers do have a higher probability of becoming an evangelist for sustainable brands. The studies in past have highlighted the importance of consumer consciousness; however, there is need to delve deep into the psychological mechanisms that drive sustainable behaviour. Exploring the psychological aspects will provide broader perspective to understand sustainable behaviour. Based on the discussions above, we predict that sustainability-consciousness consumers significantly impact consumer evangelism, leading us to the following hypothesis:

H1: Consumers' sustainability consciousness significantly impacts consumers' evangelism.

2.2 Sustainability Consciousness and Sustainable Purchase Intention

Greendex (2012) stated that consumers of India are becoming conscious of the ecosystem and are willing to change their behaviour to protect it. Interestingly, Indian consumers are more conscious than their counterparts in the United Kingdom and the United States, along with Brazil, Russia and several other countries. Additionally, Raj et al. (2023) explored that post-COVID-19 consumer have become more sustainability conscious and have higher intention to purchase sustainably. According to Danciu (2015), consumers who are informed and conscious about sustainability change their purchase behaviour accordingly. Chang and Fong (2010) too endorsed that consumers prefer sustainable products. Earlier, Kumar et al. (2018) advocated that sustainability consciousness impacts purchase intention towards sustainable products positively.

In addition, Chen and Chang (2012) believed sustainability-conscious consumers have higher sustainable purchase intention because they have environmental knowledge and awareness as opposed to consumers who are not sustainability conscious. Panda et al. (2020) presented a favourable association between sustainability consciousness and sustainable purchase intention. The above literature confirms the correlation between sustainability consciousness and sustainable purchase intention; however, it will be interesting to investigate this relationship in cultural factors unique to India, which will contribute more significantly to the intention to purchase sustainable products in Indian context. Understanding these underlying drivers could provide valuable insights for businesses and policymakers aiming to promote sustainable consumption in India. Based on the discussions above, we posit:

H2: Consumers' sustainability consciousness significantly impacts consumers' sustainable purchase intention.

2.3 Sustainable Purchase Intension and Consumers' Evangelism

Riivits-Arkonsuo et al., (2014) suggested evangelism results from a strengthened and powerful emotional affiliation between a brand and the customer. In fact, it is the consumers, who nurture this relationship and not the brand. A consumer does not need to buy any particular brand to become an evangelist. Thus, sustainable purchase intention and consumer evangelism have no significant correlation based on the literature reviewed. On the contrary, Collins et al. (2015) specified evangelists have higher purchase intention for future purchases than non-consumer evangelists. However, Panda et al. (2020) did show a positive association between sustainable purchase intention and consumers' brand evangelism for sustainable products. Based on the discussions above, we posit.

H3: Sustainable purchase intention significantly impacts consumers' evangelism.

Li et al. (2020) studied the impact of sustainable purchase intention on consumers' evangelism. It is suggested in the paper that it will be interesting to study if there is any mediating effect of sustainable purchase intention on consumer sustainability consciousness and consumers' evangelism. Additionally, Li et al. (2020) suggested considering sustainable purchase intention as a mediator of consumer sustainability consciousness and consumers' evangelism therefore, we also propose:

H4: Sustainable purchase intention will have a significant mediating effect on the relationship between consumer sustainability consciousness and consumers' evangelism.

2.4 Post-Purchase Dissonance and Consumers' Evangelism

Lee et al. (2010) suggested that if a consumer is satisfied with a product purchased, it would result in favourable post-purchase outcomes, like loyalty, favourable word of mouth (WoM) communication and re-purchase intent. Jan et al. (2013) highlighted that a satisfied consumer is more likely to become loyal and thereby spread positive WoM about the product. Solomon et al. (2006) suggested that preference for sustainability depends on the effectiveness of the product. Consequently, the above arguments lead us to the subsequent hypothesis:

H5: Post-purchase dissonance will have a significant impact on consumers' evangelism.

Hess (2013) and Rozanski et al. (1999) drew attention to retaliation that consumer evangelists may exhibit in case of any kind of betrayal, disappointment or transgressions from the brand. P. Becerra and Badrinarayanan (2013) suggested exploring the impact of post-purchase dissonance on consumer evangelism. Additionally, we predict that post-purchase dissonance would significantly moderate the relationship that exists between consumers' sustainability consciousness and evangelism. And hence, we posit:

H6: Post-purchase dissonance will significantly moderate the relationship between consumers' sustainability consciousness and consumers' evangelism.

Conceptual Framework Development: Fig. 1 shows the theoretical model.

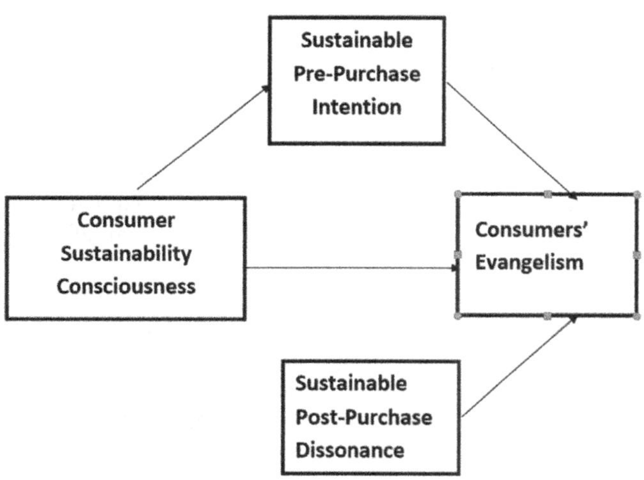

Fig. 1. Conceptual Framework. *Source:* Author.

3. RESEARCH METHODOLOGY

Both face and content validity were conducted, as per the suggestions by Zamanzadeh et al. (2015) in order to check if the instruments used were reliable and valid with the Indian populous. We availed the services of 6 panel experts and 12 lay experts to obtain and validate our results. Based on the same, we made minor modifications to items, whereby the impact score of one item (CE6) was found to be less than the threshold suggested by Zamanzadeh et al. (2015). However, since the impact score of the item was 1.2 which is very close to 1.5 (Zamanzadeh et al., 2015), hence retained it in the pilot study. Following this, we conducted a pilot study with 66 respondents for more accuracy and to decrease problems that might influence the final results. Notably, a few items with Cronbach's alpha value below 0.70 were dropped out of the final study, while all other items greater than the threshold value of 0.70 were retained. Average variance extracted (AVE) values were more than 0.5, while Hetrotrait-Monotrait (HTMT) ratio values were below 0.85, thus demonstrating convergent validity and discriminant validity respectively for the items retained.

3.1 Respondents' Profile

We selected the sample size using G*power (Ringle, 2015). In order to observe an effect size of $f^2 = 0.15$ with 80% power (at alpha = 0.05, two-tailed) in Smart partial least square (PLS) analysis, G*Power suggests a sample size of 68 participants. We noted from the literature that it is advantageous to double or even triple this sample size (Cohen et al., 1998; Hair et al., 2014; Ringle et al., 2015). So, we finally had 227 participants selected for the study. The participants included students from India's capital, Delhi. Delhi was selected for study as it is the emergent centre of modern education, heart of country, is recognized as great cities of the world (Rani, 2021). Students being future consumers could impact consumption patterns in the future, as recommended by Seegebarth et al. (2015). Moreover, they are informed and have some acquaintance on sustainability. It might have been challenging for an uninformed participant to comprehend the idea of sustainability, eventually may cause difficulty in replying to questions on many variables related to the purchase of sustainable products (Vermeir & Verbeke, 2006).

3.2 Instruments and Questionnaire Design

Four scales were adopted to undertake the study. Consumers' sustainability consciousness, sustainable purchase intention, consumers' evangelism and post-purchase dissonance were measured by adopting scales of Gericke et al. (2019), Carvalho et al. (2016), Metzler et al. (2007) and Sweeney et al. (2000), respectively. We also adopted a smaller version of the sustainability consciousness questionnaire and dropped a few items after expert advice and a pilot study of 30 respondents.

The final questionnaire included five sections: background information like name, age, gender qualification and a filter question regarding purchase. We measured them on a five-point Likert scale ranging from 1 (Strongly disagree) to 5 (Strongly agree). We emailed questionnaires to students with a letter that stated the aim of the study while ensuring the privacy of the responses. Importantly, from 227 circulated questionnaires, we received all of them, and they were useable.

4. DATA ANALYSIS AND FINDINGS

4.1 Demographic Profile

Table 1 shows demographic profile. Fifty-four per cent participants belong to age group 17–21 years, while approximately 46% were between 22 and 26 years. Students selected for study belong to two categories, graduates and post-graduate. Out of these categories, 54% of respondents were graduates or in their pre-final year, and approximately, 78.7% respondents were post-graduates. Notably, out of 227 respondents, 91 respondents were women, while 136 were men.

Using smart-PLS version 3.2.7, the analysis was undertaken in three stages. At stage one, we conducted an assessment of the outer model or measurement model to find if the model had construct reliability, along with both convergent and discriminant validities. In the second stage, we tested the structural model or inner model to check the relationship between endogenous and exogenous variables. At this stage, we also tested the predicting power of the model. Finally, we conducted higher order assessments to examine both the mediating and moderating relationships between the variables. Smart-PLS was used because we wanted to test the prediction power of the model, and PLS-SEM had higher statistical power than Covariance based structured equation modelling (CBSEM) (Hair et al., 2017). In addition, PLS-SEM was also found effective in the case of non-normal data (Hair et al., 2017).

4.2 Measurement Model Assessment

Assessment of the measurement model begins with examining the indicator loading. Indicator loading confirms the strength and reliability of the measurement model (Hair et al., 2019). Further, Hair et al. (2019) suggested that loadings should be above 0.708. Table 1 shows that values of all the indicators are above 0.708, confirming thereby the reliability of the instrument. Next, we measured composite reliability using Cronbach's alpha, Rho A and composite reliability. Composite reliability measures the extent to which each item shows internal consistency. According to Hair et al. (2019), values of composite reliability should lie between the range of 0.70 and 0.90. The Table 1 also displays all the values of Cronbach's alpha, Rho A and composite reliability within a given range Heir et al. (2016). Further, we assessed convergent validity to examine the AVE value, which is suggested to be above 0.50 (Heir et al., 2016). Table 2 shows all AVE values are above 0.50, thus demonstrating convergent validity.

As our next step, we looked to examine discriminant validity, a measure that illustrates the extent to which one construct is distinct from others within the given structural model.

Table 1. Demographic Profile.

Demographic Characteristics	Category	Number	Percentage
Age	17–21	123	54.1%
	22–26	104	45.7%
Education qualification	Graduate	123	54.1%
	Post-graduate	104	78.7%
Gender	Male	136	59.9%
	Female	91	40.0%

Source: PLS-SEM output.

Table 2. Measurement Model, Item Loading, Construct Reliability and Convergent Validity.

Construct	Items	Loading (>0.5)	Cronbach's Alpha (>0.7)	rho_A (>0.7)	Composite Reliability (>0.7)	Average Variance Extracted (>0.5)
Consumer evangelism	CE1	0.857	0.935	0.936	0.935	0.743
	CE2	0.909				
	CE3	0.856				
	CE4	0.878				
	CE5	0.808				
Consumer sustainability consciousness	CSC11	0.796	0.945	0.946	0.945	0.611
	CSC16	0.808				
	CSC19	0.796				
	CSC20	0.841				
	CSC21	0.772				
	CSC22	0.81				
	CSC3	0.77				
	CSC4	0.718				
	CSC5	0.734				
	CSC6	0.772				
	CSC7	0.775				
Post-purchase dissonance	PPD10	0.85	0.947	0.953	0.945	0.776
	PPD16	0.926				
	PPD2	0.914				
	PPD4	0.987				
	PPD9	0.702				
Sustainable purchase intention	SPI10	0.863	0.939	0.939	0.939	0.718
	SPI12	0.806				
	SPI14	0.815				
	SPI2	0.858				
	SPI5	0.873				
	SPI9	0.867				

Source: PLS-SEM output.

We used the HTMT ratio to assess it. HTMT ratio is a ratio of correlation within the constructs to the correlation between the construct. We show that the HTML criterion is fulfilled as all values were below 0.85, the threshold (Hair et al., 2019), ascertaining thereby discriminant validity of the model. Table 3 shows discriminant validity via HTMT.

Table 3. Discriminant Validity Via HTMT.

	Consumer Sustainability Consciousness	Post-purchase Dissonance	Sustainable Purchase Intention	Consumer Evangelism
Consumer sustainability consciousness				
Post-purchase dissonance	0.187			
Sustainable purchase intention	0.792	0.198		
Consumer evangelism	0.615	0.238	0.658	

Source: PLS-SEM output.

4.3 Structural Model Assessment

The section above confirms both the validity and reliability of the measurement model. The structural model analysis assessed the significance of the path coefficient and tested the hypothesis. The significance of path coefficient and hypothesis testing was done using PLS algorithms and a bootstrapping procedure using 5,000 subsamples with no significant changes. Table 4 shows the result of the structural model analysis; notably, apart from H4, all other hypotheses were accepted. Further, there is a significant effect of consumer sustainability consciousness on consumer evangelism ($\beta = 0.256, p = 0.002$). Moreover, there seemed to be a significant effect of consumer sustainability consciousness on sustainable purchase intention ($\beta = 0.748$, $p = 0.000$). Similarly, sustainable purchase intention significantly affects consumers' evangelism ($\beta = 0.494, p = 0.006$); thus, all *H1*, *H2* and *H3* were accepted. However, post-purchase dissonance does not significantly affect consumers' evangelism ($\beta = 0.256$, $p = 0.066$); thus, *H5* was not accepted.

In the sample, the explanatory power of the model was examined using R^2. Values of R^2 for sustainable purchase intention is 0.628 and for consumer evangelism is 0.461, showing substantial to moderate effects respectively (Heir et al., 2017). Furthermore, we examined the predictive power of the model by blindfolding procedure, as suggested by Heir et al. (2017). Values of Q^2 were above 0. Thus, the model holds predictive relevance both for sustainable purchase intention ($Q^2 = 0.419$) and consumer evangelism ($Q^2 = 0.331$). Additionally, we also examined f^2, effect size to assess the impact on the of endogenous construct in case of removing any predictor construct. f^2 values were 1.70 (large effect), 0.04 (small effect), 0.02 (small effect), and 0.13 (medium effect) Heir et al. (2017). This mean removal of consumer sustainability consciousness from model will have large effect on sustainable purchase intention but small effect on evangelism. Similarly, removal of post dissonance will have weak effect on consumer evangelism and moderate effect will occur if sustainable purchase intention is removed.

The PLS prediction as suggested in Heir et al. (2017) helps in the prediction of the holdout sample or out of sample. It is executed using *k*-fold cross-validation; in the current study, it is $k = 10$. Since prediction residuals were highly asymmetrical, we used mean

Table 4. Structural Path Analysis; Direct Effect.

Hypothesised Relationship	Beta	*T*-Value	*p* Value	Bias Corrected at 95% Confidence Interval		Decision	R^2	f^2	Q^2
				Lower Level	Upper Level				
H2: Consumer sustainability consciousness -> sustainable purchase intention	0.748	18.17	0	0.647	0.816	*Supported*	0.628(SPI)	1.702	0.419 (SPI)
H1: Consumer sustainability consciousness -> consumer evangelism	0.256	3.073	0.002	0.087	0.418	*Supported*	0.461(CE)	0.04	0.331(CE)
H4: Post-purchase dissonance -> consumer evangelism	0.105	1.839	0.066	0.002	0.225	*Not supported*		0.021	
H3: Sustainable purchase intention -> consumer evangelism	0.407	4.975	0	0.241	0.564	*Supported*		0.139	

Source: PLS-SEM output.

Notes: $N = 259$. Bootstrap sample size = 5,000.

absolute error (MAE) values for prediction. We compared the MAE values with the linear regression model (LM) to predict the values of the manifest variable. Table 5 shows the result of these comparisons:

Notably, since all values of PLS (MAE) were lesser than LM, we confirm that PLS does have better predictive power than LM. Consequently, the complete analysis of measurement and structural model justifies both models. The next section would cover higher order assessments, i.e. mediating and moderating effects.

Table 6 shows the results of mediating effect of sustainable purchase intention on consumer sustainability consciousness and consumers' evangelism. We conducted the mediation analysis using Hair et al. (2017) authored book 'A primer on partial least squares structural equation modeling (PLS-SEM)'. Specifically, we followed the flow chart presented in the book to obtain the results. According to the given flow chart, the indirect effect of consumer sustainability consciousness and consumers' evangelism was studied and was found to be significant (β = 0.305, p = 0.000). Subsequently, we calculated the direct effect, which was also significant (β = 0.256, p = 0.418). Finally, since all the p values were positive, it may be affirmed that sustainable purchase intention does have a complimentary partial mediation effect on the relationship between consumer sustainability consciousness and consumers' evangelism. Thus, *H4* may also be accepted.

Table 7 shows the results of moderating effect of post-purchase dissonance on the relationship between consumer sustainability consciousness and consumers' evangelism. We conducted this analysis using PLS-SEM. The analysis reveals that post-purchase dissonance does not significantly moderate the relationship between consumer sustainability consciousness and consumer' evangelism (β = − 0.02, p = 0.7); thus, *H6* was not accepted.

Further clarity can be obtained from path analysis shown in Fig. 2.

5. DISCUSSIONS

The results show that consumers' sustainability consciousness does have a significant impact on consumer evangelism *H1* (β = 0.1, p < 0.05). The finding concurs with that of many previous papers that studied sustainability consciousness. These studies also showed sustainability consciousness helps in strengthening consumer evangelism (e.g. Gaspar Ferreira & Fernandes, 2021; Kuchinka et al., 2018; Panda et al., 2020). These findings can be

Table 5. PLS Predict.

	MAE	Q^2_predict	MAE	
SPI2	0.611	0.409	0.643	−0.032
SPI5	0.564	0.466	0.57	−0.006
SPI9	0.554	0.435	0.572	−0.018
SPI10	0.588	0.449	0.614	−0.026
SPI12	0.603	0.374	0.639	−0.036
SPI14	0.597	0.399	0.622	−0.025
CE1	0.732	0.268	0.749	−0.017
CE2	0.7	0.275	0.731	−0.031
CE3	0.694	0.271	0.73	−0.036
CE4	0.691	0.264	0.722	−0.031
CE5	0.698	0.238	0.734	−0.036

Source: PLS-SEM Output.

Table 6. Structural Path Analysis: The Mediation Effect of Sustainable Purchase Intention.

	Direct Effect					Mediation Status
Hypothesised relationship	Beta	Sample mean (M)	Standard deviation (STDEV)	*T* statistics (|O/STDEV|)	*p* values	
Consumer sustainability consciousness -> consumer evangelism	0.256	3.073	0.002	0.087	0.418	Complimentary partial mediation
	Indirect Effect					
	Beta	Sample mean (M)	Standard Deviation (STDEV)	*T* statistics (|O/STDEV|)	*p* values	
Consumer sustainability consciousness -> consumer evangelism	0.305	0.305	0.065	4.705	0	

Source: PLS-SEM output.

Notes: $N = 227$, Bootstrap Sample = 5,000.

Table 7. Structural Path Analysis: The Moderation Effect of Post-Purchase Dissonance.

	Moderating Effect					
	Beta	Sample mean (M)	Standard deviation (STDEV)	*T* statistics (|O/STDEV|)	*p* values	Moderation status
Moderating effect 1 -> consumer evangelism	0.02	0.02	0.056	0.367	0.714	No moderation

Source: PLS-SEM output.

Notes: $N = 227$, Bootstrap Sample = 5,000.

attributed to strong commitment of consumer towards sustainability and the satisfaction they experience from contributing positively to society. Consecutively, they are inclined to talk and endorse sustainable products and consider good for the well-being of humanity. However, further, for hypothesis *H2* ($\beta = 0.82$, $p < 0.05$), the result shows that consumers' sustainability consciousness significantly impacts sustainable purchase intention. This finding concurs with studies of Danciu (2015), Chen and Chang (2012), Kumar et al. (2017) and Panda et al. (2020). Consumers who prefer sustainability are motivated to purchase sustainable products because such purchases are in line with their personal values, altruistic propensities and positive emotions. Such purchases help them express their self-worth within their social networks and provide a sense of satisfaction. Further, the current analysis also confirms that sustainable purchase intention does significantly impact consumer evangelism *H3* ($\beta = 0.23$, $p < 0.05$). This aligns with past studies of Collins et al. (2015) and Panda et al. (2020), who showed a positive association between sustainable purchase intention and consumers' evangelism for sustainable products. However, marketers need to develop a strong emotional bond with a specific brand, leading to evangelism (Riivits-Arkonsuo et al., 2014). Strong connection with brand motivates consumers to speak favourably about it. Additionally, their affection drives them to proactively support sustainable brand and position themselves as intelligent buyers. We also came up with a novel finding that sustainable purchase intention does have a significant mediating effect on the relationship between consumer sustainability consciousness and consumers' evangelism, *H4* ($\beta = 0.49$,

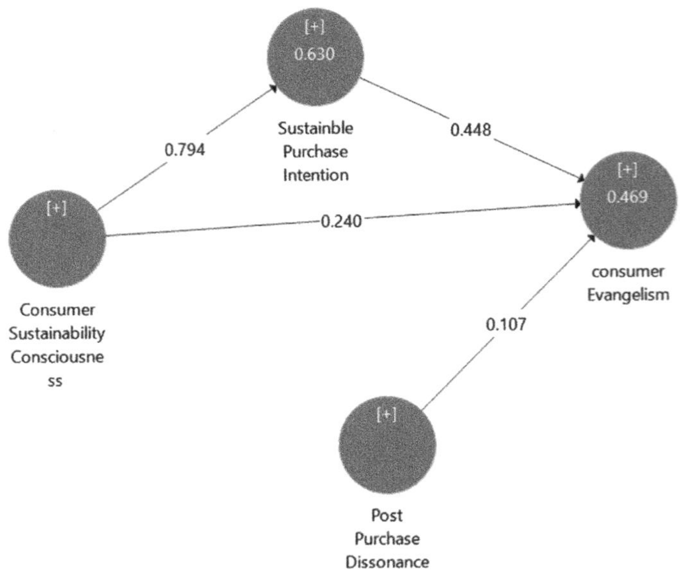

Fig. 2. Moderating Effect of Post-Purchase Dissonance. *Source:* PLS-SEM output.

$p < 0.05$). However, this study shows that post-purchase does not significantly impact consumers' evangelism *H5* ($\beta = 0.25$, $p < 0.05$), contradicting thereby the findings of Lee et al. (2010) and Jan et al. (2013). This is probably because of the changes in culture as our study was conducted in the Indian context. Furthermore, consumer utilizes various cognitive strategies to forget any type of dissonance. Therefore, neither does it impact evangelism and nor mediate the relationship. Thus, it is confirmed that post-purchase dissonance has no significant moderating effect on the relationship between consumers' sustainability consciousness on consumers' evangelism *H6* ($\beta = 0.36$, $p < 0.05$).

6. CONCLUSION

Consumers' sustainability consciousness has been enhanced, while consumers' tastes and preferences have been changing. Marketers have to be more proactive and cater to the needs of these consumers without disappointing them or making false claims. Consumer evangelism is a great way to promote sustainable brands so, with appropriate strategies, marketers could ensure effecting a successful change.

Although this study helped add value to available literature, it has a few limitations. It required the respondents to have a basic understanding of the sustainability concept, hence gathering data was complex. Secondly, the participating students were believed to be less cognitive with lower clarity of attitude (Balderjahn et al., 2013). Nevertheless, Vermeir and Verbeke (2006) showed us through their study that students may be used as participants, as they are future consumers, and therefore, they do have more clarity about sustainability.

Future research could be undertaken on another set of respondents to test differences between the sets of respondents. Social media is a platform where consumers freely communicate and vent their views on grading a subject. Future studies could thereby explore how marketers can use social media to co-create a brand. Studies could also look at exploring the role of demographic variables in the current findings too.

7. THEORETICAL, MANAGERIAL IMPLICATIONS AND FUTURE RESEARCH

7.1 Theoretical Implications

Technological advancement has provided an enormous opportunity for consumers to communicate and spread their opinion regarding a product or brand (Kumar et al., 2018). Consumers today search and provide reviews regarding a product or service on social media platforms. Additionally, consumers' buying behaviour depends on the information they come across; they use it to evaluate a product. Extant literature also suggested that consumers value the information they get from their known or trusted sources than from the company directly or through self-research (Panda et al., 2020). Thus, consumer evangelism helps in co-creating a brand, especially in the case of sustainable products, where there is massive scepticism about exaggerated claims and promises about sustainable products (Panda et al., 2020). However, as noted earlier, extant literature has been limited in terms of correlating consumers' sustainability consciousness and consumer brand evangelism.

Furthermore, this chapter provides a theoretical framework that displays the impact of sustainable purchase intention and post-purchase dissonance relationship between consumers' sustainability consciousness and brand evangelism. As depicted, the relationship between consumers' sustainability consciousness and consumer evangelism is serially mediated by sustainable intention. Literature has suggested that consumers become conscious and have sustainable purchase habits (de Medeiros & Ribeiro, 2017). Thus, the theoretical model presented in this chapter is essentially an extension to the theory of planned behaviour (TPB) model (Ajzen, 1991) while elaborating upon the decision-making process regarding consumers' ethical behaviour (Sidique et al., 2010). The inclusion of sustainable purchase intention as a mediating variable had bridged-value action gap.

7.2 Managerial Implications

All firms look for competitive advantage by meeting the needs of their customers and securing their long-term loyalty (Kumar et al., 2017; Sidique et al., 2010). Firms in recent times have been facing a lot of pressure from consumers for adopting sustainability in their operations. Therefore, to cater to the needs of sustainability consciousness consumers, it is essential for marketers to know and understand their purchase behaviour (Kumar et al., 2017, 2018; Wang et al., 2018). This study also suggests that marketers should run campaign that enhances consumers' sustainability consciousness that will in turn guide future purchase behaviour which in turn develops consumer evangelist. These evangelists speak for the brand and make stronger communication. This study also provides a theoretical framework to understand the impact of consumers' sustainability consciousness on sustainable purchase intention and consumers' evangelism. In addition, the framework also explains the mediating effect of sustainability purchase intention and moderating effect of consumers' post-purchase dissonance on the relationship between consumers' sustainability consciousness and consumer evangelism. The findings also suggest that consumers' sustainability consciousness is greatly impacted by evangelists of a sustainable brand. Importantly, his relationship is mediated by sustainable purchase intention. This finding specifically has many practical implications for marketers. For instance, marketers could target consumers' sustainability consciousness for promoting sustainability products. They may focus on sustainability features in their advisements and other promotional activities. Uber India, for instance, bats for sustainability in their campaign named #parksNotparking, solving a social issue (Area absorbed because of parking space). Hindustan Unilever, too, has been spreading awareness for equal access to resources by each section of society, thereby using resources carefully without wasting them. Thus, firms such as these have been attempting to spread awareness about sustainability and attract consumers.

8. LIMITATION AND FUTURE RESEARCH

Although the students as respondents had been accepted by many authors, the current study was restricted to urban students only. Another limitation of the current study is that it is not specific to any sector. Considering these limitations, future research may include different set of respondents. Furthermore, researchers may study given relationships with respect to specific sectors. Future research can also study demographical impact on established results.

REFERENCES

(2020). *Meet the 2020 consumers driving change*. Www.ibm.com. https://www.ibm.com/thought-leadership/institute-business-value/report/consumer-2020#

Ajzen, I. (1991). The theory of planned behavior. *Organizational Behavior and Human Decision Processes*, *50*, 179–211.

Balderjahn, I., Buerke, A., Kirchgeorg, M., Peyer, M., Seegebarth, B., & Wiedmann, K. P. (2013). Consciousness for sustainable consumption: Scale development and new insights in the economic dimension of consumers' sustainability. *AMS review*, *3*(4), 181–192.

Becerra, E. P., & Badrinarayanan, V. (2013). The influence of brand trust and brand identification on brand evangelism. *The Journal of Product and Brand Management*, *22*(5/6), 371–383. https://doi.org/10.1108/jpbm-09-2013-0394

Bido, D., da Silva, D., & Ringle, C.(2014). Structural equation modeling with the Smartpls. *Brazilian Journal of Marketing*, *13*(2).

Carvalho, B. L. D., Salgueiro, M. D. F., & Rita, P. (2016). Accessibility and trust: The two dimensions of consumers' perception on sustainable purchase intention. *The International Journal of Sustainable Development and World Ecology*, *23*(2), 203–209.

Chang, N., & Fong, Ch. (2010). Green product quality, green corporate image, green customer satisfaction, and green customer loyalty. *African Journal of Business Management*, *4*, 2836–2844.

Chen, Y. S., & Chang, C. H. (2012). Enhance green purchase intentions: The roles of green perceived value, green perceived risk, and green trust. *Management Decision*, *50*(3), 502–520.

Cherrier, H., Black, I. R., & Lee, M. (2011). Intentional non-consumption for sustainability: Consumer resistance and/or anti-consumption? *European Journal of Marketing*, *45*(11/12), 1757–1767. https://doi.org/10.1108/03090561111167397

Choi, Y. (2010). Religion, religiosity, and South Korean consumer switching behaviors. *Journal of Consumer Behaviour*, *9*(3), 157–171.

Cohen, S., Frank, E., Doyle, W. J., Skoner, D. P., Rabin, B. S., & Gwaltney, J. M. (1998). Types of stressors that increase susceptibility to the common cold in healthy adults. *Health Psychology*, *17*(3), 214–223. https://doi.org/10.1037/0278 6133.17.3.214

Collins, N., Hanna, G., Mizerski, D., & Murphy, J. (2015). Identifying customer evangelists. In *Brand meaning management*. Emerald Publishing Limited.

Cornelissen, G., Pandelaere, M., Warlop, L., & Dewitte, S. (2008). Positive cueing: Promoting sustainable consumer behavior by cueing common environmental behaviors as environmental. *International Journal of Research in Marketing*, *25*(1), 46–55.

Danciu, V. (2015). Successful green branding, a new shift in brand strategy: Why and how it works. *Romanian Economic Journal*, *56*, 47–64.

de Medeiros, J. F., & Ribeiro, J. L. D. (2017). Environmentally sustainable innovation: Expected attributes in the purchase of green products. *Journal of Cleaner Production*, *142*, 240–248.

Gadenne, D., Sharma, B., Kerr, D., & Smith, T. (2011). The influence of consumers' environmental beliefs and attitudes on energy-saving behaviours. *Energy Policy*, *39*(12), 7684–7694.

Garcıa-Gallego, A., & Georgantzıs, N. (2011). Good and bad increases in ecological awareness: Environmental differentiation revisited. *Strategic Behavior and the Environment*, *1*(1), 71–88.

Gaspar Ferreira, A., & Fernandes, M. E. (2021). Sustainable advertising or ecolabels: Which is the best for your brand and for consumers' environmental consciousness? *Journal of Marketing Theory and Practice*, *30*(1), 20–36. https://doi.org/10.1080/10696679.2021.1882864

Gericke, N., Boeve-de Pauw, J., Berglund, T., & Olsson, D. (2019). The sustainability consciousness questionnaire: The theoretical development and empirical validation of an evaluation instrument for stakeholders working with sustainable development. *Sustainable Development*, *27*(1), 35–49.

Greendex. (2012). Consumer choice and the environment – A worldwide tracking Survey – Full report. http://environment.nationalgeographic.com/environment/greendex/2012-survey/. Accessed on 7 May 2018.

Ha, H., & Janda, S. (2012). Predicting consumer intentions to purchase energy-efficient products. *Journal of Consumer Marketing*, *29*(7), 461–469.

Hair, J. F., Matthews, L. M., Matthews, R. L., & Sarstedt M. (2017). PLS-SEM or CB-SEM: Updated guidelines on which method to use. *International Journal of Multivariate Data Analysis*, *1*(2), 107. https://doi.org/10.1504/ijmda.2017.10008574

Hair, J. F., Risher, J. J., Sarstedt, M., & Ringle, C. M. (2019). When to use and how to report the results of PLS-SEM. *European Business Review*, *3*(1), 2–24.

Hair Jr, J. F., Sarstedt, M., Hopkins, L., & Kuppelwieser, V. G. (2014). Partial least squares structural equation modeling (PLS-SEM). *European Business Review*, *26*(2), 106–121. https://doi.org/10.1108/ebr-10-2013-0128

Haller, K., Lee, J., & Cheung, J. (2020). *Meet the 2020 consumers driving change*. IBM Institute for Business Value. https://www.ibm.com/downloads/cas/EXK4XKX8. Accessed on March 29, 2021.

Helliwell, J., Layard, R., & Sachs, J. (2012). World happiness report 2012. [online]. http://www.earth.columbia.edu/sitefiles/file/Sachs%20Writing/2012/World%20Happiness%20 Report.pdf. Accessed on 21 May 2017.

Hess P. N. (2013). *Economic growth and sustainable development*. Routledge. https://doi.org/10.4324/9781315722467

Jan, M. T., Abdullah, K., & Shafiq, A. (2013). The impact of customer satisfaction on word-of-mouth: Conventional banks of Malaysia investigated. *International Journal of Information Technology and Computer Science*, *10*(3), 14–23.

Kahle, L. R., & Gurel-Atay, E. (Eds.). (2013). *Communicating sustainability for the green economy*. ME Sharpe.

Khan, S. N., & Mohsin, M. (2017). The power of emotional value: Exploring the effects of values on green product consumer choice behavior. *Journal of Cleaner Production*, *150*, 65–74.

Kilbourne, W., & Pickett, G. (2008). How materialism affects environmental beliefs, concern, and environmentally responsible behavior. *Journal of Business Research*, *61*(9), 885–893.

Kuchinka, D. G., Balazs, S., Gavriletea, M. D., & Djokic, B. B. (2018). Consumer attitudes toward sustainable development and risk to brand loyalty. *Sustainability*, *10*(4), 997.

Kumar, A., Luthra, S., Khandelwal, D. K., Mehta, R., Chaudhary, N., & Bhatia, S. (2017). Measuring and improving customer retention at authorised automobile workshops after free services. *Journal of Retailing and Consumer Services*, *39*, 93–102.

Kumar, A., Mangla, S. K., Luthra, S., Rana, N. P., & Dwivedi, Y. K. (2018). Predicting changing pattern: Building model for consumer decision making in digital market. *Journal of Enterprise Information Management*, *31*(5), 674–703. https://doi.org/10.1108/JEIM-01-2018-0003

Lee, J., Hsu, L., Han, H., & Kim, Y. (2010). Understanding how consumers view green hotels: How a hotel's green image can influence behavioral intentions. *Journal of Sustainable Tourism*, *18*(7), 901914.

Li, H., Inzamam, U. H., Hira, N., Gadah, A., Wedad, A., Ahsan, N., & Javaria, H. (2020). How environmental awareness relates to green purchase intentions can affect brand evangelism? Altruism and environmental consciousness as mediators. *Revista Argentina de Clinica Psicologica*, *29*, 811–825.

Li-Ming, A. K., & Wai, T. B. (2013). Exploring consumers' green purchase behaviour towards online green advertising. *The Macrotheme Review*, *2*(7), 60–81.

Manchanda, P., Arora, N., Nazir, O., & Islam, J. U. (2023). Cultivating sustainability consciousness through mindfulness: An application of theory of mindful-consumption. *Journal of Retailing and Consumer Services*, *75*, 103527.

Metzler, K., Pichler, E. A., & Hemetsberger, A. (2007). Who is spreading the word? The positive influence of extraversion on consumer passion and brand evangelism. *Marketing Theory and Applications*, *18*(1), 25–32.

Nguyen, P. H., Nguyen, D. N., & Nguyen, L. A. T. (2023). Quantitative insights into green purchase intentions: The interplay of health consciousness, altruism, and sustainability. *Cogent Business & Management*, *10*(3), 2253616.

Panda, T. K., Kumar, A., Jakhar, S., Luthra, S., Garza-Reyes, J. A., Kazancoglu, I., & Nayak, S. S. (2019). Social and environmental sustainability model on consumers' altruism, green purchase intention, green brand loyalty, and evangelism. *Journal of Cleaner Production*. https://doi.org/10.1016/j.jclepro.2019.118575

Panda, T. K., Kumar, A., Jakhar, S., Luthra, S., Garza-Reyes, J. A., Kazancoglu, I., & Nayak, S. S. (2020). Social and environmental sustainability model on consumers' altruism, green purchase intention, green brand loyalty and evangelism. *Journal of Cleaner Production*, *243*, 118575.

Paul, J., Modi, A., & Patel, J. (2016). Predicting green product consumption using theory of planned behavior and reasoned action. *Journal of Retailing and Consumer Services*, *29*, 123–134.

Peattie, K., & Charter, M. (2003). Green marketing. *The Mark. Book*, *5*, 726–755.

Prakash, G., Choudhary, S., Kumar, A., Garza-Reyes, J. A., Khan, S. A. R., & Panda, T. K. (2019). Do altruistic and egoistic values influence consumers' attitudes and purchase intentions towards eco-friendly packaged products? An empirical investigation. *Journal of Retailing and Consumer Services*, *50*, 163–169.

Prakash, G., & Pathak, P. (2017). Intention to buy eco-friendly packaged products among young consumers of India: A study on developing nation. *Journal of Cleaner Production*, *141*, 385–393.

Pinto de Moura, A., Cunha, L. M., Castro-Cunha, M., & Costa Lima, R. (2012). A comparative evaluation of women's perceptions and importance of sustainability in fish consumption: An exploratory study among light consumers with different education levels. *Management of Environmental Quality: An International Journal*, *23*(4), 451–461.

Raj, V. A., Rai, S. S., & Jasrotia, S. S. (2023). Sustainable purchase intentions towards organic food during Covid-19 pandemic: An exploratory study on Indian consumers. *Social Responsibility Journal*, *20*(2), 243–260.

Rani, S. (2021). Urban sustainability and good governance in Delhi metropolitan region. In *Resource management, sustainable development and governance* (pp. 507–518). Springer.

Rennollet, I., Schmidkonz, C., & Kraft, P. (2020). The role of purpose in consumer choice: A comparison between baby boomers and millennials in Germany with a focus on sustainability and consciousness. *World Review of Entrepreneurship Management and Sustainable Development*, *16*(3), 241–261.

Riivits-Arkonsuo, I., Kaljund, K., & Leppiman, A. (2014). Consumer Journey from First Experience to Brand Evangelism. *Research in economics and business: Central and eastern Europe*, *6*(1).

Ringle, C., Da Silva, D., & Bido, D. (2015). Structural equation modeling with the SmartPLS. *Journal of Marketing*, *13*(2).

Ringle, C. M. (2015). Partial least squares structural equation modelling (PLS-SEM) using SmartPLS 3. Computational data analysis and numerical methods VII WCDANM. Portugal.

Rozanski, H. D., Baum, A. G., & Bradley T. (1999). Brand zealots: Realizing the full value of emotional brand loyalty. *Strategy and Business*, 51–63.

Sachayansrisakul, N. (2016). Positive influences of 'Buddhism' on successful female entrepreneurs. *World Review of Entrepreneurship Management and Sustainable Development*, *12*(2–3), 352–362.

Sidique, S. F., Lupi, F., & Joshi, S. V. (2010). The effects of behavior and attitudes on drop-off recycling activities. *Resources, Conservation and Recycling*, *54*(3), 163–170.

Smilansky, S. (2017). *Experiential marketing: A practical guide to interactive brand experiences*. Kogan Page Publishers.

Solomon, M., Bamossy, G., Askegaard, S., & Hogg, M. K. (2006). *Consumer behavior: A European perspective* (3rd ed.). Prentice Hall.

Sweeney, J. C., Hausknecht, D., & Soutar, G. N. (2000). Cognitive dissonance after purchase: A multidimensional scale. *Psychology and Marketing*, *17*(5), 369–385.

Seegebarth, B., Peyer, M., Buerke, A., Balderjahn, I., Kirchgeorg, M., & Wiedmann, K.-P. (2015). What does sustainable consumption really mean? A three dimensional measurement approach. In *Looking Forward, Looking Back: Drawing on the Past to Shape the Future of Marketing: Proceedings of the 2013 World Marketing Congress*. Springer International Publishing.

Vermeir, I., & Verbeke, W. (2006). Sustainable food consumption: Exploring the consumer 'attitude-behaviour intention' gap. *Journal of Agricultural and Environmental Ethics*, *19*(2), 169–194. https://doi.org/10.1007/s10806- 005-5485-3

Vermeir, I., & Verbeke, W. (2008). Sustainable food consumption among young adults in Belgium: Theory of planned behaviour and the role of confidence and values. *Ecological Economics*, *64*(3), 542–553.

Wang, L., Wong, P. P. W., Narayanan, E., & Chee, W. M. (2018). Green hotel selection of Chinese consumers: A planned behavior perspective. *Journal of China Tourism Research*, *15*(2), 192–212. https://doi.org/10.1080/19388160.2018.1553743

White, K., Habib, R., & Hardisty, D. J. (2019). How to SHIFT consumer behaviors to be more sustainable: A literature review and guiding framework. *Journal of Marketing*, *83*(3), 22–49.

Yadav, G., Mangla, S. K., Luthra, S., & Rai, D. P. (2019). Developing a sustainable smart city framework for developing economies: An Indian context. *Sustainable Cities and Society*, *47*, 101462.

Zamanzadeh, V., Ghahramanian, A., Rassouli, M., Abbaszadeh, A., Alavi-Majd, H., Nikanfar, A. R. (2015). Design and implementation content validity study: Development of an instrument for measuring patient-centered communication. *Journal of Caring Science*, *4*(2), 165–178. https://doi.org/10.15171/jcs.2015.017

DIGITAL INNOVATIONS AND THEIR EFFECT ON USER INTERACTION IN FITNESS APPS: A COMPREHENSIVE REVIEW AND FUTURE RESEARCH DIRECTIONS

Adarsh Chandra Nigam[a] and Ruby Soni Chanda[b]

[a]*Stanton Chase, India*
[b]*Professor, Symbiosis Institute of Management Studies, Symbiosis International University, Pune, India*

ABSTRACT

The utilization of mobile fitness applications (apps) is on the rise, making user retention and engagement critical factors in the commercial success of these apps. However, research in this area is limited and fragmented. The objective of this study is to conduct a thorough review of the available literature on the effects of digital innovations, gamification, artificial intelligence (AI) and machine learning (ML) on user engagement with fitness mobile apps. The findings reveal the relationships between gamification, the use of AI/ML and technology adoption on user engagement, interaction and intent to use. Additionally, the study highlights the importance of understanding how user experience, customer experience and brand experience impact customer retention and contribute to the overall success of mobile fitness apps. Furthermore, the study also identifies the gaps in the current research and recommends further studies to be conducted in these areas. Future research is encouraged to incorporate elements from the experience domains to provide consumers with engaging interactions and improve retention and commercial success for mobile fitness apps.

Keywords: Fitness apps; user engagement; gamification; AI/ML; user retention

1. INTRODUCTION

The results of the Fourth Industrial Revolution include significant changes in the way society interacts with digital technology and the internet. With a global penetration rate of 67%, it is

Resilient Businesses for Sustainability
Advanced Series in Management, Volume 34B, 113–135

Published under exclusive licence by Emerald Publishing Limited
ISSN: 1877-6361/doi:10.1108/S1877-63612024000034B010

estimated that there were 5.22 billion mobile devices with internet access as of January 2021 (We Are Social, 2021). Mobile applications are now at the forefront of this trend, with 91% of the time spent on mobile devices dedicated to app usage, accounting for 55.7% of all online traffic worldwide. This translates to an average daily usage of 4.2 hours per person, a 20% increase from 2019. Global app downloads reached 218 billion in 2020, generating 134 billion USD in revenue (App Annie the State of Mobile, 2021). In 2022, Statista.com's most current predictions predict that 255 billion mobile apps will have been downloaded globally.

Digitization and the sports industry have both evolved to become more organized and professional in their strategies, resources, staff and business procedures (Xiao et al., 2017). In recent years, various businesses have introduced wearable technology and mobile apps that enable individuals to monitor their personal health information. The 'quantified self' phenomenon, where people track their behavioural, physiological, biochemical and other types of health markers, has been made possible by these mHealth gadgets and apps. With a projected compound annual growth rate (CAGR) of 8.5%, the Indian market for sports and fitness equipment will grow from its 2021 valuation of USD 1,934 million to USD 3,065 million by 2027. This growth is driven by the increasing adoption of digital and virtual fitness services (IMARC, 2022).

While a fitness app's functionality may attract initial users, long-term value is generated by the adoption of healthy behaviours (Siepmann & Kowalczuk, 2021). For fitness applications, businesses creating wearable technology and businesses offering ancillary services, sustained engagement is becoming a significant challenge (Ledger & McCaffrey, 2017). What these businesses may be overlooking is the importance of habit formation, social incentives and goal reinforcement. Additionally, personalized and customized features, gamification and social support can also play a role in increasing user engagement and retention. Unfortunately, many fitness applications on the market suffer from poor user experience (UX), making it difficult for consumers to maintain engagement over time (Molina & Sundar, 2018). Therefore, it is crucial for health and fitness app businesses to understand how to increase user retention and make their apps more engaging. Furthermore, it's critical to identify which technological developments will be crucial for the long-term survival of the fitness industry and which ones should be dismissed as fads. This highlights the need for research in identifying effective strategies and features that can enhance user engagement and retention in fitness mobile apps.

The significance of habit formation, social incentives and goal reinforcement may be overlooked by businesses in the fitness industry. Despite the abundance of fitness applications available on the market, many of them suffer from poor UX and design flaws that prevent users from forming lasting habits and staying engaged for an extended period of time. This highlights the need for businesses to prioritize UX and design in their development and marketing strategies, in order to increase user retention and engagement. By understanding the importance of habit formation, social incentives and goal reinforcement, fitness applications can be made by businesses that better cater to the needs and preferences of their consumers.

Through the use of a Systematic Literature Review (SLR), this study aims to identify the connection between important digital trends and user engagement in fitness apps. SLR is a methodical approach that allows for the identification, selection, assessment and synthesis of knowledge on a specific topic. This approach is considered to be more rigorous, transparent and thorough than other forms of unstructured literature reviews (Denyer & Tranfield, 2009; Tranfield et al., 2003). Our study specifically aims to locate, compile and critically evaluate a number of research publications or papers using this systematic approach, providing a comprehensive understanding of the connection between digital trends and user engagement in fitness apps.

2. BACKGROUND

2.1 Key Issues and Conceptualization

2.1.1 Digital Disruption in Fitness Industry

Digital Disruption in the Fitness Industry: Technology has become a pervasive aspect of modern life, continuously shaping and transforming the way we conduct business. Key technological advancements such as artificial intelligence (AI), robots, additive manufacturing, automation, cloud computing, mobile and data analytics have brought about new and innovative ways to understand customer behaviour and improve connectivity. Among these, mobile health technologies (mHealth) have the potential to greatly benefit public health by providing easy access to personal health information and remote monitoring. Smartphone users are increasingly utilizing mobile fitness apps to manage their well-being, track progress and set goals (Wang & Collins, 2021). The health and fitness industry are experiencing steady growth, with total industry revenue projected to reach 46.62 billion dollars in 2022. The industry is projected to continue growing at a CAGR of 6.14% between 2022 and 2026, as competition to create innovative fitness technology intensifies. The digital disruption in the fitness industry also presents opportunities for personalization, gamification, social support and integration with wearables, which can enhance user engagement and retention. Moreover, the use of data analytics and machine learning (ML) can aid in the delivery of personalized and effective fitness programmes. Additionally, AI-powered chatbots and virtual personal trainers can provide users with real-time feedback, personalized recommendations and a human-like interaction which makes the experience more engaging and interactive. The incorporation of such technologies can help in creating a more personalized and interactive experience for the users and increase their engagement with the app.

The fitness industry is constantly evolving with the introduction of new technology innovations, making it difficult for fitness experts to determine which ones will have a long-term impact on their company's performance and which should be disregarded as fleeting fads. To evaluate the effectiveness of these technologies, it's crucial to have a deep understanding of user behaviour and to develop a strategy that can retain and engage mobile app users. Kamboj and Sarmah (2018a, 2018b) argue that a shift from a transactional to a relational perspective is necessary to ensure long-term customer loyalty. This means focusing on creating a positive UX and fostering a sense of community among users. Additionally, businesses should also consider data privacy, security and ethics in their technology implementation. By carefully evaluating and incorporating the right technology innovations, fitness businesses can improve user engagement and increase the chances of long-term success.

It is exciting to see how technology is being used more and more in the fitness industry, particularly in light of the COVID-19 outbreak. Since last year, the fitness industry has responded to digital innovative solutions in a wide variety of ways beyond the introduction of fitness items like health bands and mobile applications for tracking health. International Health, Racquet and Sportsclub Association (IHRSA) Global Report 2022 states that more than two years after its environment underwent an irrevocable transformation, the health and fitness industry has started to show positive signs of recovery. Prior studies discovered that the efficacy of an app may be impacted by its functions. Yet, the impact of different combinations of app features on how consumers interact with apps has not been thoroughly examined in studies.

Additionally interactive, smartphone apps provide a direct connection with the user (Roy et al., 2017). As a result, more consumers download mobile apps. Although mobile apps are regularly downloaded, it has been observed that 25% of them are uninstalled right away. Additionally, Only 26% of them are utilized just once. This demonstrates that for businesses, maintaining mobile apps is a challenge. Furthermore, despite soaring global sales of wearable tech, an Endeavour Partners survey found one-third of users quit within six months. On the other hand, apps that employ AI to instruct users promise to deliver a similar UX to having a trainer right next to them (Chung et al., 2018). The future of fitness is data-driven (Bhargava & Nabi, 2020). These apps will use AI/ML and data science to provide real-time, customized workout programmes that adapt to users' performance, helping them achieve their goals. Nowadays customers are highly connected via social and professional platforms (Marsden & Chaney, 2013); therefore, relationship between a consumer's location, sociability and mobility provides a unique perspective about them (Jain et al., 2018).

2.1.2 Gamification for Fitness Apps

Gamification, 'application of game design ideas in non-gaming environments', is becoming more and more popular as a business tool (See Fig. 1). Interactive and gamified designs may be seen in sports, fitness, wellness and even financial service apps. In a gamified app, a user can earn points, badges, leaderboard ranking, levels and be part of community challenges and social interaction (Miller et al., 2016). These social and gamification designs fulfil users' requirements for social interactions and recognition within their communities (Lim et al., 2015).

Wang and Collins (2021) suggested that fitness applications with gamification and motivational elements were more popular among users with higher body mass indexes (BMIs) than those with educational or tracking capabilities. They also pointed out that rather than individual functionalities, the success of an app is influenced by the many combinations of its features. They grouped mobile fitness applications from the iPhone app store in their systematic evaluation of such apps into four types such as 'Tutor, Recorder, Game Companion, Cheerleader'. These offer special functionalities that combine education, tracking, social, gamification and motivation. However, there hasn't been much focus in academic research or management practice on the difficulties in creating, putting into practice, managing and optimizing gamification initiatives. The link between gamification

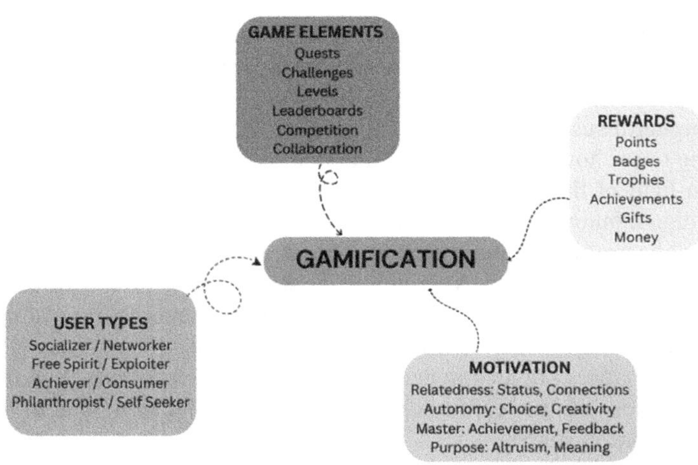

Fig. 1. Gamification. *Source:* Illustrated by authors.

and customer experience (CX) as well as brand experience-based constructs must be analyzed to increase understanding of gamification in the fitness sector.

2.1.3 User Engagements in Fitness Apps

Recent studies highlight the importance of extrinsic elements, such as surroundings, types of training and accessibility, that interfere with the use of applications to improve sporting behaviours, user interaction or motivation (Barkley et al., 2020; Canhoto & Arp, 2017). User engagement is essential to a mobile app's long-term and commercial success. To increase user engagement and brand loyalty, the fitness app must give a personalized UX, tailored to each user, in real time. User engagement has been measured using a variety of indicators, including dwell time. However, there is still much to learn about how to accurately estimate user engagement in the context of fitness apps. Do users' dwell times vary depending on the situations in which they use their mobile app, such as the time of day, and on the situations in which they use their wearable devices? Such inquiries might assist fitness app owners to optimize where they position services and advertisements (Tian et al., 2022).

3. METHODOLOGY

In this study, we conducted a SLR based on the methodology proposed by Denyer and Tranfield (2009). Our review process comprised five key phases: '(i) Framing the Research Question(s): We defined precise research questions to guide our review; (ii) Searching for Research Evidence/Studies: A comprehensive search strategy, following PRISMA guidelines, was employed to identify relevant literature; (iii) Selecting and Evaluating the Studies: We established rigorous inclusion and exclusion criteria in line with PRISMA and assessed the quality of selected studies; (iv) Analyzing and Synthesizing the Data: Data from the chosen studies were systematically analyzed and synthesized; (v) Drawing the Findings and Discussion: The outcomes of our review were interpreted and discussed in the context of our research questions'. We describe how these five phases have been implemented in the specific context of this study in the sections that follow.

3.1 Formulation of the Research Question(s)

The research questions are defined as the initial phase of an SLR. These have to depict the scope and aim of the investigation. The goal of the investigation is situated at the intersection area between gamification and technology adoption as well as the use of AI/ML concepts (digital disruptions) about user engagements towards the commercial success of fitness apps. The main ideas' definitions should be unambiguously defined; therefore, Fig. 2 displays the central themes and the areas where the mentioned papers are located.

In light of these fundamental ideas and to understand the connections between digital disruptions, the below mentioned issues have broadly been identified as the research questions (gamification, technology adoptions, and use of AI ML) and user involvement through the discovery of research field-specific agreements and conflicts.

RQ1. How does gamification impact the users of mobile fitness apps?

RQ2. What is the relationship between technology adoption and user behaviour in fitness apps?

RQ3. How do AI and ML technologies affect user experiences in fitness apps?

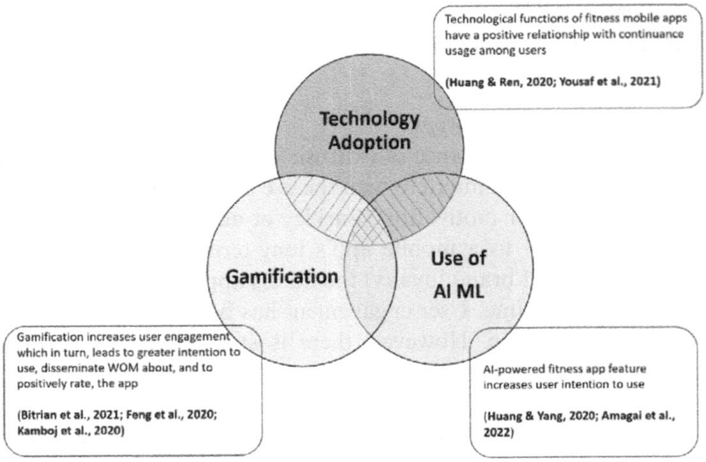

Fig. 2. Central Theme and Research Objective of the Literature Review. *Source:* Illustrated by authors.

RQ4. What is the importance of 'User Engagement' in the commercial success of fitness apps?

RQ5. What gaps and challenges remain for future research in this domain?

3.2 Identification of Studies

The studies in this instance were found using Web of Science (WoS), Scopus and EBSCO Host, three of the most pertinent scholarly databases in the field. Additionally, due to the different syntaxes among the databases, it was required to modify the search string for each one. Table 1 lists the keywords that were employed. According to the options provided by the various databases, either in the article's title, abstract or keywords, it was agreed that the specified sets of keywords should be used.

The works were chosen and judged according to predetermined inclusion and exclusion criteria. The journal quality and publication period of the publications served as the initial inclusion criterion. This was restricted to works that were peer-reviewed and released from 2018 to 2022. The titles, abstracts and keywords of the chosen papers were then examined to see if they matched the research questions. The works were then thoroughly read, and

Table 1. Keywords and Search Strings.

Keywords	
(A) Gamification	'gamification + fitness app', 'Gamification + user engagement', 'gamification + customer loyalty', 'gamification + user retention'
(B) Technology Adoption	'Technology adoption + fitness app', 'technology affordance + user engagement', 'Technology adoption + customer loyalty', 'technology adoption + user retention'
(C) AI/ML	'AI ML + fitness app', 'AI ML + fitness app', 'AI ML + user engagement', 'AI ML + customer loyalty', 'AI ML + user retention'

Source: Illustrated by authors.

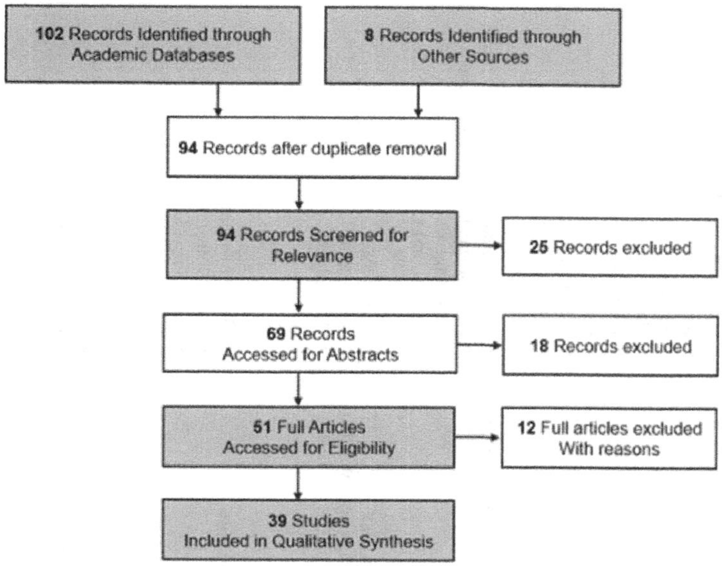

Fig. 3. PRISMA Flow Diagram of Inclusion of Articles. *Source:* Illustrated by authors.

research papers that weren't pertinent to the research problem (false positives) were eliminated. Finally, the search produced a total of 39 probable sources.

The screening and article selection process is graphically summarized by the Preferred Reporting Items for Systematic Reviews and Meta-Analyses (PRISMA) flow chart (Moher et al., 2010). The flow of data through the several phases of a systematic review is depicted in a chart (Fig. 3), and it illustrates how many records were found, how many were included and excluded.

4. LITERATURE REVIEW

4.1 Review of Impact of Gamification on Fitness App Users

Gamification consistently enhances user engagement and intention to use in fitness and health-related apps. Key factors include perceived value, habit formation and satisfaction, which influence users' desires to limit app use. Additionally, gamified apps often lead to cognitive immersion, making users more willing to share personal information with businesses. The positive effects of gamification are seen in increased user engagement and improved app ratings and reviews. Apps incorporating incompatible components for intrinsic motivation and making apps more sociable by enhancing emotional and social value are effective strategies. Inconsistencies arise in the impact of gamification on different apps and user groups. The effectiveness of gamification can vary between apps and features, affecting users' purchase intentions, brand engagement and emotional experiences. Different gamification elements may impact users' information sharing and ongoing use of health and fitness apps. Emerging patterns from the above review (Table 2) include the importance of customization and the use of incompatible components to boost intrinsic motivation in fitness gamification apps. The idea of making apps more sociable and enhancing emotional and social value is gaining prominence. Insights into corporate

Table 2. Impact of Gamification on Fitness App Users.

Author	Publisher	Key Findings	Target App	Variables Used
Huang et al. (2019)	Emerald	This paper utilized a bootstrap analysis to incorporate 'regret, habit and perceived value' into gamification apps. It examined the impact of these factors on users' desire to limit their use.	Fitness gamification apps	• Confirmation • Perceived Usefulness • Regret • Satisfaction • Habit • Intention
Trang and Weiger (2021)	Elsevier	Users of gamified apps were more willing to divulge personal data to businesses. Gamified apps' motivational experiences lead to cognitive immersion.	Gaming Apps: Sport, Health, Educational apps	• Gamification • CognitiveAbsorption • Personal Information Disclosure
Bitrián et al. (2021)	Elsevier	According to this quantitative study, user engagement has been increased through gamification, which in turn improves user intention to use, and positively rate and review the app	Users of the Fitbit app from the United States	• Motivational Affordance • Psychological Outcomes – (User Engagement) • Behavioural Outcomes
Feng et al., 2020	Elsevier	This qualitative research supported the idea that apps with incompatible components might improve user engagement and loyalty by boosting intrinsic motivation than apps using commensurate elements.	Fitness gamification app: Walkup App, WeRun App, WeChat App.	• Autonomy. • Competence • Relatedness
Tu et al. (2019)	Elsevier	The authors suggested making the apps more sociable by enhancing emotional value and increasing social value may increase their usefulness and be more successful in encouraging users to engage in physical exercise.	Fitness gamification apps: Walkup App, WeChat Sports	• Game Elements • User Motivation • Value Provided
Kamboj et al. (2020)	JECO	This study considered as a guide to app creators on how to develop apps that keep users interested in a variety of hedonic objects, facilitating their continued usage of the gaming apps.	Gamification in mobile apps: Candy crush, Temple run, Bubble shooter and Mario etc	• Perceived usefulness • Convenience • Enjoyment • Customer Engagement • Intention
Yadav (2022)	themedicon.com	This link between gamified engagements on applications for health and fitness and	Branded health and fitness apps	• Brand Engagement • Positive Emotions

		users' purchase intents was analyzed quantitatively, along with the role that brand engagement and pleasant emotions played in moulding it.		• Experience • Purchase Intention
Wang et al. (2021)	JMIR	This study investigated the elements users' intentions must keep utilizing mHealth apps in addition to the process and progression of their sentiments regarding the impact that gamification has on their continued use of such applications.	mHealth Apps	• Satisfaction • Intrinsic Motivation • Relatedness • Autonomy • Competence
Lu and Ho (2020)	MDPI	This quantitative study presented insightful information on corporate sustainability for sectors affected by the functioning of an app-based company and users' gaming behaviour and arouse favourable emotions to heighten brand stickiness.	Nike Run Club (NRC) app	• Fun • Rules • System • Presentation • Dynamics
Esmaeilzadeh (2021a, 2021b)	AISLE	Highlighted how gamification aspects could enhance users' propensity to share information via the applications and their continuous willingness to utilize apps for health and fitness.	Health and fitness apps: 'Fitocracy, Fooducate, MyFitnessPal, My Diet Coach, RunKeeper, Just 6 weeks, and JEFIT Workout'	• Dependence • Relatedness • Emotion • Intention to use • Identity

Source: Illustrated by authors.

sustainability and brand stickiness based on users' gaming behaviour and emotions are emerging as significant patterns. Gamification aspects that enhance users' propensity to share information and their continuous willingness to use health and fitness apps are gaining attention.

4.2 Review on the Effect of Technology Adoption on Fitness App Usage

The literature consistently indicates that various factors influence user engagement and continued use of fitness apps. These include interactivity, navigability, customization, relatedness, competence and autonomy in fitness tracker apps. In addition, technology self-efficacy plays a significant role in users' continued use of fitness apps. Real-world objective data, such as mindfulness and peer support, contribute to engagement. Users' perceptions of the benefits and drawbacks of technology readiness affect their decisions to use health and fitness apps. The acceptance and investment models significantly affect long-term use of health and fitness apps, with trust, social influence and health valuation as crucial predictors. While the literature (Table 3) reveals common trends in technology adoption, there are inconsistencies in the variables and factors that affect users of different fitness apps. The effectiveness of these factors can vary based on the specific app and its features and users' preferences and perceptions. In addition, there may be variations in the impact of technology readiness and perceived usefulness on user intentions to use health and fitness apps. The literature also explores the role of larger social and institutional factors, which can introduce additional variability. Emerging patterns from the review (Table 3) suggest that businesses can use technology to meet the needs of their customers and publicize their offerings. The significance of social and institutional factors in health technology is gaining attention, filling a gap in the literature. Research into user modelling, personalization and behaviour modification interventions is contributing to user-centred design, focusing on enhancing health and well-being. Additionally, gamification mechanisms are seen as facilitators of information technology identity fulfilment and beneficial user behavioural outcomes.

4.3 Use of AI/ML in Fitness Apps and Its Effect on Users

The literature on the use of AI and ML in fitness apps highlights several recurring trends. AI is increasingly employed in fitness apps to create personalized interaction marketing, offering customized solutions to users. There is a growing focus on the development and evaluation of food computing apps, which utilize AI to track nutrition effectively. Researchers delve into the factors influencing public perception of AI-powered weight loss and health management apps, considering personal innovativeness, effort expectancy and hedonic motivation. Fitness instructor applications are incorporating on-device computer vision AI to enhance user interaction. AI is also used to create AI-generated characters, supporting individualized learning and well-being. Furthermore, AI aids in achieving fitness goals by using data from wearable sensors and smart devices. AI and ML integration in fitness apps shows varying effects on user engagement and satisfaction due to diverse app approaches. For instance, the effectiveness of AI in personalized interaction marketing may differ across fitness apps. Public perception of AI in weight loss and health management apps can vary based on factors such as personal innovativeness and effort expectancy. The literature (Table 4) reveals emerging patterns that indicate the transformative potential of AI and ML in the fitness app landscape. AI is increasingly utilized in food computing apps for nutrition tracking. On-device computer vision AI is being

Table 3. Effect of Technology Adoption on Fitness App Usage.

Authors	Publisher	Key Findings	Target App	Variables Used
Zhou et al. (2022)	Taylor and Francis	Discussed the connection between psychological requirements and technological affordances to anticipate user engagement and fitness tracker use.	Fitness Tracker Apps	• Interactivity • Navigability • Customization • Relatedness • Competence • Autonomy
Yousaf et al. (2021)	Elsevier	This quantitative study examined the variables that affect users of fitness applications' post-adoption usage satisfaction, continued use and health satisfaction. It also discovers that technology self-efficacy is a significant component on user's continued use of an application.	Fitness Apps: Strava, Apple Watch, Android Smartwatch.	• Post-adoption technology self-efficacy • Post-adoption user interface quality • Usage satisfaction • Continual usage • Health satisfaction
Amit et al. (2019)	J Med	This study analyzed real-world objective data on user engagement and reported on the usage and retention metrics.	Mental Health Apps: Headspace, Calm, Daylio, Prana Breath, 7 Cups, Abide, Lets Meditate	• Mindfulness • Peer support • Anxiety • Depression
Chiu and Cho (2021)	Emerald	This study determined how individuals' perceptions of the benefits and drawbacks of technology readiness influence their decisions to use health and fitness applications.	Fitness Applications	• Optimism • Innovativeness • Discomfort • Insecurity • Intention to use
Byun et al. (2018)	IGI	This study's results imply that businesses can use technology as a significant instrument to not only publicize their offerings but also meet the needs of their customers.	Sports Brand Application: 'Nike Run Club, Runtastic, MyASICS Run Training'	• Intention to use • Perceived usefulness • Perceived ease of use • Perceived enjoyment • Actual usage
Chiu and Cho (2020)	Elsevier	The parameters of the investment model and the technology acceptance model have an effect on how long health and fitness applications are used.	Health And Fitness Apps: 'Apple Health, Samsung Health, My Fitness Pal, Nike Run Club'	• Perceived usefulness • Perceived ease of use • Satisfaction • Intention to use • Intention to continue • Commitment

Table 3. *(Continued)*

Authors	Publisher	Key Findings	Target App	Variables Used
Beldad and Hegner (2018)	Taylor and Francis	Factors from the technological acceptance model along with trust, social influence and health valuation were used to predict the long-term use of fitness applications.	Fitness App Runtastic, MyFitnessPal, Freeletics, and 7 Minutes Workout	• Perceived usefulness • Perceived ease of use • Injective social norms • Descriptive Social norms • Intention to continue • Trust, health valuation
Windasari et al. (2021)	Elsevier	By taking into account the significance of larger social and institutional factors, this quantitative study fills a gap in the body of literature on health technology and involvement of dieticians.	Fitness Apps, Wearable fitness tracker	• Choice • Involvement • Self efficacy • Satisfaction • Intention to continue
Rockmann (2019)	Core	This paper elucidated the 'evil side' of IT use in fitness applications, and describing the motivational affordances' need-relevant properties.	Fitness Apps: Strava App	• Self-monitoring • Rewards • Social recognition • Competence satisfaction • Competence thwarting
Mejova and Kalimeri (2019)	ACM	This paper contributed to the user modelling and personalization research into the user-centred design of persuading technologies and behaviour modification interventions to enhance health and well-being.	Fitness Apps: MapMyRun, MapMyRide, Spak People, MapMyFitness, etc.	• Demographics • Values • Morals • Domains • App Cats
Esmaeilzadeh (2021a, 2021b)	JMIR	The fulfilment of information technology identity and beneficial user behavioural results could be facilitated by gamification mechanisms.	Health and Fitness App: 'Fitocracy, Fooducate, MyFitnessPal, My Diet Coach, RunKeeper, Strava, and JEFIT Workout'	• Emotion energy • Dependence • Relatedness • Info sharing tendency • Intention • Perceive gamification tendency

Source: Illustrated by authors.

Table 4. Use of AI/ML in Fitness Apps and Its Effect on Users.

Author	Publisher	Key Findings	Target App	Variables Used
Kumar et al. (2019)	Sage	In this article, AI was analyzed in the context of personalized interaction marketing, a tactic for creating, distributing and offering clients customized solutions.	Fitnessapp	• Customer experience • Personalized engagement
Samad et al. (2022)	Elsevier	The implementation, efficacy and performance evaluation of food computing apps are the main areas of focus of this study, which looks into the development of AI and the considerable increase in the use of apps for tracking nutrition.	Food computing apps: KetoDiet, Meal Tracker, Nutrition Tracker, Calorie Calculator.	• Intention to use
Huang et al. (2021)	TELEMEDICINE and e-HEALTH	This study aimed to develop and test a theoretical model of factors affecting public perception of an AI-powered weight loss and health management app.	Health and fitness apps. m-Health apps, smart phone and smart watches	• Personal innovativeness • Behavioural intention • Effort expectancy • Facilitating conditions • Hedonic motivation • Habit • Network externality
Garbett et al. (2021)	ACM	This qualitative work recognized the trend of fitness instructor applications using 'on-device computer vision AI' and investigated how consumers interact with these technologies.	Fitness-related instructional apps: 'Fitness Ally: AI Workouts Coach, Onyx Home Workout, VAY Fitness Coach, Kaia Personal Trainer, Zenia'	• User interaction
Pataranutaporn et al. (2021)	Nature	The characters in this work were created by AI to support individualized learning and well-being.		• Human–AI interaction
Molina and Myrick (2021)	Taylor and Francis	This study focused on the user motivations to learn more about the relationship between technology and fitness and found that design techniques might be applied in fitness tracking apps.	Fitness App. BodySpace	• Inspired by others • Desire to regain • Desire for improved appearance • Desire for improved well-being • Job-related demands

Table 4. *(Continued)*

Author	Publisher	Key Findings	Target App	Variables Used
				• Stress relief and mental benefit
Patel and Trivedi (2020)	EQM, Researchberg	The aim of this investigation was to analyze the many commercial applications of AI (AI-powered customer service, predictive modelling, ML-powered personalization and integration of natural language processing) before conducting an empirical test to see whether such applications boost customer loyalty.	Healthcare apps	• Customer loyalty
Smyth et al. (2022)	Springer	This study demonstrated how data routinely gathered by the most recent generation of wearable sensors, smart watches and mobile fitness apps aids users in achieving their fitness objectives.	Apps for marathon runners	• User experience design

Source: Illustrated by authors.

integrated into fitness instructor applications to enhance user interaction. AI-generated characters are becoming key components in supporting individualized learning and well-being. The application of AI and ML in fitness tracking apps is being explored to enhance user motivation and engagement. AI is also gaining ground in healthcare apps, particularly in enhancing customer loyalty. Wearable sensors, smartwatches and mobile fitness apps are increasingly relying on AI and ML to help users achieve their fitness goals, highlighting the importance of UX design in this context.

4.4 Review on User Engagement in Fitness Apps

From the above literature (Table 5), we can observe that gamification consistently enhances user engagement and retention, making it a valuable strategy. Furthermore, user-centred design principles and a focus on behaviour design emerge as crucial for improving user interaction and satisfaction. The studies also emphasize the significance of recognizing and nurturing user commitment phases, from initial trials to habit formation, as this plays a pivotal role in the success of fitness apps. Inconsistencies in the research findings become apparent in several areas. Firstly, while gamification consistently enhances engagement in fitness apps, its influence on users' real-world goals and long-term benefits exhibits variability. Different users may experience varying degrees of success in achieving their objectives. Secondly, studies focusing on gamification's impact on children's behaviour provide inconclusive results, underscoring the necessity for age-specific considerations and tailored strategies in this context. Lastly, the diverse preferences of users regarding the UX in fitness apps highlight the absence of a one-size-fits-all approach. Customizable and personalized experiences are crucial to accommodate these varying preferences effectively. Tailored user retention strategies, customized to individual exercise self-efficacy and preferences, are gaining importance. Augmented reality (AR) is becoming another significant factor influencing user persistence and intentions in mobile apps, with confirmation theory playing a relevant role. The adoption of mobile health (mHealth) apps is increasingly grounded in strong theoretical foundations and a focus on UX. Continual evolution of user-centred design principles is crucial in app development for a user-centric approach.

5. SUMMARY OF THE LITERATURE

From the above systematic review, we can see that more than 60% of those who utilize exercise equipment do so to complete their routines. The current research also concluded that the majority of users believed that the gamified applications encouraged them to reach their daily physical practice objectives. We have identified the following relationships from the review (Table 6). The fact that only a small percentage of users used the programmes for prolonged times despite the seeming large numbers of app installations and daily active minutes of usage is also crucial to understand. The research, however, is not consistent about the impact of technology adoption or gamification from user intention to use and user intention to continue to further towards sustainable usage or CX and brand experience (BX) of users directly.

Table 5. User Engagement in Fitness Apps.

Author	Publisher	Key Findings	Target App	Variables Used
Wang et al. (2019)	Springer	This article described the three phases of a fitness app that serve to increase user loyalty: the initial trial phase, the habit-forming phase and the habit-maintaining phase.	Fitness Apps; Walkup App. Mi Sports App Joy Run App Hot Fitness App	• User loyalty
Li et al. (2021)	Taylor and Francis	The quantitative study methodically investigated how real-world objectives and long-term usage plans for users of mobile fitness apps were affected by gamification narrative mechanisms.	Mobile Fitness app.	• Perceived concentration • perceived understanding • perceived control • Perceived curiosity • Perceived challenge • Real-world purpose
Verhulsdonck and Shalamova (2020)	Sage	This article presented the case that technical communicators needed behavioural design because it enables the usage of digital assets, which are an essential part of the UX.	Apple Watch fitness tracking app	• Context • Habits • Other people Incentives • Congruence • Emotions • Salience
Alsaleh and Alnanih (2019)	Science Publications	The results of this research provided clarity on how to use technology to manage children's behaviour and boost gamification improves user awareness, focus and usability.	Healthcare Gamification	• Gamibetes • Mobile application • Parentpage • Childpage • Healthcare • Motivation
Carlsson et al. (2018)	Chalmers	This work performed a UX analysis, essentially a workout application that focuses on gamification and user experience components.	Gym workout application. Skull crusher, Triceps extension, Biceps Curl, Dumbbell Press	• User experience
Huang and Ren (2020)	Elsevier	This study used technological acceptance and investigated the effect of exercise self-efficacy in predicting existing. In order to better understand how to boost user retention rates, we may assess users' desire to continue using the apps.	Fitness apps	• User retention • Intention to continue

Li et al. (2020)	Elsevier	This study extends the expectation of using the confirmation theory to look at potential elements that might affect user persistence and increasing usage intention decisions regarding the post-adoption of mobile apps using augmented reality.	Health benefits apps. Pokémon GO	• Confirmation • Technical feature • Perceived benefit • Use intention • Perceived risks
Wang and Collins (2021)	Elsevier	The adoption of mHealth was supported by knowledge of eHealth and smartphone use. App development should be more theoretically informed and UX-focused.	Mobile fitness applications	• Fitness app function preference • Attitude • Perceived behavioural Control • Subjective norms • Adoption intent
Feng and Wei (2019)	MDPI	This study used the UX Curve approach to assess how the fitness app's UX has evolved over time.	Mobile fitness application	• Pragmatic quality • Hedonic identity quality • Hedonic stimulation quality • Attractiveness
Wang et al. (2022)	MDPI	This research emphasized on identifying the variables that affected fitness software users' behaviour based on the 'Unified Theory of Acceptance and Use of Technology (UTAUT).'	Fitness apps	• Use behaviour • Behavioural Intention • Perceived cost • Perceived risk • Performance expectancy

Source: Illustrated by authors.

Table 6. Summary of Relationships.

LR Themes	Summary of Relationships
Gamification for fitness apps-	Gamification → Intention to use
	Gamification → User Engagement
Use of AI/ML in fitness apps	Use of AI ML → Personalized Communication
	Use of AI ML → User Intercation
Technology adoption in fitness apps	Technology adoption → Intention to use
	Technology adoption → Intention to Continue

Source: Illustrated by authors.

6. GAPS EXPLORED AND AGENDA FOR FUTURE RESEARCH

- Previous fitness app studies have employed diverse definitions when identifying affordances and have applied different ways of using them in research. The plurality of the affordance definitions and uses raises the need for the clarification and foundation of common terms, which can lead to more advantageous future applications.
- Most of the studies have randomly drawn the sample from the online subject pool of mobile app users, which was not a typical sample of users of fitness apps, even though the demographics and socio-economic class of the subject pool showed a diversified pattern. Future research is advised to use more rigorous sample techniques, if resources permit, to improve generalizability.
- Many studies were focusing on intention to use and intention to continue, yet they have ignored conducting a longitudinal study. The longitudinal study will enable researchers to follow developments or changes in the statistics of the target over a period of time. Future research is recommended to employ longitudinal research designs to clarify the function of user interactions in the usage of mobile fitness apps.
- The intention of a person to carry out a behaviour is the most immediate and significant predictor of that behaviour, according to the theories of reasoned action and planned behaviour (Ajzen & Fishbein, 1980; Fishbein & Ajzen, 1975; Sheeran, 2002, p. 1). Numerous human actions, particularly physical exercise, have provided scientific evidence for this claim (Sheeran & Orbell, 2000). Therefore, it is crucial to track user behaviour and to analyze how users interact with the fitness app rather than just analyzing the focal outcome variable as done in the majority of the studies.
- User retention for digital healthcare solutions is still a major challenge. Therefore, a successful retention strategy is becoming more important for every online business. Understanding which customers or consumers are most likely to cease using the service

or product (churn) is essential for many firms' ability to expand. However, the existing studies have ignored focus on these directions in the context of marketing.

- The statement that user involvement in digital healthcare solutions is supported by a large body of literature. But current business statistics show that a startling 80% of users will abandon an app within just 90 days (Barello et al., 2016). Despite having the greatest user retention rates of any app category, health and fitness apps frequently have low engagement and significant user churn. Beyond user involvement and user intention to continue, existing studies fall short. Thus, future studies should concentrate on how to keep people happy through personalized and engaging communication by leveraging technology. Retaining users of fitness applications requires rewarding devoted users.
- The recent development of on-device AI computer vision and chatbot systems has made it possible for a growing number of AI fitness-related educational apps. However, human–computer interaction research on these technologies has not yet been done.
- In the context of today, the 'rewarding user' scale needs to be changed. Users can earn extra money for performing their daily workouts or taking part in specific fitness challenges thanks to online fitness platforms that reward users for maintaining their fitness levels. It adheres to the P2E (Play to Earn) practice of giving players cryptocurrency rewards for participating in games. A recent trend known as 'move-to-earn' includes a variety of goods and services that reward users for being active. As a result, future research must strive to both encourage fitness by lowering obesity and sedentary behaviour and to allow consumers to make money while enhancing their health.

Using published literature and identified gaps, we suggest a framework comprising three elements of experience – user, customer and consumer (as depicted in Fig. 4) – for guiding future research. Accordingly, the meaning of experience and its association with users, customers and brand image of a company must be examined from diverse perspectives in forthcoming studies, particularly in the domain of mobile fitness apps.

CX can be thought of as the experience's process, while UX is the experience's circumstances. In the fiercely competitive consumer market, the quality of goods and services has become homogenized; therefore, enhancing CX has recently become a marketing strategy concern for differentiation. Price, features, quality and customer service, which

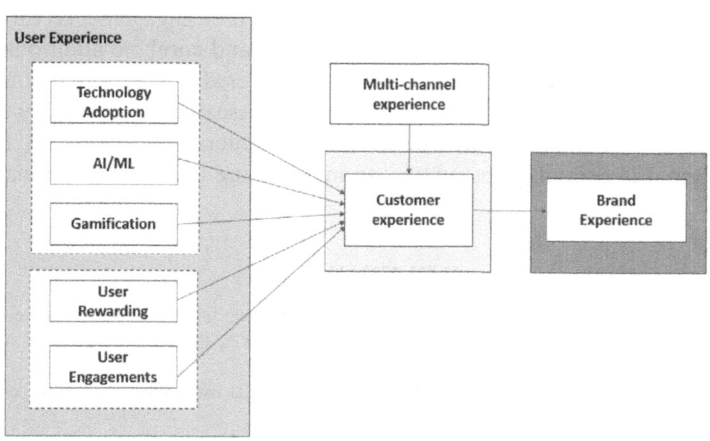

Fig. 4. Proposed Framework for Future Research. *Source:* Illustrated by authors.

were once the main points of differentiation, are no longer effective. Experiential marketing, which has become a new marketing approach or paradigm, is founded on the experience economy idea put forth by Pine and Gilmore (1998, 1999) and the strategic experiential model by Schmitt (1999). CX and UX are thought to have an impact on BX. BX is the perception of the customer at each point of brand encounter (Alloza, 2008).

A similar definition of BX was presented by Brakus et al. (2009), by whom it was described as 'subjective, internal consumer responses and behavioural responses evoked by brand-related stimuli that are part of a brand's design and identity, packaging, messaging, and locations.' The contact between the customer and the brand as well as the consumer's behavioural and psychological reactions that might be affected by the encounter experience are highlighted in those definitions of BX. Those characteristics of BX can correspond to Dewey's two primary concepts of experience, interaction and continuity (1934). According to the provided definitions of BX, we describe it as the interaction between consumers and a brand that encompasses all aspects of the brand and aims to enhance its value. The ultimate objective of BX is to increase the brand's equity.

7. CONCLUSIONS AND IMPLICATIONS

Thanks to advancements that make it easier to practice and adhere to a fitness regimen, technology is increasingly being used in sports and fitness. Beyond compliance, it's critical to recognize technology as a facilitation tool. While the future can be anxiety-inducing, the best strategy for any business is to keep an eye on the changing landscape. A thorough analysis of fresh opportunities can result in significant rewards and long-term success. Our findings show that there is still a need for empirical research on how digital disruption affects the use of fitness applications for modern users in the context of UX. Additionally, we discovered how extensive and contradictory the existing research is on gamification for fitness apps.

The majority of the study that has already been done on gamification for fitness apps was based on user interactions and user intention to use, which produced an equal number of results with supporting and contradictory evidence, making it inconclusive. The impact of gamification and the use of AI, ML and other technological functions to map UX, CX and BX in fitness apps has not received any research attention, even though numerous models and scales have been proposed for measuring 'user engagements' for mobile app users. To provide uniqueness to gamification research and combine additional constructs towards UX, CX and BX, the present study has offered a conceptual foundation for further investigation. As a result, this study advises researchers to employ components from the experience domains, which offer consumer interaction points for the product, service and brand in everyday encounters, to make future studies more valuable.

REFERENCES

Ajzen, I., & Fishbein, M. (1980). *Understanding attitudes and predicting social behavior*. Prentice-Hall.

Alloza, A. (2008). Brand engagement and brand experience at BBVA, the transformation of a 150 years old company. *Corporate Reputation Review*, *11*(4), 371–379.

Alsaleh, N., & Alnanih, R. (2019). Mapping gamification mechanisms to user experience factors for designing user interfaces. *Journal of Computer Science*, *15*, 736–744.

Amit, B., Frederick, M., Stav, E., & Kane J. M. (2019). Objective user engagement with mental health apps: Systematic search and panel-based usage analysis. *Journal of Medical Internet Research*, *21*(9), e14567.

App Annie the State of Mobile 2021. (2021). https://www.appannie.com/en/go/state-of-mobile-2021/. Accessed on 15 February 2021.

Barello, S., Triberti, S., Graffigna, G., Libreri, C., Serino, S., Hibbard, J., & Riva, G. (2016). eHealth for patient engagement: A systematic review. *Frontiers in Psychology*, *6*, 2013. https://doi.org/10.3389/fpsyg.2015.02013

Barkley, J. E., Lepp, A., Santo, A., Glickman, E., & Dowdell, B. (2020). The relationship between fitness app use and physical activity behavior is mediated by exercise identity. *Computers in Human Behavior*, *108*, 106313.

Beldad, A. D., & Hegner, S. M. (2018). Expanding the technology acceptance model with the inclusion of trust, social influence, and health valuation to determine the predictors of German users' willingness to continue using a fitness app: A structural equation modeling approach. *International Journal of Human-Computer Interaction*, *34*(9), 882–893.

Bhargava, Y., & Nabi, J. (2020). The opportunities, challenges and obligations of Fitness Data Analytics. *Procedia Computer Science*, *167*, 1354–1362.

Bitrián, P., Buil, I., & Catalán, S. (2021). Enhancing user engagement: The role of gamification in mobile apps. *Journal of Business Research*, *132*, 170–185.

Brakus, J. J., Schmitt, B. H., & Zarantonello, L. (2009). Brand experience: What is it? How is it measured? Does it affect loyalty? *Journal of Marketing*, *73*(3), 52–62.

Byun, H., Chiu, W., & Bae, J. S. (2018). Exploring the adoption of sports brand apps: An application of the modified technology acceptance model. *International Journal of Asian Business and Information Management*, *9*(1), 52–65.

Canhoto, A. I., & Arp, S. (2017). Exploring the factors that support adoption & sustained use of health & fitness wearables. *Journal of Marketing Management*, *33*(1–2), 32–60.

Carlsson, A., Engelbrektsson, F., Larsson, L., Nordström, E., & Södergren, M. (2018). *UX analysis: A workout application focusing on elements of user experience & gamification* (Bachelor's thesis).

Chiu, W., & Cho, H. (2021). The role of technology readiness in individuals' intention to use health and fitness applications: A comparison between users and non-users. *Asia Pacific Journal of Marketing and Logistics*, *33*(3), 807–825.

Cho, H., Chi, C., & Chiu, W. (2020). Understanding sustained usage of health & fitness apps: Incorporating the technology acceptance model with the investment model. *Technology in Society*, *63*, 101429.

Chung, A. E., Griffin, A. C., Selezneva, D., & Gotz, D. (2018). Health & fitness apps for hands-free voice-activated assistants: Content analysis. *JMIR mHealth & uHealth*, *6*(9), e9705.

Denyer, D., & Tranfield, D. (2009). Producing a systematic review. In *The SAGE handbook of organizational research methods* (pp. 671–689). Sage Publications.

Esmaeilzadeh, P. (2021a). The influence of gamification & information technology identity on postadoption behaviors of health & fitness app users: Empirical study in the United States. *JMIR Serious Games*, *9*(3), e28282.

Esmaeilzadeh, P. (2021b). *The effects of gamification on the post-adoption behaviors of health & fitness apps' users: The mediating role of IT identity*.

Feng, W., Tu, R., & Hsieh, P. (2020). Can gamification increase consumers' engagement in fitness apps? The moderating role of commensurability of the game elements. *Journal of Retailing & Consumer Services*, *57*, 102229.

Feng, L., & Wei, W. (2019). An empirical study on user experience evaluation & identification of critical UX issues. *Sustainability*, *11*(8), 2432.

Fishbein, M., & Ajzen, I. (1975). *Belief, attituak, intention & behavior*. Addison-Wesley.

Garbett, A., Degutyte, Z., Hodge, J., & Astell, A. (2021, June). Towards understanding people's experiences of AI computer vision fitness instructor apps. In *Designing interactive systems conference 2021* (pp. 1619–1637).

Huang, C. K., Chen, C. D., & Liu, Y. T. (2019). To stay or not to stay? Discontinuance intention of gamification apps. *Information Technology & People*, *32*(6), 1423–1445.

Huang, G., & Ren, Y. (2020). Linking technological functions of fitness mobile apps with continuance usage among Chinese users: Moderating role of exercise self-efficacy. *Computers in Human Behavior*, *103*, 151–160.

Huang, C. Y., Yang, M. C., & Huang, C. Y. (2021). An empirical study on factors influencing consumer adoption intention of an AI-powered chatbot for health & weight management. *International Journal of Performability Engineering*, *17*(5).

https://www.ihrsa.org/improve-your-club/2022-ihrsa-global-report-recognizes-fitness-industry-resilience/

https://info.localytics.com/blog/mobile-apps-whats-a-good-retention-rate

https://storyly.io/how-to-increase-user-engagement-in-wearables/

IMARC. Indian sports & fitness goods market: Industry trends, share, size, growth, opportunity & forecast 2022–2027. https://www.imarcgroup.com/indian-sports-fitness-goods-market#:~:text=Market%20Outlook%202022%2D2027%3A,8.5%25%20during%202022%2D2027

Jain, N. K., Kamboj, S., Kumar, V., & Rahman, Z. (2018). Examining consumer-brand relationships on social media platforms. *Marketing Intelligence & Planning*, *36*(1), 63–78.

Kamboj, S., Rana, S., & Drave, V. A. (2020). Factors driving consumer engagement & intentions with gamification of mobile apps. *Journal of Electronic Commerce in Organizations*, *18*(2), 17–35.

Kamboj, S., & Sarmah, B. (2018a). Construction & validation of the customer social participation in brand communities scale. *Internet Research*, *28*(1), 46–73.

Kamboj, S., & Sarmah, B. (2018b). Antecedents & consequences of employee engagement for a diverse workforce. In *Management techniques for a diverse & cross-cultural workforce* (pp. 132–148). IGI Global.

Kumar, V., Rajan, B., Venkatesan, R., & Lecinski, J. (2019). Understanding the role of artificial intelligence in personalized engagement marketing. *California Management Review*, *61*(4), 135–155.

Ledger, D., & McCaffrey, D. (2017). Inside wearables part 1: How behavior change unlocks long-term engagement. *Endeavour Partners*. https://medium.com/endeavourprtnrs/inside-wearable-how-the-science-of-human-behavior-change-offers-the-secret-to-long-term-engagement-a15b3c7d4cf3

Li, H., Gupta, A., Zhang, J., & Flor, N. (2020). Who will use augmented reality? An integrated approach based on text analytics & field survey. *European Journal of Operational Research*, *281*(3), 502–516.

Li, M., Wang, Y., Wu, Y., & Liu, H. (2021). Gamification narrative design as a predictor for mobile fitness app user persistent usage intentions: A goal priming perspective. *Enterprise Information Systems*, *15*(10), 1501–1545.

Lim, S. L., Bentley, P. J., Kanakam, N., Ishikawa, F., & Honiden, S. (2015). Investigating country differences in mobile app user behavior & challenges for software engineering. *IEEE Transactions on Software Engineering*, *41*(1), 40–64.

Lu, H. P., & Ho, H. C. (2020). Exploring the impact of gamification on users' engagement for sustainable development: A case study in brand applications. *Sustainability*, *12*(10), 4169.

Marsden, P., & Chaney, P. (2013). *The social commerce handbook: 20 secrets for turning social media into social sales*. McGraw Hill Professional.

Mejova, Y., & Kalimeri, K. (2019, June). Effect of values & technology use on exercise: Implications for personalized behavior change interventions. In *Proceedings of the 27th ACM conference on user modeling, adaptation & personalization* (pp. 36–45).

Miller, A. S., Cafazzo, J. A., & Seto, E. (2016). A game plan: Gamification design principles in mHealth applications for chronic disease management. *Health Informatics Journal*, *22*(2), 184–193.

Moher, D., Liberati, A., Tetzlaff, J., & Altman, D. G., & Prisma Group. (2010). Preferred reporting items for systematic reviews and meta-analyses: The PRISMA statement. *International Journal of Surgery*, *8*(5), 336–341.

Molina, M. D., & Myrick, J. G. (2021). The 'how' & 'why' of fitness app use: Investigating user motivations to gain insights into the nexus of technology & fitness. *Sport in Society*, *24*(7), 1233–1248.

Molina, M. D., & Sundar, S. S. (2018). Can mobile apps motivate fitness tracking? A study of technological affordances & workout behaviors. *Health Communication*, *35*(1), 65–74.

Pataranutaporn, P., Danry, V., Leong, J., Punpongsanon, P., Novy, D., Maes, P., & Sra, M. (2021). AI-generated characters for supporting personalized learning & well-being. *Nature Machine Intelligence*, *3*(12), 1013–1022.

Patel, N., & Trivedi, S. (2020). Leveraging predictive modeling, machine learning personalization, NLP customer support, & AI chatbots to increase customer loyalty. *Empirical Quests for Management Essences*, *3*(3), 1–24.

Pine, B., & Gilmore, J. H. (1998, July-August). Welcome to the experience economy. *Harvard Business Review*, 97–105.

Pine, B., & Gilmore, J. H. (1999). *The experience economy*. Harvard Business School Press.

Rockmann, R. (2019). *Don't hurt me ... no more? An empirical study on the positive & adverse motivational effects in fitness apps*.

Roy, S., Ponnam, A., & Mandal, S. (2017). Comprehending technology attachment in the case of smart phone-applications: An empirical study. *Journal of Electronic Commerce in Organizations*, *15*(1), 23–43.

Samad, S., Ahmed, F., Naher, S., Kabir, M. A., Das, A., Amin, S., & Islam, S. M. S. (2022). Smartphone apps for tracking food consumption & recommendations: Evaluating artificial intelligence-based functionalities, features & quality of current apps. *Intelligent Systems With Applications*, 200103.

Schmitt, B. H. (1999). *Experiential marketing. How to get customers to sense, feel, think, act, relate to your company & brands*. The Free Press.

Sheeran, P. (2002). Intention – Behavior relations: A conceptual & empirical review. *European Review of Social Psychology*, *12*, 1–36.

Sheeran, P., & Orbell, S. (2000). Using implementation intentions to increase attendance for cervical cancer screening. *Health Psychology*, *19*, 283–289.

Siepmann, C., & Kowalczuk, P. (2021). Understanding continued smartwatch usage: The role of emotional as well as health & fitness factors. *Electronic Markets*, *31*(4), 795–809.

Smyth, B., Lawlor, A., Berndsen, J., & Feely, C. (2022). Recommendations for marathon runners: On the application of recommender systems & machine learning to support recreational marathon runners. *User Modelling and User-Adapted Interaction*, *32*(5), 787–838.

Tian, Z., Yang, W., Zhang, T., Ai, T., & Wang, Y. (2022). Characterizing the activity patterns of outdoor jogging using massive multi-aspect trajectory data. *Computers, Environment and Urban Systems*, *95*, 101804.

Tranfield, D., Denyer, D., & Smart, P. (2003). Towards a methodology for developing evidence-informed management knowledge by means of systematic review. *British Journal of Management*, *14*(3), 207–222.

Trang, S., & Weiger, W. H. (2021). The perils of gamification: Does engaging with gamified services increase users' willingness to disclose personal information? *Computers in Human Behavior*, *116*, 106644.

Tu, R., Hsieh, P., & Feng, W. (2019). Walking for fun or for 'likes'? The impacts of different gamification orientations of fitness apps on consumers' physical activities. *Sport Management Review*, *22*(5), 682–693.

Verhulsdonck, G., & Shalamova, N. (2020). Creating content that influences people: Considering user experience & behavioral design in technical communication. *Journal of Technical Writing and Communication*, *50*(4), 376–400.

Wang, Y., & Collins, W. B. (2021). Systematic evaluation of mobile fitness apps: Apps as the tutor, recorder, game companion, & cheerleader. *Telematics and Informatics*, *59*, 101552.

Wang, J. Q., Cong, J. C., Zheng, Z. Y., Meng, Y., & Liu, C. (2019, July). An interaction design approach of fitness app. In *International conference on human-computer interaction* (pp. 348–358). Springer.

Wang, T., Fan, L., Zheng, X., Wang, W., Liang, J., An, K., & Lei, J. (2021). The impact of gamification-induced users' feelings on the continued use of mHealth apps: A structural equation model with the self-determination theory approach. *Journal of Medical Internet Research*, *23*(8), e24546.

Wang, C., Wu, G., Zhou, X., & Lv, Y. (2022). An empirical study of the factors influencing user behavior of fitness software in college students based on UTAUT. *Sustainability*, *14*(15), 9720.

We Are Social. Digital in 2021 Global Overview. (2021). https://wearesocial.com/digital-2021. Accessed on 30 January 2021.

Windasari, N. A., Lin, F. R., & Kato-Lin, Y. C. (2021). Continued use of wearable fitness technology: A value co-creation perspective. *International Journal of Information Management*, *57*, 102292.

Xiao, X., Hedman, J., Tan, F. T. C., Tan, C. W., Lim, E. T., Clemenson, T., & Hillegersberg, J. V. (2017). Sports digitalization: An overview & A research agenda. In *International conference on information (ICIS)*. Association For Information System.

Yadav, A. (2022). Gamified interaction's impact on consumers' purchasing decisions: A health and fitness apps perspective. *Medicon Engineering Themes*, *2*(5), 33–40.

Yousaf, A., Mishra, A., & Gupta, A. (2021). From technology adoption to consumption': Effect of pre-adoption expectations from fitness applications on usage satisfaction, continual usage, & health satisfaction. *Journal of Retailing & Consumer Services*, *62*, 102655.

Zhou, X., Krishnan, A., & Dincelli, E. (2022). Examining user engagement & use of fitness tracking technology through the lens of technology affordances. *Behaviour & Information Technology*, *41*(9), 2018–2033.

INFLUENCE OF DIGITAL MARKETING ADOPTION TO LEVERAGE DIGITAL FOOTFALL AND ENHANCED SALES

Sadashiva Tandur[a], Adarsh Garg[b] and Mujibur Rahman[a]

[a]*Galgotias University, India*
[b]*GL Bajaj Institute of Management and Research, India*

ABSTRACT

The primary objective of this research is to identify and analyze the influence of digital marketing practises on performance of business of manufacturing enterprises in Delhi-NCR. A quantitative and descriptive research design was implemented in this study. 368 participants from various enterprises were chosen. Questionnaires were used to collect data on the benefits and challenges which are perceived of digital marketing, as well as usage and business performance of these enterprises. SPSS v24.0 is utilized to carry out statistical analysis on the collected data. The study discovered that advantages and problems of digital marketing practices influenced the usage of digital marketing. Furthermore, the execution of digital marketing had a prominent influence on sales and total number of customers of these enterprises, and this relationship was moderated by type and size of businesses. It was discovered that using digital marketing strategies increased business profits by raising digital marketing awareness among consumers and various industries. It made digital marketing easier to implement in various businesses. However, research should be conducted for appropriate generalization in a larger scale.

Keywords: Digital marketing adoption; digital marketing; digital footfall; digital marketing challenges; business performance

1. INTRODUCTION

The current century has been taken over by 'electronic commerce'. It is the application of technologies to run business interactions; it can be within business, B2B as well as B2C. It is the application of technologies for automation of business transactions and work progress (Gan et al., 2005). The number of websites has increased from 17 million (2000) to 1 billion (2014), B2C e-commerce sales has shown growth by 20.1% with a total estimation

Resilient Businesses for Sustainability
Advanced Series in Management, Volume 34B, 137–152

Published under exclusive licence by Emerald Publishing Limited
ISSN: 1877-6361/doi:10.1108/S1877-63612024000034B011

of 1,500 trillion US$. There is a significant rise in mobile and online users worldwide, particularly from emerging markets and m-commerce. This has contributed to a considerable rise in sales (Grubor & Jaksa, 2018). These days it has become compulsory for companies to have their presence online through websites or applications if they intend to expand their business with regards to sales of merchandise. To make the most of these digital platforms, a business uses different techniques. These techniques are generally connected to the digital marketing (DM) concept. For marketing management in business, application of DM is a developmental process. Business organization slowly introduces these technology and innovations to themselves on the basis of requirements of the market (Falahat et al., 2020; Lestari et al., 2020; van de Vrande et al., 2009). Like offline cases, significance of online cases also differs between B2B and B2C business. B2B companies focus on rational buildings like online product demonstration or conducting online events. They have a less specialized online approach; most of it is like offline approach. Even though they spend large amount of budget on online events and activities, they lack an organized way of planning and prioritizing their online expenditure. Further, it also largely depends on planning of advertisement and its frequency of reach (Jensen, 2006).

Moreover, this information from e-tools benefits concerned people to take advantage in the market, in the form of company turnover or magnifying this consumption with respect of resources available (Peltier et al., 2020; Sokolova & Kefi, 2020). However, this standardization process requires adoption of certain digital habits from both supplier and consumer side of the market. These habits are governed by a degree of acceptance of technology. Hence, the reasons are still unclear about whether the company size affects adoption of technology. Therefore, deep research on quantitative level is required for similar economic and geographical units. However, previous experience does play the part in the technology adoption process by both large and small medium enterprises (SMEs) (Pollák & Markovič, 2021). Further, factors like readiness of market to utilize the social media networking and accept e-transaction also influence the platform adoption (Al-Qirim, 2007; Ifinedo, 2011; Kendall et al., 2001). Local vendors and small businesses adopt the e-platform. Other significant factors include market trend, culture, globalization and economy climate (El-Gohary, 2012; Pookulangara & Koesler, 2011; Stockdale & Standing, 2006). The challenges faced by entrepreneurial companies of any size include new skill development, collaboration, knowledge sharing and resource allocation (Constantin, 2009; Zangiacomi et al., 2020). However, very little research has been conducted keeping social media network and marketing communications in focus. Moreover, online customers are not docile observers, but they actively participate in interaction with companies. The online reviews are electronic word of mouth (WOM) which has also reported to prominently increase the performance of companies involved in hotel management (De Pelsmacker et al., 2018). Additionally, WOM is connected with generating new members and increasing traffic on the website leading to enhance the visibility of company when considered in terms of marketing (Verma, 2018). Here, the consumers can be approached from anywhere and anytime across the globe by presenting them with attractive webpage background containing good graphics, informative text and audio. It provides the consumer with improved user experience when compared to the traditional consumer approach. It has also bolster the brand value by clearing any misunderstanding of consumer concerning brand through communication of ideas, opinions and this leads to better purchase intention (Dastane, 2020). This led to the idea of consumer relationship management (CRM); it is a blend of the ultra-modern consumer feedback with quick technological changes to increase consumer purchase ability (Putney & Puney, 2013).

Compared to traditional CRM methods, now CRM has made use of DM platforms for communications, consumer services and advertisement which has so far given satisfactory results (Dastane, 2020). This has led to an increase in the number and reach of consumers and an increase in the rate of sales as well. However, a thorough study must be conducted to make accurate assumptions.

Further, the main role of DM is to evaluate, plan, implement and control projects to content the consumers' demands, requirements and wishes, thus benefiting the company. Therefore, DM is considered to play business sustainability, development and success. It is highly associated with the latest technologies for advancement of business which traditional marketing fails to serve. Nonetheless, it is considered that it affects the newer firms as opposed to established firms (Teixeira et al., 2018). An upsurge of digital marketing is related to the latest technologies like Internet of Things (IoT), smart gadgets and artificial intelligence (AI). They have significant influence on the insurgency of customer purchases and amending the future of marketing strategy (Dastane et al., 2020). However, marketers face novel problems in choosing an appropriate blend of digital marketing tools to enhance brand awareness and thus increasing sales by effective consumer interaction (Gruca, 2018). Moreover, without appropriate marketing strategies, convincing consumer to purchase and converting sales leads to sales is a highly complex process (Epstein & Yuthas, 2007). Taking note of the extensive perspectives on adoption of DM at different company size levels, our work aims to find the most appropriate determinants for adoption of DM. We aim to bridge the gap concerning the influence of DM on business size and sales and customer digital foot fall of business moreover its impact on challenges faced by different business. Additionally, this research presents an extensive overview of DM that affects subsequent business patterns which significantly rely on consumer association and are more justifiable.

This study will examine the way the concept of marketing is perceived and practised by companies for the development of SMEs in an Indian context. India is a diverse and highly populated country with a wide range of customer groups, varying from users of digital shopping to novices of internet usage. Therefore, this study will provide insights on the digital marketing adoption by SMEs for a variety of masses, which will provide future researchers to conduct comparative studies with a global perspective. Furthermore, this study will help in determining government strategies for economic growth of Small Medium Enterprises and the nation.

1.1 Research Contributions

Use of digital marketing tools had a notable effect on performance of a business suggestive of increased business performance upon the usage of digital marketing. Adoption of digital marketing had a moderate association between digital marketing usage and performance of a business. The results showed that duration, level of management, tools support and digital marketing usage had a remarkable and positive effect on performance of a business.

Multiple factors like a lack of technical information, high cost of installation and security and privacy issues were hindrance to the embracing of digital marketing. The SMEs owner should be sensitized on the benefits as well as challenges and must be trained to adopt necessary action to ensure the safety of data. In addition, the government should come up with financial aid or programs to help installation of proper IT infrastructure to support digital marketing for small businesses.

In lack of technical expertise and knowledge on digital marketing, there is a high probability that some SMEs will be using their own or conventional marketing strategies to survive. Thus, there is a growing need to identify such SMEs and explain to them the relative advantage of digital marketing on the performance of a business.

2. LITERATURE REVIEW

E-commerce adoption enables SMEs boost their overall marketing. It allows for two-way communication, which helps with sales and marketing. It facilitates the customization of customer service, hence increasing customer happiness (Abou-Shouk et al., 2013). The influence of digital marketing on SMEs' development in South Asia was studied by James (2020a,b). To accomplish this, a variety of digital marketing channels were used, including email marketing, web advertising, social media and so on, with income and market share being used as metrics. The findings revealed that digital marketing has a favourable and considerable influence on SMEs growth.

SMEs are companies that are small or medium-sized in terms of organizational structure, investment and company size (Camanzi & Giua, 2020). Moreover, SMEs are significant segment of the economy, mainly in developing nations as SMEs benefit the economy by creating jobs for the citizens, producing material and supporting export, among others (Bianchi & Abu Saleh, 2020). The presence of SMEs is crucial for any nation, yet SMEs confront unique obstacles and limits, and as a result, numerous SMEs suffer significant losses and even close their doors (Okamuro, 2020). For any enterprise, acquiring consumers and clients is critical, and investigations have shown that several SMEs suffer marketing issues and fail to meet their prospective customers. As a result, these SMEs have begun to implement digital marketing strategies (Eggers, 2020).

Currently, companies can no longer depend on conventional marketing principles, and investigations have shown that companies with higher investments in digital marketing receive greater returns (Lessmann et al., 2021). As a result, many businesses have begun to incorporate digital marketing with the assistance of digital marketing service operators or in-house marketing teams. These services are easy to quantify and manage online, making it a distinct advantage of digital marketing versus traditional marketing (Järvinen & Karjaluoto, 2015). Numerous additional services are being introduced to current digital marketing offerings periodically, enabling marketing more engaging. According to research, the need for digital marketing has risen dramatically among businesses in the last five years (Warokka et al., 2020).

Fjellström et al. (2020) investigated the way digitalization influences marketing strategies of SMEs using a qualitative approach. It was found that digital marketing tools require fewer resources, and such tools bear a constructive impact on competitive advantage. The investigation showed that SMEs develop strategy by focusing on customer preferences and it demonstrated that digitalizing a firm's marketing activities minimizes costs and enhances dynamic capabilities to gain a competitive edge.

Digital Marketing services are a quick approach to gain market share because it is easy to communicate with customers on national and international levels in the digital age. Businesses with limited resources have shown to benefit from such services and achieve greater results (Tiago & Verı́ssimo, 2014). However, according to marketing reports, digital marketing outcomes take time.

Hirvonen and Majuri (2020) aimed to understand the required capabilities to leverage digital systems efficiently in 12 manufacturing SMEs in Finland. The authors used DigiMat method to examine digital capabilities in these companies. In addition, they aimed to find the manner in which companies comprehend the usefulness and usability of this assessment technique. The findings indicated that IT infrastructure was of top priority, followed by renewal and development capabilities, though the order of priority varied among different divisions of the industry. In addition, sales and marketing and production were considered as important domains, while HR governance and collaboration were regarded as the least important. The tool assisted staff members of multiple departments in forming a collective understanding of development requirements based on the feedback received. Firms were able to focus on their development initiatives with the aid of data and visuals.

Eller et al. (2020) analyzed the effects of three key SME resources (digital strategy, employee skills and information technology) on digitalization among 193 Austrian SMEs of destination marketing companies. The authors examined how digitization affected financial performance and if digitalization affects performance through the mediating influence of resources. It was found that digitization could bear a constructive impact on SMEs' functioning, with the aforementioned SMEs resources being positively associated with digitalization. As a result, digitalization has a substantial impact on performance, and it moderates the impact of information technology. Nevertheless, it did not play a mediating role on the effect of personnel skills or digital strategy on SMEs' performance.

Sivakumar et al. (2020) aimed to determine whether mobile marketing has an impact on rural bank performance, to explore the influence of social media marketing on rural bank performance and to determine whether the use of diverse online resources has an influence on performance of rural bank. According to this study, mobile marketing allows businesses to target clients quickly and easily. Furthermore, social media marketing demonstrates that it generates greater brand identity, tailored client details and location-based data. Furthermore, information was exchanged among Web providers via various search engines.

Marketing with social media platforms is more effective in raising brand awareness, acquiring potential customers, enhancing client loyalty and expanding the customer base. SME marketing performance is shown to improve with the usage of social media networks (Dahnil et al., 2014). Marketing tactics are progressive such as the use of digital resources in reaction to changes brought about by the digital economy. There is confirmation that information and communications technology (ICT) provides economic advantages to both large and small businesses (Johnston et al., 2007) as well as how digital marketing in businesses is linked to improved performance and competitiveness (Brodie et al., 2007).

Although digital marketing presents some obstacles, it provides SMEs with more options to reinvent their business performance as well as assist in reframing client groups (Jones et al., 2015). Other research scholars mentioned that internet marketing aids SMEs in expanding their businesses, communicating more quickly, improving sales and increasing brand awareness. Emails, search engine optimisation (SEO) and search engine marketing (SEM) as well as other forms of social media are all crucial tools for digital marketing. To leverage digital marketing, SMEs must expand their expertise of the subject (Taiminen & Karjaluoto, 2015). According to another study, SMEs are shifting to social media marketing because of low expenses. Adapting social media marketing improves sales volume and increases brand awareness (Musa et al., 2016).

Digitalization is a continuous process that has improved manufacturing performance in various manners. In several areas like the IoT and AI, digitalization is only getting started in several sectors, implying that it will become an even more powerful change factor in the future years. As a result, manufacturing companies are investing heavily in digital systems (Hirvonen & Majuri, 2020).

The manufacturing sector is on the verge of a modern transformation. The rise of Industry 4.0, a new digital industrial transformation with smart manufacturing at its forefront, is transforming the way firms operate (Qu et al., 2016). Smart manufacturing is akin to a completely integrated, collaborating manufacturing environment that reacts in real time to continually evolving requirements and situations along the value chain (NIST, 2014). Smart manufacturing's technology breakthrough is dramatically transforming the basis of value design and delivery in the production setting (Lu & Weng, 2018). Smart manufacturing is defined by its connectivity and synthesis of the real and the virtual worlds (Ghobakhloo et al., 2018).

Thaha et al. (2021) conducted a systematic mapping study on digital marketing in Small Medium Enterprises, which concluded that digital marketing helps SMEs to track and respond to customers' desired needs, easily. The authors discovered that there has been a growth in digital marketing trends in Small Medium Enterprises in both advanced and emerging nations in the recent past, with a spotlight on adoption of digital marketing and business performance also categorized various sectors including single sectors such as manufacturing, food and beverage and hotel industries.

On the basis of the above literature review, four hypotheses are presented:

H1. Adoption of digital marketing significantly influences the increase in sales.
H2. Size of business affects the association betwixt digital marketing adoption and increase in sales.
H3. Adoption of digital marketing influences the increase in customers.
H4. Size of business affects the association betwixt digital marketing adoption and increase in customers.

As limited studies have been conducted so far on the advantages or problems and performance of a business including customer and sales hike of businesses, the current study was conducted to address this gap. To conduct the current study, analysis of dependent and independent variables was performed. Here, benefits and challenges which are perceived of digital marketing and its usage were used as predictor variables. The dependent variable considered is business performance. Moderating variables considered are time span of digital marketing, digital marketing adoption level and various support tools. Control variables considered are management level, business size and business type.

3. METHODOLOGY

Research Approach: To analyze and find the potential effects of digital marketing on performance of a business, their magnitude, the frequency of sales, a quantitative and deductive research approach was used. Here, general hypotheses are created and then specific conclusions are drawn using quantitative design.

Research Purpose: The explanatory study seeks to explore the way digital marketing affects the sales of enterprises, gross profit of companies, potential business opportunities at the domestic and global levels and increase of customer base. Hence, an explanatory approach has been used.

Method of Research: A quantitative technique is utilized to conduct the research. Digital marketing's impact on the sales of enterprises, gross profit of companies and potential business opportunities at domestic and global levels has been measured using quantitative analysis.

Research Design: As closed-ended questions are carefully crafted to structure the questionnaire and numerical values are assigned to the answers, wherein the respondents answer about different digital marketing platforms used by them and the benefits and drawbacks of using them, quantitative research design is used.

Research Tools: Questionnaires have been used in the present study. The answers of a closed-ended questionnaire are designed using Likert, semantic, differential and dichotomous scale measurements.

Sampling Design: The target population is specifically the organizations situated in Delhi-NCR using digital marketing tools for the growth of their businesses. In addition, a random sampling method was chosen to provide 368 individuals as sample size.

Data Analysis: SPSS v24.0 is utilized to execute statistical analysis. Logistic regression, ANOVA test, chi-squared test and correlation analysis technique are used for data analysis.

4. THEORIES USED IN THE RESEARCH

Existing theories emphasize the significance and simplicity of use of technological innovations such as digital marketing for SMEs. They also analyze the dynamics of their adoption, which are predicated on SMEs' ability to afford and incorporate them into their operations.

The Technology Acceptance Model (TAM) highlights the elements that impact end-user behaviour when it comes to information technology. It is aimed to explain computer usage through two cognitions, according to Elliott and Boshoff (2007): 'perceived usefulness' and 'perceived ease of use'. Accordingly, an individual assumes that utilizing a certain system would improve his/her performance in job is referred to as perceived usefulness. According to studies, people are motivated to embrace a technology mostly because of the features it affords them, as well as the ease with which they can gain from these services. SMEs, like other businesses, are likely to profit from digital marketing because it improves their performance at a lower cost. Sharma and Aragón-Correa (2005) found that SMEs that acknowledged digital technology gained profits.

SMEs may recognize the value of digital marketing; however, they may be unable to implement it owing to technological challenges. The notion of diffusion of innovation (DOI) is a foundational concept that underpins technology adoption research (Rogers, 1983; Yang & Jarvenpaa, 2005). It proposes that five sets of variables influence technology adoption, namely relative advantages, compatibility, complexity, observability and trialability.

In addition, research on information systems (IS) has emphasized the relevance of digitalization for technology adoption and corporate success (Rai et al., 2006; Sambamurthy et al., 2003). The adoption, usage, the effectiveness of e-commerce, in particular, has become a thriving research subject with major contributions to the literature (Mishra et al., 2007; Zhu & Kraemer, 2005).

5. RESULTS

Objective 1: To find the type and size of businesses adopting digital marketing.

Table 1 represents the distinct traits of participants. A larger number of businesses operated in B2B type (65.5%), followed by both (28.5%) and B2C (6%). 28% of enterprises

Table 1. Type of and Size of Business.

	Frequency	Percentage
Type of Business		
B2B	241	65.5
B2C	22	6.0
Both	105	28.5
Size of Business		
Micro enterprises	103	28.0
Small enterprises	134	36.4
Medium enterprises	131	35.6
Total	368	100.0

Source: Author's own.

belonged to the micro category. Small and medium enterprises amounted to 36.4% and 35.6%, respectively.

Objective 2: To explore the influence of challenges of digital marketing adoption by different types of businesses.

Table 2 presents the prediction and classification of problems of the proposed model. Logistic regression is utilized to find the influence of challenges on digital marketing adoption by different types of businesses. To find out if the novel model (independent variables included) is an advancement over the baseline model (without any independent variables included), Omnibus test of model coefficients is utilized. To find if there is a remarkable difference between the novel model and log-likelihoods of the baseline model chi-square tests is used. If the new model has a fundamentally decreased – 2 Log probability contrasted with the benchmark, then it recommends that the new model is making sense of a greater amount of the fluctuation in the result. Here, the chi-square is highly significant for B2B (chi-square = 96.646, df = 1, $p < 0.01$), B2C (chi-square = 13.905, df = 1, $p < 0.01$) and both (chi-square = 73.994, df = 1, $p < 0.01$), therefore novel model is significantly more acceptable. The coefficient of determination is represented by Nagelkerke R Square. For B2B, B2C and both types of business model explain 50.4%, 65.6% and 69.0% of the proportion of variance in the adoption of digital marketing (Table 2).

Table 3 presents results of independent variables. In the dependent variable (adoption of digital marketing), there are two categories: partial and full implementation. In the regression model, partial implementation is considered as a reference category. To determine the statistical significance, Wald test is used for each of the independent variables. ForB2B, challenge has a highly significant effect (Wald = 42.709, $p < 0.0.01$) on adoption of digital marketing and the coefficient value (β) = -3.238 implies as challenges increases the odds of getting output as fully implemented digital marketing decreases. ForB2C,

Table 2. Omnibus Tests of Model Coefficients and Model Summary.

Types of Businesses	Chi-Square	df	Sig.	−2 Log Likelihood	Nagelkerke R Square
B2B	96.646	1	0.000	159.781	0.504
B2C	13.905	1	0.000	13.616	0.656
Both	73.994	1	0.000	64.546	0.690

Source: Author's own.

Table 3. Coefficients for Impact of Challenges on Adoption of Digital Marketing.

Types of Businesses		β	Wald	Sig.	OR (95% CI)
B2B	Challenges	−3.238	42.709	0.000	0.039 (0.015–0.104)
	Constant	11.706	36.308	0.000	
B2C	Challenges	−4.776	4.902	0.027	0.008 (0.000–0.578)
	Constant	17.855	4.571	0.033	
Both	Challenges	−5.408	28.999	0.000	0.004 (0.001–0.032)
	Constant	21.746	28.475	0.000	

Source: Author's own.

challenge has a highly significant effect (Wald = 4.902, $p < 0.05$) on digital marketing adoption and the coefficient value (β) = −4.776 implies as challenges increases the odds of getting output as fully implemented digital marketing decreases and similarly for both B2B and B2C, challenge has highly significant effect (Wald = 28.999, $p < 0.0.01$) on adoption of digital marketing and the coefficient value (β) = −5.408 implies as challenges increases the odds of getting output as fully implemented digital marketing decreases.

Objective 3: To find the influence of digital marketing adoption in increasing sales and customer digital footfall.

Table 4 represents results from a simple mediation analysis using Hayes PROCESS model. Hayes' PROCESS macro was used to perform regression model. It was utilized to find the influence of adoption of digital marketing in increasing sales and customer digital footfall. R addresses the correlation coefficient ranging from −1 to +1. As the R value is 0.659 and 0.667, it means that adoption of digital marketing and sizes of business have moderate association with increasing sales and customer digital footfall. R^2 addresses the determination coefficient ranging from 0 to 1. As R^2 = 0.434 and 0.445, it implies that the adoption of digital marketing tools, size of business and moderator accounted for 43.4% of the total variation in the increase in sales with an F (3, 364) change value of 92.956 and 44.5% of the total variation in the increase in customers with an F (3, 364) change value of 97.389.

Table 4. Influence of Digital Marketing Adoption in Increasing Sales and Customer Digital Footfall.

	Increase in Sales		Increase in Customer Digital Footfall	
	β (p Value)	t Value	β (p Value)	t Value
Constant	−0.025 (0.601)	−0.523	−0.008 (0.860)	−0.177
Adoption of digital marketing	0.567 (0.000)	10.141	0.616 (0.000)	11.129
Size of business	0.116 (0.014)	2.473	0.078 (0.094)	1.678
Adoption × size of business	0.049 (0.348)	0.940	0.017 (0.750)	0.318
R	0.659		0.667	
R square	0.434		0.445	
F	92.956		97.389	
df1	3		3	
df2	364		364	
p value	0.000		0.000	

Source: Author's own.

The regression coefficient 'β' is the change in response variable for each unit change in predictor variables. The impact of adoption of digital marketing ($\beta = 0.567$, $t = 10.141$, $p < 0.01$) and size of business ($\beta = 0.116$, $t = 2.473$, $p < 0.05$) was found to be positive and significant to increase in sales. This value indicates for every one unit increase in adoption of digital marketing, there was a 0.0.567 increase in sales, and for every one unit increase in size of business, there was a 0.116 increase in sales.

Thus, H_1*: Adoption of digital marketing significantly influences the increase in sales is accepted.* However, interaction between adoption of digital marketing and size of business ($\beta = 0.049$, $t = 0.940$, $p > 0.05$) is not significant to increase in sales, and it is deduced that there is no influence of moderating variable (size of business) on the association betwixt digital marketing adoption and increase in sales. Thus, the hypothesis H_2*: Size of business moderates the association betwixt digital marketing adoption and increase in sales is not accepted.*

The impact of adoption of digital marketing ($\beta = 0.616$, $t = 11.129$, $p < 0.01$) is calculated to be significant and positive to increase in customers. This value indicates for every one unit increase in adoption of digital marketing, there was a. 0.616 increase in customers. Thus, the hypothesis H_3*: Adoption of digital marketing significantly influences the increase in customers is accepted.* However, size of business ($\beta = 0.078$, $t = 1.678$, $p > 0.05$) and interaction between digital marketing adoption and size of business ($\beta = 0.017$, $t = 0.318$, $p > 0.05$) is not significant to increase in customers. Therefore, it is deduced that there is no effect of the moderating variable (size of business) on the association betwixt digital marketing adoption and increase in customers. Thus, the hypothesis H_4*: Size of business moderates the association betwixt digital marketing adoption and increase in customers is not accepted.*

6. DISCUSSION AND CONCLUSION

This e-commerce has now become the era of digitization where there is digitized show-room, digitized advertisement through internet-based media and advanced interaction with both seller and consumers (Ajani, 2021). The function of digital market is also validated by Institute for Business Value (IBM) (Leeflang et al., 2014). However, rising use of digitization raises concerns that whether the priorities and organization of the current market can achieve even more difficult organization tasks. B2B business, which do not possess the foundation of evident quantifiable media may require a more organized and wholesome methods (Jensen, 2006). The present research is performed to analyze the influence of digital marketing on the business performance of enterprises. When embraced efficiently, digitization can benefit entrepreneurial company's performance by combining efficient marketing with entrepreneurial marketing. When entrepreneurial marketing is considered, DM becomes a necessity when performance of new companies needs to be explained. The Internet provides entry to novel markets which can improve productivity and enable collaboration between enterprises. It can also facilitate the customization of services and products. Further, it also enables a better relationship with the customer and the building of new products with the consumers (Rozhkova et al., 2020). Even though these platforms provide convenient and powerful marketing strategies. Due to the lack of awareness of techniques given by it, digitization is not fully adopted, entrepreneurs do not know this concept very well and cannot take advantage of it (Samarasinghe et al., 2016).

The challenges faced by enterprises to adopt internet networking are generally divided into certain factors like consumer preference, company management, technological problems, top decision makers, administration and the environment of the company. Further, online marketing itself faces challenges which includes problem with integrity, lack of personal interaction, lack of trust and many security reasons (Bostanshirin, 2014). Moreover, growth of the company is generally referred to the rise in demand of products and services whose results can be seen in growth of sales and investment (Janssen, 2006). The market structure and innovations significantly determine the growth of the companies (Daunfeldt & Elert, 2013). Further, marketing facilitates creating awareness about these products and services. Averse to traditional marketing techniques, DM has become increasingly accepted. Companies operationalize DM via emails, applications, content, social media, SEO, SEM, pay per click (PPC) and online marketing (Omondi, 2017). Hence, DM is able to lure a broad range of consumers; it is capable of allowing effective interaction between business and consumers and leads them to the purchase of goods and services (Dastane, 2020). Accordingly, our study also found a positive relation between sales, customer and DM. We found the significant influence of DM on the sales and customers.

In the current study, partial or full adoption of digital marketing in SMEs moderated the association betwixt digital marketing usage and enterprise performance. When the resources and cost are concerned large, businesses have considerable competitive dominance because of market advantage or the economy. Therefore, they can re-invest these resources in innovations. However, for SMEs, accessibility to technology is significantly more complex (Gherghina et al., 2020; Rosenbusch et al., 2011). An already established market with large companies has set rules for the use of these e-tools, specifically for enhancing the infrastructure. Even though technologies are accessible worldwide, infrastructure is limited because it is of local nature in the market. This affects accessibility of resources (Carnahan et al., 2010; Srivastava & Gnyawali, 2011).

Given that there are huge number of business types and sizes, the sample size in the study is comparatively tiny. Furthermore, because the emphasis is on manufacturing enterprises in Delhi-NCR, hence after evaluating marketing assets, size as well as type of enterprises and digital application of enterprises within India (except Delhi-NCR region) and outside India, generalizability should be made. As this study is quantitative where a mixed approach was implemented in which participants' opinions on various aspects of digital marketing in enterprises were gathered through qualitative interviews. Furthermore, a bigger sample size and information from individual and specific enterprises across the country would be required to broaden understanding of digital marketing practices by businesses.

The results showed SMEs' high dependence on technology and lack of necessary technical skills within organizations. Digital marketing gives a competitive advantage to the emerging business at domestic and international markets. Thus, to avail the opportunities, SMEs must increase their competitiveness by upgrading digital/technological infrastructure and by developing expertise on digital technology.

The practitioners of digital marketing strategies should plan workshops on strategies of digital marketing for SMEs to improve the awareness of existing digital market strategies at an industrial level. In addition, policymakers should work on regional as well as national policies for the integration of digital technology in SMEs. Lack of technical expertise and knowledge on digital marketing would result in a high probability of some SMEs using their own strategies or conventional marketing strategies to survive.

Thus, there is a growing need to identify such SMEs and make them mindful of the relative merits of digital marketing on the performance of a business.

Social media was found to be the most used digital marketing platform. However, digital marketing mix including mobile apps and websites can also be used to enhance their market presence, gain consumers' attention and boost consumers' experience. Additionally, SMEs can allot financial resources for hiring technology experts to generate or curate content.

7. IMPLICATIONS

Strategic Decision-Making: Managers can use research findings to make informed decisions about their digital marketing strategies.

Resource Allocation: Insights from this research can help managers allocate their budgets optimally, ensuring they invest in strategies that offer the best returns.

Adoption of Emerging Technologies: This research can guide managers in adopting and integrating emerging technologies in their digital marketing strategies, ensuring they stay on the cutting edge of innovation.

Training and Skill Development: The practical implications of research can inform training programs and skill development initiatives. This can empower employees to effectively execute digital marketing strategies.

Measurement and Metrics: This research can provide practical metrics and measurement tools for businesses to track the influence of digital marketing on digital footfall and sales, enabling data-driven decision-making.

Cross-Disciplinary Insights: The research contributions may extend beyond marketing and involve other disciplines such as economics, psychology and technology.

Consumer Behaviour Theories: Investigating the influence of digital marketing on consumer behaviour can lead to the development or refinement of consumer behaviour theories. For instance, researchers can explore how various digital marketing strategies influence the decision-making process, online reviews or the effect of personalization on consumer choices.

Digital Customer Journey Models: This study can aid the evolution of comprehensive models that describe the digital customer journey. These models can include various touchpoints, channels and interactions, providing a theoretical framework to understand how digital marketing impacts the path to purchase.

According to the obtained results in this study, it is concluded that DM highly influenced in getting benefits like high sales, number of customers and profit. However, there are certain challenges such as lack of technical framework and skills that influence DM. Further, size of business moderated the relationship of DM adoption and increase in sales and customers. However, large-scale studies need to be conducted to generalize this concept.

REFERENCES

Abou-Shouk, M., Megicks, P., & Lim, W. M. (2013). Perceived benefits and e-commerce adoption by SME travel agents in developing countries: Evidence from Egypt. *Journal of Hospitality & Tourism Research*, *37*(4), 490–515. https://doi.org/10.1177/1096348012442544

Ajani, N. M. (2021). Digital marketing in e-business. *Ijarcce*, *10*(10), 34–38. https://doi.org/10.17148/ijarcce.2021.101007

Al-Qirim, N. (2007). The adoption of eCommerce communications and applications technologies in small businesses in New Zealand. *Electronic Commerce Research and Applications*, *6*(4), 462–473. https://doi.org/10.1016/j.elerap.2007.02.012

Bianchi, C., & Abu Saleh, Md. (2020). Investigating SME importer–foreign supplier relationship trust and commitment. *Journal of Business Research*, *119*, 572–584. https://doi.org/10.1016/j.jbusres.2020.07.023

Bostanshirin, S. (2014). Online marketing: Challenges and opportunities. In *International conference on social sciences and humanities* (pp. 783–790).

Brodie, R. J., Winklhofer, H., Coviello, N. E., & Johnston, W. J. (2007). Is e-marketing coming of age? An examination of the penetration of e-marketing and firm performance. *Journal of Interactive Marketing*, *21*(1), 2–21. https://doi.org/10.1002/dir.20071

Camanzi, L., & Giua, C. (2020). SME network relationships and competitive strategies in the agri-food sector: Some empirical evidence and a provisional conceptual framework. *European Business Review*, *32*(3), 405–424. https://doi.org/10.1108/EBR-08-2019-0150

Carnahan, S., Agarwal, R., & Campbell, B. (2010). The effect of firm compensation structures on the mobility and entrepreneurship of extreme performers. *Business*, *920*(October), 1–43. https://doi.org/10.1002/smj

Constantin, C. (2009). Multi-level marketing – A tool of relationship marketing. *Economic Sciences*, *2*(51), 6.

Dahnil, M. I., Marzuki, K. M., Langgat, J., & Fabeil, N. F. (2014). Factors influencing SMEs adoption of social media marketing. *Procedia – Social and Behavioral Sciences*, *148*, 119–126. https://doi.org/10.1016/j.sbspro.2014.07.025

Dastane, O. (2020). Impact of digital marketing on online purchase intention: Mediation effect of customer relationship management. *Journal of Asian Business Strategy*, *10*(1), 142–158. https://doi.org/10.18488/journal.1006.2020.101.142.158

Dastane, O., Goi, C. L., & Rabbanee, F. (2020). A synthesis of constructs for modelling consumers' perception of value from mobile-commerce (M-VAL). *Journal of Retailing and Consumer Services*, *55*(February). https://doi.org/10.1016/j.jretconser.2020.102074

Daunfeldt, S. O., & Elert, N. (2013). When is Gibrat's law a law? *Small Business Economics*, *41*(1), 133–147. https://doi.org/10.1007/s11187-011-9404-x

De Pelsmacker, P., van Tilburg, S., & Holthof, C. (2018). Digital marketing strategies, online reviews and hotel performance. *International Journal of Hospitality Management*, *72*(July 2017), 47–55. https://doi.org/10.1016/j.ijhm.2018.01.003

Eggers, F. (2020). Masters of disasters? Challenges and opportunities for SMEs in times of crisis. *Journal of Business Research*, *116*, 199–208. https://doi.org/10.1016/j.jbusres.2020.05.025

El-Gohary, H. (2012). Factors affecting e-marketing adoption and implementation in tourism firms: An empirical investigation of Egyptian small tourism organisations. *Tourism Management*, *33*(5), 1256–1269. https://doi.org/10.1016/j.tourman.2011.10.013

Eller, R., Alford, P., Kallmünzer, A., & Peters, M. (2020). Antecedents, consequences, and challenges of small and medium-sized enterprise digitalization. *Journal of Business Research*, *112*(March), 119–127. https://doi.org/10.1016/j.jbusres.2020.03.004

Elliott, R., & Boshoff, C. (2007). The influence of the owner-manager of small tourism businesses on the success of internet marketing. *South African Journal of Business Management*, *38*(3), 15–27. https://doi.org/10.10520/EJC22337

Epstein, M. J., & Yuthas, K. (2007). Managing customer value. In *Management accounting guideline*. The Society of Management Accountants of Canada, The American Institute of Certified Public Accountants and The Chartered Institute of Management Accountants.

Falahat, M., Ramayah, T., Soto-Acosta, P., & Lee, Y. Y. (2020). SMEs internationalization: The role of product innovation, market intelligence, pricing and marketing communication capabilities as drivers of SMEs' international performance. *Technological Forecasting and Social Change*, *152*(January), 119908. https://doi.org/10.1016/j.techfore.2020.119908

Fjellström, D., Osarenkhoe, A., Pettersson, T., & Tadesse, D. (2020). The role of digitalization in SMEs' strategy development: The case of Sweden | SpringerLink. In A. Thrassou, D. Vrontis, Y. Weber, S. M. R. Shams, & E. Tsoukatos (Eds.), *The changing role of SMEs in global business*. Palgrave Macmillan. https://link.springer.com/chapter/10.1007/978-3-030-45831-7_4

Gan, L., Lee, D., Lingtay, K., & Wai, S. H. (2005). Online marketing: A boon or bane for business in Singapore? *Asia Pacific Business Review*, *11*(3), 327–347. https://doi.org/10.1080/13602380500068391

Gherghina, S. C., Botezatu, M. A., Hosszu, A., & Simionescu, L. N. (2020). Small and medium-sized enterprises (SMEs): The engine of economic growth through investments and innovation. *Sustainability*, *12*(1). https://doi.org/10.3390/SU12010347

Ghobakhloo, M., Azar, A., & Tang, S. H. (2018). Business value of enterprise resource planning spending and scope: A post-implementation perspective. *Kybernetes*, *48*(5), 967–989. https://doi.org/10.1108/K-01-2018-0025

Grubor, A., & Jaksa, O. (2018). Internet marketing as a business necessity. *Interdisciplinary Description of Complex Systems*, *16*(2), 265–274. https://doi.org/10.7906/indecs.16.2.6

Gruca, T. S. (2018, February). *Social media sentiment and firm value Chanchal B Tamrakar Tae*. Hyung Pyo College of Business and Economics University of Idaho Thomas S Gruca Tippie College of Business University of Iowa.

Hirvonen, J., & Majuri, M. (2020). Digital capabilities in manufacturing SMEs. *Procedia Manufacturing*, *51*, 1283–1289. https://doi.org/10.1016/j.promfg.2020.10.179

Ifinedo, P. (2011). Internet/e-business technologies acceptance in Canada's SMEs: An exploratory investigation. *Internet Research*, *21*(3), 255–281. https://doi.org/10.1108/10662241111139309

James, L. (2020a). Impact of digital marketing on SME growth in South Asia: A case study on Faheem Haydar Dealzmag. *SA Business Press Journal*, *9*.

James, L. (2020b, January 5). Identifying the effect of Digital Marketing channels on the growth of SME in South Asia: A case study on Faheem Haydar Dealzmag [MPRA Paper]. https://mpra.ub.uni-muenchen.de/105156/

Janssen, F. (2006). Do managers' characteristics influence the employment growth of SMEs? *Journal of Small Business and Entrepreneurship*, *19*(3), 293–315. https://doi.org/10.1080/08276331.2006.10593372

Järvinen, J., & Karjaluoto, H. (2015). The use of Web analytics for digital marketing performance measurement. *Industrial Marketing Management*, *50*, 117–127. https://doi.org/10.1016/j.indmarman.2015.04.009

Jensen, M. B. (2006). Characteristics of B2B adoption and planning of online marketing communications. *Journal of Targeting, Measurement and Analysis for Marketing*, *14*, 357–368. http://download.springer.com/static/pdf/987/art%253A10.1057%252Fpalgrave.jt.5740194.pdf?originUrl=http%3A%2F%2Flink.springer.com%2Farticle%2F10.1057%2Fpalgrave.jt.5740194&token2=exp=1485127156~acl=%2Fstatic%2Fpdf%2F987%2Fart%25253A10.1057%25252Fpalgrave.j

Johnston, D. A., Wade, M., & Mcclean, R. (2007). Does e-Business Matter to SMEs? A comparison of the financial impacts of internet business solutions on European and North American SMEs. *Journal of Small Business Management*, *45*(3), 354–361. https://doi.org/10.1111/j.1540-627X.2007.00217.x

Jones, R., Alford, P., & Wolfenden, S. (2015, November 2). *Entrepreneurial marketing in the digital age: A study of the SME tourism industry*. Global Research Symposium on Marketing and Entrepreneurship. http://eprints.bournemouth.ac.uk/22932/

Kendall, J. D., Tung, L. L., Chua, K. H., Ng, C. H. D., & Tan, S. M. (2001). Receptivity of Singapore's SMEs to electronic commerce adoption. *The Journal of Strategic Information Systems*, *10*(3), 223–242. https://doi.org/10.1016/S0963-8687(01)00048-8

Leeflang, P. S. H., Verhoef, P. C., Dahlström, P., & Freundt, T. (2014). Challenges and solutions for marketing in a digital era. *European Management Journal*, *32*(1), 1–12. https://doi.org/10.1016/j.emj.2013.12.001

Lessmann, S., Haupt, J., Coussement, K., & De Bock, K. W. (2021). Targeting customers for profit: An ensemble learning framework to support marketing decision-making. *Information Sciences*, *557*, 286–301. https://doi.org/10.1016/j.ins.2019.05.027

Lestari, S. D., Leon, F. M., Widyastuti, S., Brabo, N. A., & Putra, A. H. P. K. (2020). Antecedents and consequences of innovation and business strategy on performance and competitive advantage of SMEs. *Journal of Asian Finance, Economics and Business*, *7*(6), 365–378. https://doi.org/10.13106/JAFEB.2020.VOL7.NO6.365

Lu, H.-P., & Weng, C.-I. (2018). Smart manufacturing technology, market maturity analysis and technology roadmap in the computer and electronic product manufacturing industry. *Technological Forecasting and Social Change*, *133*, 85–94. https://doi.org/10.1016/j.techfore.2018.03.005

Mishra, A. N., Konana, P., & Barua, A. (2007). Antecedents and consequences of internet use in procurement: An empirical investigation of U.S. manufacturing firms. *Information Systems Research*, *18*(1), 103–120. https://doi.org/10.1287/isre.1070.0115

Musa, H., Rahim, N. A., Azmi, F. R., Shibghatullah, A. S., & Othman, N. A. (2016). Social media marketing and online small and medium enterprises performance: Perspective of Malaysian small and medium enterprises. *International Review of Management and Marketing*, *6*(7S), 1–5.

NIST. (2014, April 25). *Smart manufacturing operations planning and control program* [Text]. NIST. https://www.nist.gov/programs-projects/smart-manufacturing-operations-planning-and-control-program

Okamuro, H. (2020). Messages from T20 Tokyo Summit 2019: Challenges and proposals for SME policies in G20 countries. *Journal of the International Council for Small Business*, *1*(1), 45–51. https://doi.org/10.1080/26437015.2020.1714362

Omondi, O. J. (2017). Impact of digital marketing on sales growth of small and medium enterprises in Nairobi, Kenya. *Erepository.Uonbi.Ac.Ke*, 1–57. http://erepository.uonbi.ac.ke/bitstream/handle/11295/103209/

Olonde_Impact of Digital Marketing on Sales Growth of Small and Medium Enterprises in Nairobi, Kenya.pdf?sequence=1%0Ashorturl.at/wzADT

Peltier, J. W., Dahl, A. J., & Swan, E. L. (2020). Digital information flows across a B2C/C2C continuum and technological innovations in service ecosystems: A service-dominant logic perspective. *Journal of Business Research*, *121*(April 2019), 724–734. https://doi.org/10.1016/j.jbusres.2020.03.020

Pollák, F., & Markovič, P. (2021). Size of business unit as a factor influencing adoption of digital marketing: Empirical analysis of SMEs operating in the central European market. *Administrative Sciences*, *11*(3). https://doi.org/10.3390/admsci11030071

Pookulangara, S., & Koesler, K. (2011). Cultural influence on consumers' usage of social networks and its' impact on online purchase intentions. *Journal of Retailing and Consumer Services*, *18*(4), 348–354. https://doi.org/10.1016/j.jretconser.2011.03.003

Putney, A., & Puney, M. (2013). A study on the role of customer relationship management (CRM) in the Indian banking sector. *International Journal of Management and Business Studies*, *3*(2), 88–89.

Qu, T., Lei, S. P., Wang, Z. Z., Nie, D. X., Chen, X., & Huang, G. Q. (2016). IoT-based real-time production logistics synchronization system under smart cloud manufacturing. *The International Journal of Advanced Manufacturing Technology*, *84*(1), 147–164. https://doi.org/10.1007/s00170-015-7220-1

Rai, A., Patnayakuni, R., & Seth, N. (2006). Firm performance impacts of digitally enabled supply chain integration capabilities. *MIS Quarterly*, *30*(2), 225–246. https://doi.org/10.2307/25148729

Rogers, E. M. (1983). *Diffusion of innovations* (3rd ed.). Free Press.

Rosenbusch, N., Brinckmann, J., & Bausch, A. (2011). Is innovation always beneficial? A meta-analysis of the relationship between innovation and performance in SMEs. *Journal of Business Venturing*, *26*(4), 441–457. https://doi.org/10.1016/j.jbusvent.2009.12.002

Rozhkova, D., Rozhkova, N., & Blinova, U. (2020). Digital universities in Russia: Prospects and problems. In *Advances in intelligent systems and computing: Vol. 1114 AISC*. https://doi.org/10.1007/978-3-030-37737-3_23

Samarasinghe, G. D., Suwandaarachchi, C. M., & Ekanayaka, E. M. R. K. (2016). *Impact of social media on business performance: Empirical study on apparel fashion brand retailers in Sri Lanka.*

Sambamurthy, V., Bharadwaj, A., & Grover, V. (2003). Shaping agility through digital options: Reconceptualizing the role of information technology in contemporary firms. *MIS Quarterly*, *27*(2), 237–263. https://doi.org/10.2307/30036530

Sharma, S. & Aragón-Correa, J. A. (2005). Corporate environmental strategy and competitive advantage. In *Corporate Environmental Strategy and Competitive Advantage* (pp. 1–318). https://doi:10.4337/9781845426859

Sivakumar, R., Chandramohan, M., & Ajaganandam, A. (2020). Repercussion of Digital Marketing on Performance of Indian Rural Banks. *Journal of Critical Reviews*, *7*(8), 2020. https://doi.org/10.31838/jcr.07.08.440

Sokolova, K., & Kefi, H. (2020). Instagram and YouTube bloggers promote it, why should I buy? How credibility and parasocial interaction influence purchase intentions. *Journal of Retailing and Consumer Services*, *53*(September 2018). https://doi.org/10.1016/j.jretconser.2019.01.011

Srivastava, M. K., & Gnyawali, D. R. (2011). When do relational resources matter? Leveraging portfolio technological resources for breakthrough innovation. *Academy of Management Journal*, *54*(4), 797–810. https://doi.org/10.5465/AMJ.2011.64870140

Stockdale, R., & Standing, C. (2006). A classification model to support SME e-commerce adoption initiatives. *Journal of Small Business and Enterprise Development*, *13*(3), 381–394. https://doi.org/10.1108/14626000610680262

Taiminen, H. M., & Karjaluoto, H. (2015). The usage of digital marketing channels in SMEs. *Journal of Small Business and Enterprise Development*, *22*(4), 633–651. https://doi.org/10.1108/JSBED-05-2013-0073

Thaha, A., Maulina, E., Muftiadi, R. A., & Alexandri, M. (2021). Digital marketing and SMEs: A systematic mapping study. *Library Philosophy and Practice (e-Journal)*, *5113*. https://digitalcommons.unl.edu/libphilprac/5113

Teixeira, S., Martins, J., Branco, F., Gonçalves, R., Au-Yong-Oliveira, M., & Moreira, F. (2018). A theoretical analysis of digital marketing adoption by startups. *Advances in Intelligent Systems and Computing*, *688*, 94–105. https://doi.org/10.1007/978-3-319-69341-5_9

Tiago, M. T. P. M. B., & Veríssimo, J. M. C. (2014). Digital marketing and social media: Why bother? *Business Horizons*, *57*(6), 703–708. https://doi.org/10.1016/j.bushor.2014.07.002

van de Vrande, V., de Jong, J. P. J., Vanhaverbeke, W., & de Rochemont, M. (2009). Open innovation in SMEs: Trends, motives and management challenges. *Technovation*, *29*(6–7), 423–437. https://doi.org/10.1016/j.technovation.2008.10.001

Verma, D. (2018). A critical review of digital marketing digital marketing view project financial reforms view project. *International Journal of Management, IT & Engineering*, *8*(10), 321–339. http://www.ijmra.us

Warokka, A., Sjahruddin, H., Sriyanto, S., Noerhartati, E., & Saddhono, K. (2020). Digital marketing support and business development using online marketing tools: An experimental analysis. *International Journal of Psychosocial Rehabilitation*, *24*(1), 1181–1188. https://doi.org/10.37200/IJPR/V24I1/PR200219

Yang, G., & Jarvenpaa, S. L. (2005). Trust and radio frequency identification (RFID) adoption within an alliance. In *Proceedings of the 38th Annual Hawaii International Conference on System Sciences* (pp. 208a–208a). https://doi.org/10.1109/HICSS.2005.643

Zangiacomi, A., Pessot, E., Fornasiero, R., Bertetti, M., & Sacco, M. (2020). Moving towards digitalization: A multiple case study in manufacturing. *Production Planning & Control*, *31*(2–3), 143–157. https://doi.org/10.1080/09537287.2019.1631468

Zhu, K., & Kraemer, K. L. (2005). Post-adoption variations in usage and value of e-business by organizations: Cross-country evidence from the retail industry. *Information Systems Research*, *16*(1), 61–84. https://doi.org/10.1287/isre.1050.0045

A STUDY ON THE IMPACT OF COVID-19 TOWARDS E-COMMERCE IN INDIA

Dave K. A.

St. Joseph's College of Commerce (Autonomous), India

ABSTRACT

COVID-19 is one of people's glooming disasters that brought the entire world to a standstill. To reduce the effect, a countrywide lockout was announced. Stock and distribution chains were affected on a larger scale. Due to the pandemic, purchasing habits of people have changed. It is also evident that individuals are choosing to shop online. As per recent researches, consumer buying behaviour has transformed as a result of the contagion. Due to which, many businesses are revolutionizing to adjust to the new reality. This study was taken up to scrutinize the effect of Corona Virus Disease of 2019 on changes in customer buying behaviour towards E-commerce. This study has offered detailed information on new ways of buyer shopping. It suggests that during the COVID-19 pandemic, consumers have become more accepting of internet shopping, experts in webrooming and with time they are mastering the art of online shopping as well as tuned to online payment methods and are accepting to live with ease in an economy of cashless e-transactions.

Keywords: E-commerce; COVID-19; pandemic; consumer behaviour; webrooming and online payment methods

1. INTRODUCTION

Coronaviruses are an assorted group of diseases. It can form basis for an individual to catch chills and fever. Domestic animals and mammals such as bats, camels and cattle are infected by this virus. As per, virologists' early strains of COVID-19 are believed to have originated in bats and at Wuhan's open-air fresh produce and live animal markets; SARS-CoV-2 might have infected people. Viruses from diverse animals can exchange genetic factor in packed places. When a virus goes through substantial alterations, it possibly starts tainting and spreading among humans. SARS-CoV-2 infected humans having zero straight connection with faunas, but as it was highly contagious, it first spread in China and then across the globe. A pandemic had occurred consequently due to the

Resilient Businesses for Sustainability
Advanced Series in Management, Volume 34B, 153–168

ISSN: 1877-6361/doi:10.1108/S1877-63612024000034B012

worldwide transmission of this deadly virus. The utmost shared indicators of COVID-19 were fever, dry cough and fatigue. However, these otherwise regular symptoms could go from being undetectable in a person to becoming as fatal as taking away a life in no time. Initially, infected individuals were contagious for an average 10 days and they could transfer the virus even if they were asymptomatic. Many strains with different degrees of infection and lethality have resulted from this virus' genes.

2. COVID-19'S IMPACT AT A GLOBAL LEVEL

The pandemic inflicted mayhem on every country's socio-economic structure, thereby resulting in the nastiest trying times that countries witnessed in the longest time since World War II. Global stock interruption and alarmed buying led to extensive supply shortages of food and medicines mainly. According to the worldwide lockdowns, a positive sign witnessed by human kind was dropping levels of water, air and soil pollution. Schools, colleges, offices, parks, touristy places and other publicly accessed areas were closed completely or in partial leading to huge losses in the Travel, Tourism and Hospitality industries. Most events were either annulled, deferred or it simply went on a virtual mode. Political turmoil arose as fake messages spread through various media forms, people did not know what to believe and what to ignore. The pandemic raised concerns about cultural and topographical differences, health impartiality and finding an ethical balance between public health and individual human rights. The repercussions of COVID-19 have disturbed the global economy and international trade beyond repair. Various issues like pay cuts, trans-bounded travel restrictions, pandemic induced changes in consumer demands and resultant fast paced changing market activities have catapulted the uncertainty in which businesses and customers are thriving in even in the current scenario. Apprehensions over the pandemic shattered stock indices of many developed countries, causing them to fall to their lowest levels since recession in the years 2006–2008. Cargo shipments witnessed strikingly high waiting time. Global labour revenue reduced by 10.7% (ILO, 2022).

3. COVID-19'S IMPACT ON INDIA'S ECONOMY

The bearing of this pandemic on India was no different from the global scenario, as India recorded the second highest number of cases in the world. Most of the industries struggled to get minimum domestic business orders and exports had plummeted, however, a few prominent industries such as IT, ITeS, Pharmaceutical, ed-tech, etc., witnessed an unexpected high growth as well.

3.1 Agriculture and Food

For India, agriculture is its mainstay and is clearly a priority sector in terms of GDP. As a result, there has been a bare minimum effect on this industry. Unrestricted inter and intra state movement of fruits, vegetables, dairy products and other food items including meat was permitted even during the peak of the pandemic (Times of India, 2020).

3.2 Tourism and Air Travel Industry

These two industries offer an approximate 2.49% and 9.23% of India's GDP (Kesari & Kesharwani, 2021). It is a known fact that this industry was brutally affected by the pandemic with huge financial crunches leading to the labour force being cut down by 70% and was the last ones to recover post-pandemic.

3.3 Pharma Sector

Meanwhile, the jerk of coronaviruses helped the pharmaceutical sector of India witness shooting growth of $55 billion (Deshpande, 2020), as it is the world's largest manufacturer of broad pharma products. Acute shortage of raw materials concerning global shut down compelled Indian organizations to innovate in a remarkable time frame and they successfully managed to make masks, PPE kits, made sure the availability of oxygen, medicines and vaccines for its citizens and over a period of time began to export to other needing countries.

3.4 Oil and Gas

The Indian oil and gas industry is the world's third-largest consumer owing to its massive population. It accounts for 5.2% of global oil demand (IEA, 2021). The lockdown pulled down the demand for petrol and diesel as plying of two-wheelers, cars and commercial vehicles dropped. Goods and passenger mobility fell to its lowest levels. This was more or less a global scenario which led to crude oil prices falling around this time, but the government increased central excise duties to compensate for the revenue losses induced by the pandemic.

3.5 E-Commerce

Electronic commerce is regarded as a highly disruptive technology across the globe as it has the capability of changing the shape of any industry that you name under the sun. Almost every item or service can be availed with the help of this technology. This online way of doing business has been making its presence felt in the Indian market since mid-2000s, and with COVID-19, it only zoomed at a rocket speed.

4. COVID-19'S IMPACT ON THE E-COMMERCE TRADE

The outbreak of the pandemic all over the world has changed the way in which persons in India acquire goods and services alongside how they perceive e-commerce as a business. India's unbending lockdown curbs clubbed with a purchaser's increasing reluctance to step out of the house for even something as small as a packet of milk which underwrote a storming evolution of E-commerce. The costumers' shopping habits drifted from physical store locations to the internet portals for anything and everything right from daily needs to labelled items and services. Pandemic actually led to a surge in the number of first-time users towards online shopping. COVID-19 was unlike anything human kind had ever seen before. As the nations of the world came to a standstill, it is rational to accept that internet way of businesses turned out to be a blessing in disguise, allowing the mankind to remain inside their homes and yet get everything delivered at their doorsteps. IBEF i.e. India Brand Equity Foundation predicts that online business sector of India will reach $200 billion by 2026, up from $30 billion in 2017 (Kumar & Kumar, 2021). On the flip side, the pandemic actually resulted in slowdown of work in various industries during the nationwide lockdown which resulted in layoffs, slash in pays and financial crunch which resulted in E-commerce being used by consumers only for bare necessities (Gu et al., 2021). This stunted the growth of the e-businesses for a temporary period at least as online sales of apparel, eyewear and accessories were down by almost 19% on an average. Only FMCG, agricultural products and health and pharmaceutical items recorded increases of an average 34% (Mishra & Peermohamed, 2021). Consequences of COVID-19 hurt customer demand that otherwise was inflicted through impulsive buying both in urban and rural India. The online shopping behaviour displayed by people during the pandemic, made the e-commerce industry believe that people will begin to dodge physical store shopping and drove unprecedented expectations of a demand revival (Galhotra & Dewan, 2020). However, it may be noted that while People may be getting comfortable with the idea of online shopping, nonetheless, they are yet to get comfortable with the idea of shopping items of luxury and fashion. As such, a total of four lockdowns in India showcased differing trends in shopper's behaviour when buying through e-commerce platforms or completing transactions of services such as electricity, internet bills, phone recharges, water bills, etc., online. The COVID-19 pandemic, which lasted for some time, had a huge negative financial effect on economies. Around this time, buyers used varied online purchasing methods to circumvent any contact with humans. Consumers, actually, have a strong desire to use their sense organs to know a product, which is lone accessible at brick-and-mortar stores. Hence, it further led to the boom in webrooming among consumers. Through webrooming, some consumers will remain hooked onto buying online after sourcing information from digital and social media platforms and then there would be the other kind who will buy from a physical store but after gathering enough information through online means.

5. STATEMENT OF PROBLEM

The coronavirus has struck each and every sector in the world even the FMCG saw a decline in its sales. E-commerce is the only industry that flourished during the same period with the increase in its sales higher than ever (Tran, 2020). Since there was a lockdown in place, people were forced to make their purchases online which was the key factor for the boom in the E-commerce sector. According to the characteristics and needs of shoppers in the digital era, there are four consumer attitudes. Pure-offline buying, pure-online buying, showrooming and webrooming are the four consumer behaviours. As per industry stalwarts, internet commerce was and supposedly is the greatest backing that was available to individuals in cities, towns and villages during the lockdowns. E-commerce faces a number of hurdles in India, which the authors believe that the pandemic has allowed it to reach its full potential throughout and beyond. The sample size taken into consideration in the study is from the city of Bengaluru considering all demographics. Since Bengaluru city used E-commerce the most in comparison to any other city in the country (Kesari & Kesharwani, 2021), it is apt to consider the city for the study. This paper made a conscious attempt to understand the preferred digital platforms and products ordered during the lockdown phases. The study further delved into understanding if the trend of online shopping which strengthened during the pandemic has become a lifestyle habit.

6. NEED AND IMPORTANCE OF STUDY

Technology has gradually displaced different human activities, including buying, resulting towards the emergence of internet buying. As one of the deadliest viruses, the pandemic influenced consumer spending, the way people select and shop for goods and services. As a result, before and during the COVID-19 pandemic, there is a noteworthy shift in consumer purchasing patterns. The aforesaid research purposes to identify the pandemic consequence on customer spending in the area of electronic commerce. The study intensively monitors and assesses consumers' shifts in online buying behaviour in the pre-COVID, during the lockdown and post-COVID environments.

7. OBJECTIVES OF THE STUDY

- To assess consumer behaviour while making purchases during lockdown and post-lockdown.
- To study the frequency and necessity of online purchases as drivers for change in consumer behaviour.
- To comprehend the association between electronic commerce purchases in relation to the shift towards online payment modes.

8. HYPOTHESES

H0. In India, COVID-19 did not have an influence on shopper conduct towards e-retail.
H1. In India, COVID-19 had an influence on shopper conduct towards online e-retail.

H0. There was no association between upsurge in online payment methods and COVID-19 in India.
H1. There was an association between the upsurge in online payment methods and COVID-19 in India.

9. RESEARCH METHODOLOGY

Results of the statistical study come from a survey conducted for about two months duration. The input from diverse respondents in Bengaluru is analyzed using a basic survey method through questionnaire in order to evaluate the shift in customer buying behaviour towards internet shopping because of COVID-19 lockdowns. This study mainly focused on primary data for analysis purposes. A structured questionnaire was developed. Since whole research is understood by the data that is collected, sampling design plays an important role in understanding the entire study. Through including those aged 18 and above, the target populace of the study is reduced to 32,76,098 as this is the number of e-commerce users in the city of Bengaluru. The information is backed by appropriate evidence (Salman, 2020). After accounting for 5% margin error and 95% confidence level, a sample size of 385 was computed using Cochran's Rule. Simple Random Sampling was adopted and other characteristics such as having shopped before and during the pandemic were taken into account when selecting the sample. For analysis, the researcher applied descriptive statistics to get a sense of the data distribution and to find correlations between variables. Inferential statistics was applied to prove hypotheses. The findings of the analysis were acquired using IBM SPSS 21's numerous statistical tools.

10. AN ANALYSIS ON THE IMPACT OF COVID-19 ON CONSUMER BEHAVIOUR TOWARDS E-COMMERCE DURING LOCKDOWN AND THEREAFTER

A total of 385 people were surveyed within Bengaluru's city limits for this study. Frequency, price, availability of product, necessity and manner of payment were the primary characteristics identified as the foundation for a movement in customer behaviour towards E-commerce. The research aimed to know if there was any difference between the E-shopping trend before the pandemic and how it evolved throughout the pandemic and thereafter.

- Assessing the consumer level of satisfaction while making online purchase during the lockdown.
- Analyzing the frequency and necessity of online purchase during lockdown.
- Understanding the relationship between online purchase and shift towards online payment modes.

10.1 Assessing the Consumer Level of Satisfaction While Making Online Purchase during the Lockdown

The following analysis is done in order to study the consumer satisfaction towards e-commerce while shopping during lockdown and also to identify what are their thoughts towards e-commerce replacing traditional brick and mortar stores. In order to conduct this study, Regression test was conducted.

H0. There is no impact of level of satisfaction while shopping virtually and proposition that E-commerce played a vital role during pandemic to fulfil purchase needs.
H1. There is an impact of level of satisfaction while shopping virtually and proposition that E-commerce played a vital role during pandemic to fulfil purchase needs.

From Table 1, the significant value for the satisfaction level for shopping online is 0.012 which is less than the significant value of 0.05. As per the proposed hypothesis, it shows there is significant impact between level of satisfaction and proposition that E-commerce played a vital role during pandemic to fulfil purchase needs. Hence, the researchers accept alternative hypothesis when tested using regression analysis.

In order to understand if respondents feel that the online stores are going to replace the offline stores, a regression test was conducted with a framed hypothesis.

H0. There is no impact of level of satisfaction while shopping virtually and thoughts on whether E-commerce would replace traditional shopping.
H1. There is an impact of level of satisfaction while shopping virtually and thoughts on whether E-commerce would replace traditional shopping.

From Table 1, the significant value for the satisfaction level for shopping online is 0.051 which is more than the significant value of 0.05. As per the proposed hypothesis, it shows there is no significant impact between level of satisfaction and thoughts on whether E-commerce would replace traditional shopping. Hence, the researchers accept the null hypothesis.

Table 1. Showing Impact of Consumer Satisfaction While Shopping Virtually on E-Commerce Playing Vital Role during the Pandemic: Regression Test.

Model	Sum of Squares	df	Mean Square	*F*	Sig.
Regression	16.623	2	8.312	6.507	0.002[b]
Residual	487.912	382	1.277		
Total	504.535	384			

Model	Unstandardized Coefficients *B*	Unstandardized Coefficients Std. Error	Standardized Coefficients Beta	*t*	Sig.
	2.530	0.199		12.723	0.000
Would you agree to the proposition that E-commerce played a vital role during pandemic to fulfil your purchase needs?	0.131	0.052	0.131	2.536	0.012
Do you feel E-commerce would replace traditional in person shopping?	0.104	0.053	0.101	1.955	0.051

Source: Primary data.

The test was conducted in order to understand if there was any association between challenges faced by customers during their purchase and their level of satisfaction using anova one way test.

H0. There is no association between challenges of making online purchases during lockdown and satisfaction while shopping virtually.

H1. There is an association between challenges of making online purchases during lockdown and satisfaction while shopping virtually.

From Table 2, the significant value for the satisfaction level for shopping online is 0.724 which is more than the *p*-value of 0.05 (5% of significant value). Hence, the researchers accept the null hypothesis by conducting one-way anova test.

10.2 Analyzing the Frequency and Necessity of Online Purchase during Lockdown

The study is conducted between the variables' gender and frequency since it can have an impact on the consumer behaviour towards e-commerce.

Table 2. Showing Association Between Challenges Faced during Online Purchase and Level of Satisfaction: anova One Way Test.

		Sum of Squares	df	Mean Square	*F*	Sig.
What was your satisfaction level while shopping virtually?	Between Groups	55.508	48	1.156	0.865	0.724
	Within Groups	449.027	336	1.336		
	Total	504.535	384			

Source: Primary Data.

H0. There is no association between gender and frequency of shopping online.
H1. There is an association between gender and frequency of shopping online.

From Table 3, the significant value for the satisfaction level for shopping online is 0.588 which is more than the *p*-value of 0.05 (5% of significant value). Hence, researcher accepts null hypothesis (Table 4).

In order to identify any connotation between respondents' age and their frequency of shopping online during the lockdown since it can have an impact on the consumer behaviour towards e-commerce. This study was conducted using Chi-square test.

H0. There is no association between age and regularity of shopping virtually.
H1. There is an association between age and regularity of shopping virtually.

From Table 4, *p*-value 0.05 is equal to 5% significant value. Since *p*-value is 0.05, alternate hypothesis is accepted.

This analysis was conducted to assess any association between the occupation of the respondents and their frequency of the shopping. The study is conducted since respondents

Table 3. Showing Association Between Gender and Frequency of Virtual Shopping during the Lockdown: One Way anova Test.

		Sum of Squares	df	Mean Square	*F*	Sig.
Has pandemic lockdown increased the frequency of shopping online?	Between Groups	0.427	1	0.427	0.294	0.588
	Within Groups	557.406	383	1.455		
	Total	557.834	384			

Source: Primary data.

Table 4. Showing Association Between Age and Frequency of Virtual Shopping during the Lockdown: Chi-Square Test.

	How Would You Describe the Frequency of Your Online Shopping During the Lockdown?					
Age	Frequently	Regularly	Occasionally	Rarely	Never	Total
18–25	24	33	51	6	18	132
26–35	8	36	34	3	16	97
36–45	12	29	51	4	21	117
46 and above	3	9	12	5	10	39
Total	47	107	148	18	65	385
	Value	df	Asymp. Sig. (2-sided)			
Pearson chi-square	21.049[a]	12	0.050			
Probability ratio	18.721	12	0.095			
Linear-by-linear association	6.331	1	0.012			
N of valid cases	385					

Source: Primary data.

with various occupation backgrounds might differ in their frequency of making online purchase which might affect the consumer behaviour towards E-commerce.

H0. There is no association between occupation and frequency of virtual shopping.
H1. There is an association between occupation and frequency of virtual shopping.

Table 5 shows the results of Chi-square test. Since the *p*-value 0.207 is more than 0.05 that means 5% significant value. Therefore, occupation has no connection with the frequency of virtual shopping.

The study was conducted to understand if the respondents face any challenges while making their purchase online and if those challenges had an impact on their frequency of making purchases online. Therefore, in order to conduct this test, anova one-way test was conducted.

H0. There is no association between challenges of making online purchases during lockdown and frequency of shopping online.
H1. There is an association between challenges of making online purchases during lockdown and frequency of shopping online.

From Table 6, the significant value for the satisfaction level for shopping online is 0.055, which is more than the *p*-value of 0.05 (5% of significant value). Hence, the researcher accepts null hypothesis.

The study is conducted to understand if there exists any association between the monthly income of the respondents and the frequency of online shopping. The test is conducted since there might be possibility that the frequency of online shopping might be affected by the disposable income available to the respondents. Therefore, to understand this, chi-square test was conducted.

H0. There is no association between monthly income and virtual shopping frequency.
H1. There is an association between monthly income and virtual shopping frequency.

Table 5. Showing Association Between Occupation and Frequency of Virtual Shopping: Chi-Square Test.

	How Would You Describe the Frequency of Your Online Shopping?					
Occupation	Frequently	Regularly	Occasionally	Rarely	Never	Total
Student	19	24	40	3	11	97
Private employee	13	35	42	3	19	112
Govt employee	9	29	39	6	14	97
Business	6	19	26	6	22	79
Total	47	107	148	18	65	385
	Value	df	Asymp. Sig. (2-sided)			
Pearson chi-square	20.303[a]	16	0.207			
Likelihood ratio	19.708	16	0.234			
Linear-by-linear association	9.641	1	0.002			
No of valid cases	385					

Source: Primary data.

Table 6. Showing Association Between Challenges Faced during Online Purchase and Frequency of Virtual Shopping: anova One-Way Test.

		Sum of Squares	df	Mean Square	*F*	Sig.
Has pandemic lockdown increased the frequency of shopping?	Between Groups	91.990	48	1.916	1.382	0.055
	Within Groups	465.843	336	1.386		
	Total	557.834	384			

Source: Primary data.

Table 7 exhibits chi-square test. Since the *p*-value of 0.019 is less than 0.05 at 5% significant value; it is concluded that there is a connection between monthly income and the respondent's virtual shopping frequency.

10.3 Understanding Relationship Between Online Purchase and Shift Towards Online Payment Modes

The table exhibits the relationship between age and modes of payment used by the respondents in prior to lockdown. This study is done to understand the extent of internet modes of payment used by the respondents before the epidemic and if there is any impact of age over the results.

H0. There is no association between age and payment modes prior the lockdown.
H1. There is an association between age and payment modes prior the lockdown.

Table 8 shows the Chi-square Test and a *p*-value of 0.00 which is less than 0.05 at 5% significance value. It is concluded that there is an association between age and payment modes used prior the COVID-19 pandemic.

Table 7. Showing Association Between Monthly Income and Frequency of Virtual Shopping: Chi-Square Test.

	How Would You Describe the Frequency of Your Online Shopping?					
	Frequently	Regularly	Occasionally	Rarely	Never	Total
Up to 15,000	18	19	37	3	10	87
15,000–30,000	6	36	41	6	25	114
30,000–50,000	13	42	56	5	24	140
50,000+	10	10	14	4	6	44
Total	47	107	148	18	65	385

	Value	df	Asymp. Sig. (2-sided)
Pearson chi-square	24.159[a]	12	0.019
Likelihood ratio	23.597	12	0.023
Linear-by-linear association	0.137	1	0.712
N of valid cases	385		

Source: Primary data.

Table 8. Showing Association Between Age and Modes of Payment Used Prior to Lockdown: Chi-Square Test.

Age	Prior to Lockdown What Were the Various Modes of Payment Methods Used					Total
	Cash on Delivery	UPI Payment	Cards	Net Banking	Card on Delivery	
18–25	37	56	17	12	10	132
26–35	15	38	24	13	6	96
36–45	18	34	40	24	1	117
46 and above	7	15	8	5	4	39
Total	77	143	89	54	21	384

	Value	df	Asymp. Sig. (2-sided)
Pearson chi-square	35.326[a]	12	0.000
Likelihood ratio	37.539	12	0.000
Linear-by-linear association	6.063	1	0.014
N of valid cases	384		

Source: Primary data.

This study is the continuation of the previous test conducted. The previous study exhibits the results of online payment modes used by respondents prior to the lockdown whereas this study aims to understand the modes of payment used during the lockdown. The purpose of this analysis is to understand if respondents' age affected the usage of online modes of payment during the lockdown. Therefore, Chi-square test is used to conduct the study.

H0. There is no association between age and payment modes availed throughout lockdown.

H1. There is an association between age and payment modes availed throughout lockdown.

In Table 9, the p-value 0.003 is less than 0.05 at 5% significant value. It is therefore confirmed that there is an association between age and modes of payment availed during the lockdown.

The study is conducted in order to understand the relationship between the monthly income and the payment methods used prior to lockdown. Respondents who come under different income groups may choose different payment methods according to their preference and for many other reasons. Therefore, the test is conducted to understand if there is any relationship between monthly income and payment methods used prior to COVID-19 pandemic.

H0. There is no association between monthly income and payment modes prior lockdown.

H1. There is an association between monthly income and payment modes prior lockdown.

Table 9. Showing Association Between Age and Modes of Payment Availed during the Lockdown: Chi-Square Test.

	During the Lockdown What Were the Various Modes of Payment Used					
Age	Cash on Delivery	UPI Payment	Cards	Net Banking	Card on Delivery	Total
18–25	26	61	28	12	5	132
26–35	12	28	40	16	1	97
36–45	10	40	36	24	7	117
46 and above	4	14	14	4	3	39
Total	52	143	118	56	16	385

	Value	df	Asymp. Sig. (2-sided)
Pearson chi-square	29.758[a]	12	0.003
Likelihood ratio	30.472	12	0.002
Linear-by-linear association	12.106	1	0.001
N of valid cases	385		

Source: Primary data.

Table 10 shows the results of chi-square test conducted on modes of payment used prior to lockdown and the *p*-value of 0.04 is less than 0.05 which is at 5% significance value. Alternate hypothesis is accepted.

The above test is conducted in order to study the relationship between the monthly income and the payment modes used during the lockdown. This is done to understand if there is any way that the monthly income would have impacted the online payment modes during the lockdown since the respondents has their own preferences for various reasons.

Table 10. Showing Association Between Monthly Income and Modes of Payment Used Prior to Lockdown: Chi-Square Test.

	Prior Lockdown What Were the Various Modes of Payment Method?					
	Cash on Delivery	UPI Payment	Cards	Net Banking	Card on Delivery	Total
Up to 15,000	26	35	12	8	6	87
15,000–30,000	20	47	29	14	4	114
30,000–50,000	21	46	34	28	10	139
50,000+	10	15	14	4	1	44
Total	77	143	89	54	21	384

	Value	df	Asymp. Sig. (2-sided)
Pearson chi-square	21.788[a]	12	0.040
Likelihood ratio	21.968	12	0.038
Linear-by-linear association	4.033	1	0.045
No of valid cases	384		

Source: Primary data.

H0. There is no association between monthly income and payment modes availed during lockdown.
H1. There is an association between monthly income and payment modes availed during lockdown.

Table 11 exhibits the *p*-value 0.000 and it is less than 0.05 that means 5% significant value. Therefore, there is an association between monthly income and modes of payment availed during lockdown.

11. SUMMARY OF FINDINGS, SUGGESTION AND CONCLUSION

The research aimed to see how the pandemic affected customer purchase behaviour when it came to e-shopping. This chapter discusses the findings of the analysis, offers suggestions and wraps it up with a conclusion. The deductions are based on the findings, and recommendations are based on the researcher's best estimates.

12. FINDINGS

- The age group of majority of the respondents was between 18 and 25, which was 34.8%. Since this age group is more prone to online purchases and active online, the responses are higher from this age group.
- More than 50% of the respondents were males.
- Majority of them are literates, and 28% of respondents' highest qualification is an Undergraduate degree, and while 62% have done higher degree and doctorates. While 10% of the respondents have completed their primary education. This implies that

Table 11. Showing Association Between Monthly Income and Modes of Payment Availed during the Lockdown: Chi-Square Test.

	During the Lockdown What Were the Various Modes of Payment Used?					
	Cash on Delivery	UPI Payment	Cards	Net Banking	Cards on Delivery	Total
Up to 15,000	22	44	10	9	2	87
15,000–30,000	11	39	46	13	5	114
30,000–50,000	13	47	47	27	6	140
50,000+	6	13	15	7	3	44
Total	52	143	118	56	16	385

	Value	df	Asymp. Sig. (2-sided)
Pearson chi-square	37.714[a]	12	0.000
Likelihood ratio	38.838	12	0.000
Linear-by-linear association	15.260	1	0.000
N of valid cases	385		

Source: Primary data.

mobile phones are accessible by all kinds of population and online purchases are made by all demographics.

- The respondents are very well distributed between students, private employee, government employees and business people, which again prove that majority of the population are moving towards online purchases.
- Cumulative majority earned above Rs. 15,000–Rs. 50,000 (66%) which can be understood as the earners are more inclined towards online purchases.
- 68% of respondents had made online purchase prior to lockdown which was constant even during the pandemic (66%) which shows that people did not change their purchasing behaviour on general terms.
- Majority of the population (38%) were occasional buyers which meant they made a purchase once in 2–4 months.
- Before the pandemic, the respondents' most preferred mode of payment was Cash on Delivery and cards which was 20% and 24% respectively. But during the lockdown, this trend changed as 38% of respondents preferred UPI payment.
- The most bought products online were electronic items, apparels, medicines and groceries.
- It seems almost 60% respondents' cap on spending on online purchase was Rs. 1,000–Rs. 4,000 rupees.
- 30% of the respondents were satisfied with online shopping.
- There has been an increased occurrence of online shopping owing to lockdown.
- Few main reasons to prefer online purchase were government imposing lockdown and closure of offline stores and to avoid crowd in the essential stores.
- Majority (76%) respondents approved the proposition that online businesses played a pivotal part during epidemic to fulfil their purchase needs.
- Pandemic helped consumers believe online payment methods are trustworthy.
- Respondents agree that online shopping during pandemic and various risks of cash transaction have influenced people to move towards cashless transaction.
- When compared to offline shopping, where the chance of contact is extremely high, respondents believe that online shopping is considerably safer.
- Regardless of the fear of a pandemic, the study finds that customer preference for internet shopping is on the rise.
- Few of the problems or challenges faced by the users during online purchases were non-availability of products online, risks of COVID infection during delivery, speed of internet connection and delivery time.
- 27% of the respondents agree that E-commerce is going to replace traditional in-person shopping, while 33% of the respondents remain neutral regarding such proposition. The remaining 40% of the respondents are comfortable practicing webrooming.

13. SUGGESTIONS

- It is seen that the frequent online buyers are of the income level of Rs. 15,000–Rs. 40,000. Therefore, the online vendors need to come up with the strategy to attract the higher income population as well since they still prefer offline purchases which can be assumed as the purchase of the premium products.
- It is identified massive online discounts attract more buyers and therefore increases the traffic on the apps. Therefore, many more apps must come up with such promotional

highly discounted well marketed sales. Apps like Flipkart and Amazon must increase the number of sales during the year as well (Shashidhar, 2019).
- The online shopping apps must also concentrate on those buyers who make purchases in bulk in their offline purchases and try to get them into the online space.
- Online buyers cannot feel the product before making the purchase so the online shopping apps must come up with some strategy to attract such rigid customers.
- They must come up with a provision of providing free shipment to closer locations, and this will help and improve the sale in remote locations since most of the manufacturing is done in remote areas.
- The pandemic has made people more focused towards health and hygiene, therefore the E-commerce platform must grab this opportunity as soon as possible.

The respondents through the questionnaire brought out the issues they faced while buying online, and the following suggestions were made:

- Online sellers must ensure that customers do not face any delays in receiving their orders.
- Online sellers should make sure that the safety of their customers is their first priority.
- Online sellers should ensure that customers receive timely refunds for cancelled orders.
- Online retailers should aim to keep all of the things that customers want in stock.

14. CONCLUSION

COVID-19 is one of humanity's darkest disasters, bringing the entire world to a standstill. After being found in over 200 countries, WHO declared a pandemic. In terms of health and infrastructure, India is a developing country; nevertheless, the country's economy has suffered. To lessen the impact, a nationwide lockout was enacted. Supply chains were affected on a larger scale. Consumers' purchase patterns for products and services have changed in an era of new norms. Consequently, the pandemic altered public purchasing ways. It's also evident that individuals prefer to shop online. Above all, online buying is practical and the way of the future. The pandemic has established the practise of wearing masks and sanitizing frequently; in the near future, online purchasing will also become popular. Consumer buying behaviour has been studied extensively over the years, and marketing experts have shown a keen interest in this research, recognizing the importance of consumer buying behaviour. COVID-19 influenced worldwide customer behaviour, and this has had an effect on economies around the world. All scales of businesses are adapting to the present reality. It's worth noting that technology has grown in value for consumers and businesses alike. This study examined the bearing of COVID-19 on changes in buyer's attitude towards electronic commerce, as well as how COVID-19 influenced those habits. Consumer behaviour pre and throughout the COVID-19 is explored. This study has offered detailed information on consumer purchasing habits and suggests that during the COVID-19 pandemic, consumers have become more accepting of internet shopping which is more of a way of living than a mere occasional online purchase. Also, online payment methods have become much more acceptable by the consumers and are comfortably embracing the reality of living in the Indian economic eco-system which is filled with cashless digital transactions.

REFERENCES

Deshpande, S. (2020, October 4). *Impact of Covid-19 on Indian economy*. TOI. https://timesofindia.indiatimes.com/readersblog/midweekread/impact-of-covid-19-on-indian-economy-26770/

Galhotra, B., & Dewan, A. (2020). Impact of COVID-19 on digital platforms and change in e-commerce shopping trends. In *2020 fourth international conference on I-SMAC (IoT in social, mobile, analytics and cloud) (I-SMAC)* (pp. 861–866). https://doi.org/10.1109/I-SMAC49090.2020.9243379

Gu, S., Ślusarczyk, B., Hajizada, S., Kovalyova, I., & Sakhbieva, A. (2021). Impact of COVID-19 pandemic on online consumer purchasing behavior. *Theoretical and Applied Electronic Commerce Research*, *16*(6), 2263–2281. https://doi.org/10.3390/jtaer16060125

IEA (International Energy Agency). (2021, October 1). *World energy outlook 2021*. IEA 50. https://www.iea.org/reports/world-energy-outlook-2021

ILO (International Labour Organisation). (2022, July 21). *Annual report 2021*. https://www.ilo.org/publications/annual-report-2021

Kesari, R., & Kesharwani, A. (2021). After covid -19 pandemic: E-commerce revolution in India gets its second wind. *International Journal of Economics and Management Studies*, *8*(2), 123–129. https://doi.org/10.14445/23939125/ijems-v8i2p118

Kumar, P. P., & Kumar, R. (2021). An empirical study on impact of e-commerce on retail business sales (grocery, electronics, apparels, drugs and furniture) due to covid-19 in India. *Journal of University of Shanghai for Science and Technology*, *23*(08), 771–783. https://doi.org/10.51201/jusst/21/08440

Mishra, D., & Peermohamed, A. (2021, May 21). *E-Commerce fails to escape ongoing Covid-19 wave unlike last year*. ET. https://economictimes.indiatimes.com/tech/technology/second-covid-19-wave-rocks-ecommerce-boat-hits-consumer-spends/articleshow/82807434.cms

Salman, S. H. (2020, June 11). *India's e-commerce market to see 300 mn shoppers by 2025*. https://www.live-mint.com/industry/retail/india-s-e-commerce-market-to-see-300-mn-shoppers-by-2025-11591894031861.html

Shashidhar, A. (2019, October 31). *Reliance, Amazon, Flipkart battle royale for digital dominance in India*. Business Today. https://www.businesstoday.in/latest/corporate/story/reliance-amazon-flipkart-battle-royale-digital-dominance-india-234858-2019-10-31

Times of India. (2020, June 25). *How is government turning around agriculture sector post Covid-19 lockdown*. TOI. https://www.businesstoday.in/latest/corporate/story/reliance-amazon-flipkart-battle-royale-digital-dominance-india-234858-2019-10-31

Tran, L. (2020). Managing the effectiveness of e-commerce platforms in a pandemic. *Journal of Retailing and Consumer Services*, 253–268. http://www.elsevier.com/locate/jretconser

A BIBLIOMETRIC ANALYSIS ON LUXURY MARKETING IN INDIA: 2010–2021

Charul Agrawal[a] and Taranjeet Duggal[b]

[a]*Amity University, India*
[b]*Manav Rachna International Institute of Research and Studies, India*

ABSTRACT

The study aims to study the extent of research done in luxury marketing in an emerging economy like India by conducting a bibliometric analysis. A period of 21 years has been considered to present a comprehensive picture for results and analysis. Key findings indicate the gaps and scope of further research for academics in India and abroad. The findings indicate a dearth of research by scholars and academicians in luxury, counterfeit and masstige, especially when there is a surge of the upper middle class in India. More specifically, Indian-grown luxury brands also present a massive scope for future research.

Keywords: Luxury; luxury brands; India; masstige; domestic luxury brands

1. INTRODUCTION

From time immemorial, man has been subjected to the pleasures of luxury. From the forbidden fruit to the GUCCI perfume of today, pursuing luxury has always held him bewildered. Atwal and Williams (2017) point out that although there is disagreement about what constitutes a luxury brand, the progression of luxury over time – first embraced by the elite and affluent, then relentlessly rewritten and transformed for mainstream consumers – raises new problems for marketers. When discussing one standard definition of a luxury brand, Rodrigues and Borges (2021) indicate that the old definition of luxury is unclear, and the new definition of luxury should consider democratizing the term luxury. Kapferer (2017) attributes the vagueness of defining Luxury brands to the loss of distinctness that was initially possessed by these brands and which has now become insignificant when it comes to the management of Luxury brands. According to the research done by Özbölük (2021), the new meaning of the term luxury has been outlined.

Resilient Businesses for Sustainability
Advanced Series in Management, Volume 34B, 169–183

ISSN: 1877-6361/doi:10.1108/S1877-636120240000034B013

He talks about the increasing importance of consumer experience and gives two critical aspects of luxury, which are the need for uniqueness and freedom at the same time. The study of Turunen and Turunen (2018) also concluded that luxury does not only result from consumer behaviour but also the product's inherent qualities; thus, from the standpoint of consumption, the essence of luxury needs to be grasped. They further emphasize elements of earlier literature about the use of luxury items and stress the significance of social symbolic connotations. The concept of luxury has undergone many transformations, and it holds different meanings in different countries. Eng and Bogaert (2010) reveals that cultural and psychological aspects are crucial in impacting India's consumption of luxury goods. India's luxury consumption conveys social status and prestige.

Many direct and indirect factors have a bearing on the purchase decision of these luxury goods. Lloyd and Cheah (2015) confirms that brand recognition affects customer's willingness to purchase luxury goods. He further emphasizes that social influence also has a significant bearing. Pino et al. (2019) compared an emerging economy like India and a mature market like the US. They concluded that compared to their US counterparts, Indian consumers with higher status consumption are more likely to purchase branded luxury goods. Kapferer and Valette-Florence (2018) undertook a study with 1,286 affluent Westerners and 60 luxury brands to establish a dual effect of brand penetration on the desirability of Luxury. Mamat et al. (2016) conducted a study with Malaysian consumers and concluded that household income and the functional value of the product influence the purchase intention. Farrag (2017) conducted a study on the consumers of Qatar. The results revealed that purchase attitudes and intentions for luxury brands are significantly influenced by fashion engagement, brand consciousness, social comparison and experience demands. Aliyev and Wagner (2018) conducted a study on consumers' perceptions regarding the advertisements of luxury cars. The study revealed that Europeans are more focused on the object in consideration, whereas Asians notice the advertisement background more. Fionda and Moore (2009) have undertaken a qualitative approach and identified nine essential attributes that help consumers form a favourable brand proposition; in fact, some consumers will not shy from buying a fake to create an impression. Heine et al. (2018) have studied the significant dimensions of luxury brand personality, such as tradition, modesty, elitism and sensuality. The author has also highlighted the merits of personality-based brand management.

Brun and Castelli (2013) highlight that the definition of luxury is complex and needs a thorough method for categorizing premium buyers to reveal distinct consumer profiles to understand distinct personal and social motivations for purchase. Marketers also need to make their efforts to lure the consumer.

Ghosh and Varshney (2013) assert that though significant study has been done on the luxury market and the characteristics of luxury consumers, there is a dearth of comprehensive and integrated research on Luxury Consumption. According to Husic and Cicic (2009), Luxury consumption has not been studied in detail, and the underlying assumptions must be explored. The study by Jain (2019) also supports that despite India being home to the largest share of the millennial population, there need to be more studies dedicated to luxury consumption, particularly related to millennials. There is a need to understand the research trends in luxury marketing, particularly in a developing economy like India. For the same, it is required that a comprehensive and retrospective cyber metric analysis is conducted of the various documents that have been published, which includes Research papers, thesis, conference papers, books, book chapters, review papers and peer-reviewed journal articles in a renowned database like Scopus.

A wide range of keywords need to be selected for conducting such analysis. The scope of the current study is to study all the academic work comprising journal articles, conference papers, book chapters, etc.

2. RESEARCH METHODOLOGY

The authors have attempted to study both qualitative and quantitative dimensions of the selected theme, the study of the luxury market in India. According to Roig-Tierno et al. (2017), bibliometric analysis – a qualitative and quantitative technique – is a research methodology expanding worldwide. It enables scholars to access one another's contributions to a field. The current study aims for cyber metric analysis with retrospective effect to evaluate and identify the recent and relevant publications, their changing trends and patterns in the theme from 2000 to 2021. The authors believe that Scopus presents a repository of reputed publications, which include books, articles and research papers.

The authors have tried to accomplish the current research with the articles and papers already published in Scopus for 21 years, i.e. from 2000 to 2021. All the publications considered for the study have been indexed in Scopus, a multi-disciplinary database encompassing works of repute from Applied Sciences, Dentistry, Medical, Humanities, Business Management, Agriculture, Psychology, etc.

The authors have adopted an inductive review approach as the information received from the Scopus database was thoroughly classified and analyzed to arrive at the results presented in the later sections.

The review process adopted by the authors has been depicted in Fig. 1, which exhibits how the study moved forward during the entire review process.

The initial step was keyword identification, which helped select the study's relevant publications. Since this paper aims to review all the published articles in Luxury Marketing in India, the authors chose the following keywords in the initial phase.

'Luxury' and 'India'. With this, the Scopus yielded 387 results. As the data were massive, there were possibilities that some irrelevant studies could be included in the initial results. Year 2000 was the base year for the study for two main reasons. Firstly, very few studies were conducted before 2000 on luxury brands, especially keeping Indian consumers in consideration. Secondly, the authors wanted to give attention to the recent papers, which is why the year 2000, also the start of a new century, was selected. A time gap of 20 years was found suitable as quite considerable work has been done in this domain globally. India, an emerging economy where consumers have increased disposable income, is more prone to buying luxury brands.

In the subsequent step, short surveys, notes, editorials, book reviews, books and book chapters, conference papers and thesis have all been excluded. The result was a total of 250 articles. In the further step, all the articles related to environmental science, humanities, agriculture, psychology, CSR, medicine, material science, economics, decision sciences and chemical engineering were excluded. Only articles from the Business Management and Accounting journals were considered, resulting in 132 articles. Lastly, the following inclusion criteria were adopted to get the final 128 articles.

- Only fully published articles were considered for the study.
- All papers in other language other than English were excluded.
- Only papers from 2000 to 2021 have been considered.

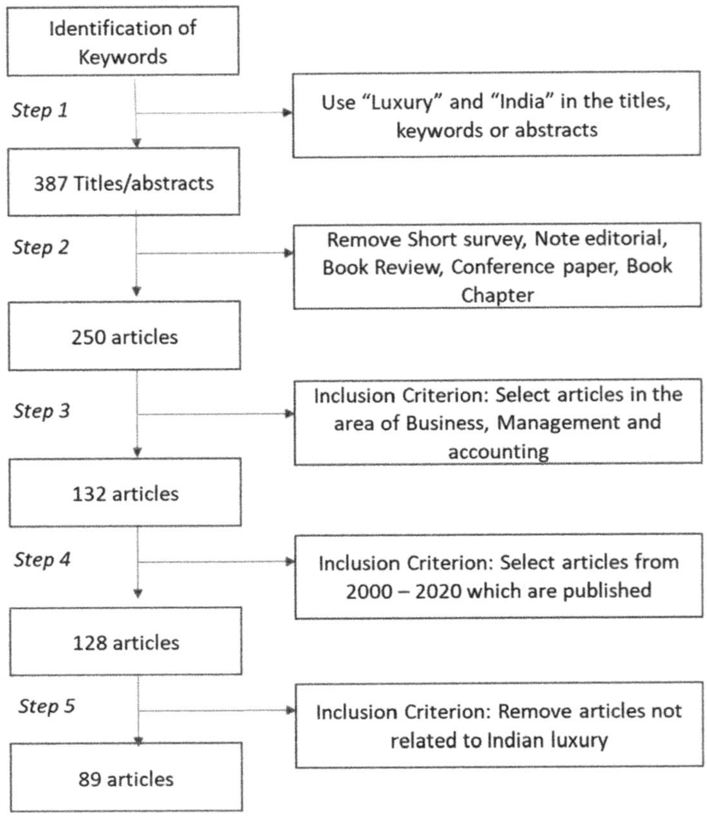

Fig. 1. Flowchart of Research Steps. *Source:* Authors' own work.

The above three exclusion criteria resulted in 128 articles. The authors analyzed the titles, abstracts and keywords of all 128 articles to identify the most relevant study on luxury marketing in the Indian market. A total of 39 articles were further found irrelevant as they were not related to the Indian market or Indian consumers.

The final 89 articles were carefully studied and analyzed by the authors in detail, and the findings have been presented in the next section.

3. RESULTS OF THE STUDY

3.1 Yearly Trend

Fig. 2 shows the trend of the publication from the year 2000 onwards. It becomes evident from the chart that the research publications show an increasing trend basically from the year 2013. The research publications before 2013 were few and not very prominent, suggesting that luxury marketing in India was still nascent. In the past eight years, there has been significant growth in the number of publications from one paper to 25 papers in 2021. The number of publications was 16 in 2020, which was further low in 2019. In 2019, only nine publications were there in the study. This increasing trend exhibits an increasing

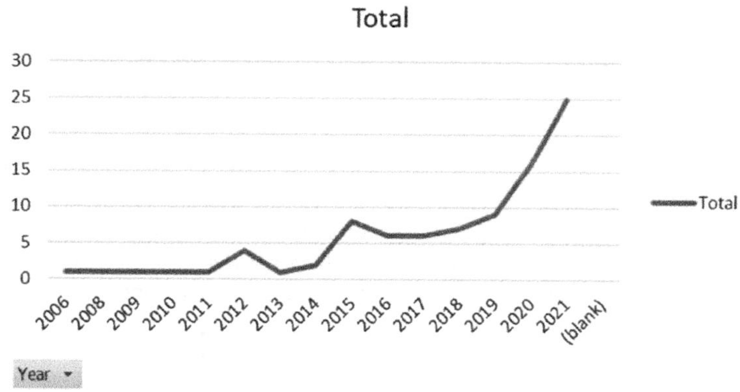

Fig. 2. Yearly Trend of Publications. *Source:* Authors' own work.

interest among the researchers who have selected Indians and Indian consumers for the study under luxury marketing.

3.2 Journal Analysis

The analysis reveals that all the 89 journals selected for the study come from 48. Fig. 3 summarizes the result. The figure shows the top 9 journals which have contributed the most significant number of publications. The *Indian Journal of Marketing* and *Fashion Marketing and Management* have maximum publications (7 papers), followed by the *Journal of Retailing and Consumer Services* (6 papers).

Both *Worldwide Hospitality and Tourism Services* and the *Journal of Business Research* have contributions of 5 papers each. A total of 3 papers have been contributed by the

Fig. 3. Journal-Wise Distribution. *Source:* Authors' own work.

International Journal of Applied Business and Economic Research, International Journal of Hospitality Management, Journal of Global Fashion Marketing and *Journal of Product and Brand Management.*

3.3 Keyword Analysis

The Scopus database lists the keywords indexed by the authors for their research work. Fig. 4 exhibits the keywords used by the authors of the selected 89 publications. As per the chart given below, it is visible that *India, Consumer behaviour, luxury brands* and *hotels* are the prominent clusters formed. It shows that these are the most popular keywords used by the authors.

Table 1 shows the top 10 keywords and their frequencies for more straightforward interpretation.

3.4 Authors and Their Affiliation Analysis

Though it is very natural that since all the selected 89 papers related to luxury marketing in India, the maximum share is that of the Indian researchers, substantial contributions can be seen from researchers worldwide. More than 160 authors have contributed to these selected 89 papers. All the selected articles are under co-authorship except Bothra (2014), Goyal (2020), Jain (2018, 2019, 2020, 2021a), Jain and Mishra (2020), Khare (2014), Laldinliana (2012), Menon (2021), Nagar (2016), Shukla (2012), Singh (2017, 2019) and Willis (2006).

The remaining 74 selected articles have either two or more two authors.

Some publications are exclusively from foreign authors such as Cheah et al. (2016), Haldorai et al. (2020), Mohsin and Lockyer (2010), Pino et al. (2019), Rehman et al. (2021), Willis (2006) and Yu and Hudders (2021).

Foreign researchers have not fully explored the Indian luxury market. Very few studies form a part of the selected articles. There is ample scope in the Indian market as the purchasing power has increased. Social media has accentuated the levels of awareness among Indian consumers, and India can be an opportune region for the study of luxury brands by Indian researchers. From the entire data of 89 articles, the overall contribution

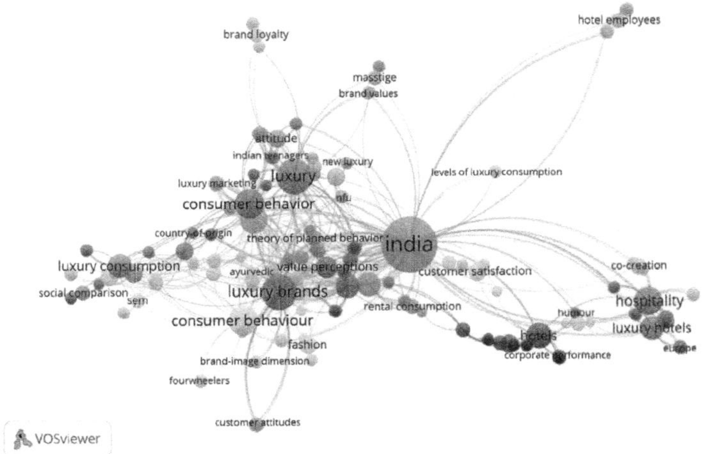

Fig. 4. Cluster of Keywords. *Source:* Authors' own work.

Table 1. Top 10 Keywords.

Rank	Keyword	Frequency
1	Luxury	69
2	Brand	51
3	Consumer	36
4	India	32
5	Marketing	20
5	Value	20
6	Hotels	18
7	Intention	15
7	Consumption	15
8	Social	15

Source: Authors' own work.

from the industry is weak. Only Arora and Chatterjee(2017) from CISCO and Luxe Analytics which is a luxury market research firm has nine contributions (Jain, 2019, 2020, 2021; Jain et al., 2021; Jain & Mishra, 2018; Kumaran & Seal, 2017; Mishra et al., 2021; Shankar & Jain, 2021). The current selection also has three contributions from Trident Bandra Kurla, Mumbai, which is a 5-star rated property offering luxury accommodation in Mumbai (Bharwani et al., 2019; Bharwani & Mathews, 2021a, 2021b).

Some selected papers have also been written in collaboration between Indian and foreign researchers.

3.5 Content Analysis

The authors have identified themes based on which all the selected 89 articles have been categorized. For this purpose, the research articles were studied deeply to extract the core theme on which they were based. The following themes have been identified with the corresponding research papers (Table 2).

The above themes emerge as the primary focus areas of the selected articles for the study. However, there were few papers which could not be placed in any of the above categories as they did not focus on one particular theme.

4. THEMATIC ANALYSIS

Out of all the 89 articles considered for detailed study, it can be concluded that some significant themes emerge and also that there are some domains where only a few articles could be matched.

The findings from each theme have been briefly explained below.

4.1 Theme 1: Indian Hospitality Industry

Many research articles belong to the category of Indian luxury hotels. In the case of the service industry, hotel resorts in India represent a fair share of the luxury segment essentially booked by Indian consumers. Most of the articles falling under this area have the employees of the Luxury hotels in focus. The corporate social responsibility practices undertaken by the hotels have been studied by Nazir et al. (2021), Nazir and Islam (2020a,

Table 2. Themes and Corresponding Papers.

S No.	Theme	Research Papers
1.	Hospitality industry, where luxury hotels resorts have been studied	(Bharwani et al., 2019; Bharwani & Mathews, 2021a; Bharwani & Mathews, 2021b; Bhat & Sharma, 2021; Dhiman & Arora, 2020; Haldorai et al., 2020; Mathew et al., 2020; Nazir et al., 2021; Nazir & Islam, 2020a; Nazir & Islam, 2020b; Roy et al., 2020; Senthil Kumaran & Seal, 2020; S. Sharma & Mishra, 2019; A. Singh, 2019; Banerjee & Biswas, 2018; Datta & Singh, 2018; Sarmah et al., 2017; Kiessling et al., 2009; Mohsin et al., 2013, 2015; Mohsin & Lockyer, 2010; Shankari & Suja, 2008)
2.	Factors which influence the consumers to make a purchase decision	Rehman et al., 2021; Menezes et al., 2021; Shahid et al., 2021; Sanyal et al., 2021; Shankar & Jain, 2021; Jacob et al., 2020; S. Jain, 2020; S. Jain & Mishra, 2020; Neerattiparambil & Belli, 2020; S. Jain & Mishra, 2020; Kautish et al., 2020; Sharda & Bhat, 2019; S. Jain, 2019; Ajitha & Sivakumar, 2019; V. Jain & Schultz, 2019; Pasricha & Jain, 2019; Pino et al., 2019; S. Jain & Mishra, 2018; Sharda & Bhat, 2018; D. E. Schultz & Jain, 2018; S. Ajitha & Sivakumar, 2017; S. Jain & Khan, 2017; S. Jain et al., 2017; Cheah et al., 2016; Srivastava et al., 2016; D. Schultz & Jain, 2015; Fain et al., 2015; Akila et al., 2015; Khare, 2014; Laldinliana, 2012; Gupta et al., 2012; Khare & Handa, 2011)
3.	Specific brands have been studied.	(Sondhi & Basu, 2021; Shetty et al., 2021; Jayanti & Raghunath, 2018; Arora & Chatterjee, 2017; Thakur et al., 2015; Thakur & Kaur, 2015, 2021)
4.	Luxury value perceptions	(Shukla & Purani, 2012; Yu & Hudders, 2021; Shukla & Purani, 2012)
5.	Masstige brands	(Das et al., 2021; Goyal, 2020)
6.	Post-purchase behaviour of luxury shopping	(Jhamb et al., 2020; Pasricha & Jain, 2019)
7.	Brand personality, commitment and loyalty	(Jaywant Singh et al., 2021; Beig & Khan, 2022; Jasrai et al., 2016; Thakur & Kaur, 2016)
8.	Others	(S. Jain et al., 2021; V. Jain, 2018; Jaspreet Singh, 2017; Nagar, 2016; Swaminathan & Viswanathan, 2016; Swaminathan & Viswanathan, 2015; Bothra, 2014; Willis, 2006)

Source: Authors' own work.

2020b) and Sharma and Mishra (2019) about employee engagement and firm performance respectively (Mohsin et al., 2015). Moreover, Mohsin et al. (2013) have discussed the reasons for staff resignations or turnover in Indian luxury hotels. Organizational enthusiasm is the standard variable noticed in both the research articles.

The selected articles have also emphasized co-creation concerning technology (Bhat & Sharma, 2021) and smartphone apps (Sarmah et al., 2017).

4.2 Theme 2: Factors Which Have an Impact on Consumer Behaviour

The majority of the research work has been in the Indian context concerning the factors which impact consumers' intention to go for luxury brands. Certain factors were quoted repeatedly in the theme like the Need for Uniqueness has been studied by Das et al. (2021), Jebarajakirthy and Das (2021), Khare and Handa (2011) and Ajitha and Sivakumar (2019). Social media has also emerged as an essential factor, though only (Jain & Schultz, 2019; Menon, 2021) have tried to focus it on Indian consumers.

Many studies have drawn a comparison pattern between the Indian Consumers and those of other countries. Pillai and Nair (2021) Have concluded that while India is a collectivist country as compared to the UK, which has a more individualistic social orientation, has more impact on consumer purchase intention. Shukla and Rosendo-Rios (2021) have made comparison with China, which is also an emerging market like India. However, another author (Rehman et al., 2021) has compared two entirely different cultures, Saudi Arabia and India, showing the impact of religion and the personal and functional value of the purchase.

Findings also indicate that certain sections of the consumers have also been studied in particular. Generation Y has been studied by Jain (2020, 2021). Both have concluded that subjective norms are an essential parameter for luxury fashion among Gen Y consumers in India. Only two papers were a part of the study; hence, there is more scope to study Gen Y Indian consumers.

4.3 Theme 3: Masstige Brands

A significant gap can be observed in masstige brands, the scaled-down versions of the luxury brands. These masstige brands are basically 'prestige for masses'. Only two studies (Das et al., 2021; Goyal, 2020) have so far been conducted in the context of Indian origin. Both researchers have touched upon two entirely different subjects (Goyal, 2020) and discuss masstige vs luxury (Das et al., 2021), focusing on how effective desire, which is made up of discomfort and guilt, leads to intention and finally towards masstige engagement.

4.4 Theme 4: Post-Purchase Consumer Behaviour

Another domain where very few researchers have focused is post-purchase behaviour. Compared to the number of studies conducted on what impacts or motivates a consumer for luxury shopping, post-purchase actions have not been studied much. Jhamb et al. (2020) conducted their study in a city in western India, concluding that sensory and intellectual experiences considerably impact post-purchase behaviour. In contrast, Jain (2019) studied the post-purchase behaviour among Delhi consumers related to Ayurvedic cosmetics, where he concluded that sense of power and sense of power were key determiners. Both have concluded that there is a dearth of quality research in the Indian context regarding post-purchase behaviour.

4.5 Theme 5: Individual Brands

Some popular luxury brands are also part of the study as they have become popular with Indian Consumers. Two studies (Thakur et al., 2015 and Thakur & Kaur, 2015) have studied five global brands amongst Indian Consumers, which are Zara, Armani, Guess, Versace and Calvin Klein and concluded that in one case, emotional attachment leads to brand loyalty whereas in another case personal image and individual goals are an essential determinant for luxury purchase. There are cases of domestic brands where Sirohi (Sondhi & Basu, 2021) and its connection with women empowerment have been studied.

On the other hand, one of India's most iconic brands, Parle G (Shetty et al., 2021), which has always been associated with affordability and nutrition, has been discussed regarding how it is scaling up towards the premium segment to match its competitors.

5. SCOPE OF FUTURE RESEARCH AND CONCLUSION

The study's findings presented above lead to the following points of conclusion, and future research domains were identified.

- Since there is a significant gap in the domain of masstige brands, which are scaled-down versions of Luxury brands, the study of luxury and masstige in the Indian context can be taken up by future researchers (Purohit & Radia, 2022). They have advocated that research in masstige brands is still in the infancy stage (Kumar et al., 2020) and emphasized that the service industry from a masstige point of view has not been much explored. India is an emerging economy with increasing disposable incomes, making the middle class one of the most significant segments to buy luxury and masstige brands.
- A fair amount of research articles are available that elaborate on the factors that directly or indirectly impact the consumer's intention to buy a luxury product. However, very few studies have been conducted on post-purchase consumer behaviour in general and the Indian market. This presents a potential research topic, as studying post-purchase dissonance/satisfaction is equally significant as pre-purchase behaviour.
- The current study has indicated that the academicians have not focused on the domestically manufactured brands which can be scaled up to the category of Masstige, making it a contemporary topic which can be selected for study.
- Another area which has not been touched upon is the impact of celebrity endorsement on Indian consumers. Many articles have mentioned emotions, beliefs, self-image, etc., and how they impact the consumer's intention to buy, but none have discussed celebrity endorsement. Khan and Zaman (2021) signify that there is a need to gain customer confidence and trust regarding celebrity endorsement. Not only media celebrities but also Social media influencers and their impact on luxury purchase intention can be studied by Indian consumers.
- Another notable finding indicates that publications concerning counterfeit goods and Indian consumers are less. A very close association exists between luxury and counterfeit goods, signalling it as an essential study topic.
- The current study only deals with the publications selected from the Scopus database; inclusions from other databases like the Web of Science and Taylor and Francis would have yielded a more comprehensive picture, which future researchers can take up.
- In totality, bibliometric studies about the Indian luxury market are few which call for attention from active researchers. Cross-cultural studies can also be a subject matter for future research.

The present study attempts to integrate the published work in the domain of the luxury market concerning India. The study has both theoretical and practical implications for researchers and practitioners. From a theoretical point of view, the study adds to the existing research, thereby outlining the future research areas which can be carried on with the luxury brands. The study further accentuates a comprehensive understanding of the

Indian luxury scenario, highlighting the significant trends shaping luxury research in an emerging economy like India. From a practical perspective, the study brings forth the implications for luxury brand marketers and social media influencers who are a major driving force behind luxury purchases.

REFERENCES

Ajitha, S., & Sivakumar, V. (2017). Understanding the effect of personal and social value on attitude and usage behavior of luxury cosmetic brands. *Journal of Retailing and Consumer Services*, *39*, 103–113.

Ajitha, S., & Sivakumar, V. J. (2019). The moderating role of age and gender on the attitude towards new luxury fashion brands. *Journal of Fashion Marketing and Management*, *23*(4), 440–465. https://doi.org/10.1108/JFMM-05-2018-0074

Akila, R., Pamavathy, N., Balaji, S., & Senthilkumar, A. (2015). Brand preference and purchase behavior of B-segment passenger cars in Vellore city. *International Journal of Applied Business and Economic Research*, *13*(1).

Aliyev, F., & Wagner, R. (2018). Cultural influence on luxury value perceptions: Collectivist vs. Individualist luxury perceptions. *Journal of International Consumer Marketing*, *30*(3), 158–172.

Arora, S., & Chatterjee, R. (2017). Using experiential marketing to sell off-road vehicles in India: The Polaris way. *Global Business and Organizational Excellence*, *36*(5), 20–25. https://doi.org/10.1002/joe.21798

Atwal, G., & Williams, A. (2017). Luxury brand marketing – The experience is everything. *Advances in Luxury Brand Management*, 43–57.

Banerjee, D., & Biswas, D. (2018). Human contribution to service quality in West Bengal's luxury hotels. *Human Systems Management*, *37*(1), 7–13. https://doi.org/10.3233/HSM-171781

Beig, F. A., & Khan, M. F. (2022). Romancing the brands on social media. *Global Business Review*, *23*(3), 841–862.

Bharwani, S., & Mathews, D. (2021a). Post-pandemic pressures to pivot: Tech transformations in luxury hotels. *Worldwide Hospitality and Tourism Themes*, *13*(5), 569–583. https://doi.org/10.1108/WHATT-05-2021-0072

Bharwani, S., & Mathews, D. (2021b). Techno-business strategies for enhancing guest experience in luxury hotels: A managerial perspective. *Worldwide Hospitality and Tourism Themes*, *13*(2), 168–185. https://doi.org/10.1108/WHATT-09-2020-0121

Bharwani, S., Mathews, D., & Ghura, A. S. (2019). Business model innovation in the Indian hospitality industry: A study of the willingness to outsource specialty restaurants in luxury hotels. *Worldwide Hospitality and Tourism Themes*, *11*(4), 362–377.

Bhat, D. A. R., & Sharma, V. (2021). Enabling service innovation and firm performance: The role of co-creation and technological innovation in the hospitality industry. *Technology Analysis and Strategic Management*. https://doi.org/10.1080/09537325.2021.1919614

Bothra, N. (2014). Louis Vuitton, Gucci, and Audi: The luxury retail sector in India-will it grow or go? *Indian Journal of Marketing*, *44*(6), 51–61.

Brun, A., & Castelli, C. (2013). The nature of luxury: A consumer perspective. *International Journal of Retail & Distribution Management*, *41*(11/12), 823–847.

Cheah, I., Zainol, Z., & Phau, I. (2016). Conceptualizing country-of-ingredient authenticity of luxury brands. *Journal of Business Research*, *69*(12), 5819–5826. https://doi.org/10.1016/j.jbusres.2016.04.179

Das, M., Habib, M., Saha, V., & Jebarajakirthy, C. (2021). Bandwagon vs snob luxuries: Targeting consumers based on uniqueness dominance. *Journal of Retailing and Consumer Services*, *61*. https://doi.org/10.1016/j.jretconser.2021.102582

Das, M., Saha, V., & Roy, A. (2021). Inspired and engaged: Decoding MASSTIGE value in engagement. *International Journal of Consumer Studies*. https://doi.org/10.1111/ijcs.12726

Datta, A., & Singh, R. (2018). Determining the dimensions of organizational climate perceived by the hotel employees. *Journal of Hospitality and Tourism Management*, *36*, 40–48. https://doi.org/10.1016/j.jhtm.2018.07.001

Dhiman, P., & Arora, S. (2020). A conceptual framework for identifying key employee branding dimensions: A study of hospitality industry. *Journal of Innovation and Knowledge*, *5*(3), 200–209. https://doi.org/10.1016/j.jik.2019.08.003

Eng, T.-Y., & Bogaert, J. (2010). Psychological and cultural insights into consumption of luxury western brands in India. *Journal of Customer Behaviour*, *9*(1), 55–75.

Fain, V., Roy, S., & Ranchhod, A. (2015). Conceptualizing luxury buying behavior: The Indian perspective. *The Journal of Product and Brand Management*, *24*(3), 211–228. https://doi.org/10.1108/JPBM-07-2014-0655

Farrag, D. A. (2017). The young luxury consumer in Qatar. *Young Consumers*, *18*(4), 393–407.

Fionda, A. M., & Moore, C. M. (2009). The anatomy of the luxury fashion brand. *Journal of Brand Management*, *16*, 347–363.

Ghosh, A., & Varshney, S. (2013). Luxury goods consumption: A conceptual framework based on literature review. *South Asian Journal of Management*, *20*(2).

Goyal, A. (2020). Consumer perceived associations of masstige brands: An Indian perspective. *Journal of Promotion Management*, *27*(3), 399–416.

Gupta, S., Dasgupta, S., & Chaudhuri, R. (2012). Critical success factors for experiential marketing: Evidences from the Indian hospitality industry. *International Journal of Services and Operations Management*, *11*(3), 314–334. https://doi.org/10.1504/IJSOM.2012.045661

Haldorai, K., Kim, W. G., Chang, H. S., & Li, J. (2020). Workplace spirituality as a mediator between ethical climate and workplace deviant behavior. *International Journal of Hospitality Management*, *86*(Justin). https://doi.org/10.1016/j.ijhm.2019.102372

Heine, K., Atwal, G., Crener-Ricard, S., & Phan, M. (2018). Personality-driven luxury brand management. *Journal of Brand Management*, *25*, 474–487.

Husic, M., & Cicic, M. (2009). Luxury consumption factors. *Journal of Fashion Marketing and Management: An International Journal*, *13*(2), 231–245.

Jacob, I., Khanna, M., & Rai, K. A. (2020). Attribution analysis of luxury brands: An investigation into consumer-brand congruence through conspicuous consumption. *Journal of Business Research*, *116*, 597–607. https://doi.org/10.1016/j.jbusres.2019.07.007

Jain, V. (2018). Luxury: Not for consumption but developing extended digital self. *Journal of Human Values*, *24*(1), 25–38. https://doi.org/10.1177/0971685817733570

Jain, S. (2019). Exploring relationship between value perception and luxury purchase intention: A case of Indian millennials. *Journal of Fashion Marketing and Management*, *23*(4), 414–439. https://doi.org/10.1108/JFMM-10-2018-0133

Jain, S. (2020). Assessing the moderating effect of subjective norm on luxury purchase intention: A study of Gen Y consumers in India. *International Journal of Retail & Distribution Management*, *48*(5), 517–536.

Jain, S. (2021). Role of conspicuous value in luxury purchase intention. *Marketing Intelligence & Planning*, *39*(2), 169–185. https://doi.org/10.1108/MIP-03-2020-0102

Jain, S. (2021a). Examining the moderating role of perceived risk and web atmospherics in online luxury purchase intention. *Journal of Fashion Marketing and Management: An International Journal*, *25*(4), 585–605.

Jain, S., & Khan, M. N. (2017). Measuring the impact of beliefs on luxury buying behavior in an emerging market: Empirical evidence from India. *Journal of Fashion Marketing and Management*, *21*(3), 341–360. https://doi.org/10.1108/JFMM-07-2016-0065

Jain, S., Khan, M. N., & Mishra, S. (2017). Understanding consumer behaviour regarding luxury fashion goods in India based on the theory of planned behaviour. *Journal of Asia Business Studies*, *11*(1), 4–21. https://doi.org/10.1108/JABS-08-2015-0118

Jain, S., & Mishra, S. (2018). Effect of value perceptions on luxury purchase intentions: An Indian market perspective. *International Review of Retail Distribution & Consumer Research*, *28*(4), 414–435. https://doi.org/10.1080/09593969.2018.1490332

Jain, S., & Mishra, S. (2020). Luxury fashion consumption in sharing economy: A study of Indian millennials. *Journal of Global Fashion Marketing*, *11*(2), 171–189.

Jain, S., Mishra, S., & Mukhopadhyay, S. (2021). Critical success factors for luxury fashion brands in emerging markets: Insights from a qualitative study. *Journal of Global Fashion Marketing*, *12*(1), 47–61. https://doi.org/10.1080/20932685.2020.1845765

Jain, V., & Schultz, D. E. (2019). How digital platforms influence luxury purchase behavior in India? *Journal of Marketing Communications*, *25*(1), 41–64. https://doi.org/10.1080/13527266.2016.1197295

Jasrai, L., Thakur, A., & Kaur, R. (2016). Relationship between brand personality and attitudinal brand loyalty towards luxury fashion brands: A critique. *International Journal of Applied Business and Economic Research*, *12*, 8371–8378. https://www.researchgate.net/publication/313605225

Jayanti, R. K., & Raghunath, S. (2018). Institutional entrepreneur strategies in emerging economies: Creating market exclusivity for the rising affluent. *Journal of Business Research*, *89*, 87–98. https://doi.org/10.1016/j.jbusres.2018.03.039

Jebarajakirthy, C., & Das, M. (2021). Uniqueness and luxury: A moderated mediation approach. *Journal of Retailing and Consumer Services*, *60*. https://doi.org/10.1016/j.jretconser.2021.102477

Jhamb, D., Aggarwal, A., Mittal, A., & Paul, J. (2020). Experience and attitude towards luxury brands consumption in an emerging market. *European Business Review*, *32*(5), 909–936. https://doi.org/10.1108/EBR-09-2019-0218

Kapferer, J.-N. (2017). Managing luxury brands. *Advances in Luxury Brand Management*, 235–249.

Kapferer, J.-N., & Valette-Florence, P. (2018). The impact of brand penetration and awareness on luxury brand desirability: A cross country analysis of the relevance of the rarity principle. *Journal of Business Research*, *83*, 38–50.

Kautish, P., Khare, A., & Sharma, R. (2020). Influence of values, brand consciousness and behavioral intentions in predicting luxury fashion consumption. *The Journal of Product and Brand Management*, *30*(4), 513–531. https://doi.org/10.1108/JPBM-08-2019-2535

Khan, S. W., & Zaman, U. (2021). Linking celebrity endorsement and luxury brand purchase intentions through signaling theory: A serial-mediation model involving psychological ownership, brand trust and brand attitude. *Pakistan Journal of Commerce and Social Science*, *15*(3), 586–613.

Khare, A. (2014). How cosmopolitan are Indian consumers? A study on fashion clothing involvement. *Journal of Fashion Marketing and Management*, *18*(4), 431–451. https://doi.org/10.1108/JFMM-05-2013-0066

Khare, A., & Handa, M. (2011). Need for uniqueness as antecedent to purchase behaviour amongst Indian youth. *International Journal of Business and Globalization*, *6*(1), 15–29. https://doi.org/10.1504/IJBG.2011.037317

Kiessling, G., Balekjian, C., & Oehmichen, A. (2009). What credit crunch? More luxury for new money: European rising stars & established markets. *Journal of Retail and Leisure Property*, *8*(1), 3–23. https://doi.org/10.1057/rlp.2008.26

Kumar, A., Paul, J., & Unnithan, A. B. (2020). Masstige' marketing: A review, synthesis and research agenda. *Journal of Business Research*, *113*, 384–398. https://doi.org/10.1016/j.jbusres.2019.09.030

Kumaran, S. P., & Seal, P. P. (2017). Trends and opportunities: Room linen in hotels. *Colourage*, *64*(3), 48–49.

Laldinliana. (2012). Consumer behavior towards two wheelers and four wheelers: A study on rural and urban Mizoram. *Indian Journal of Marketing*, *42*(10), 53–59.

Lloyd, J., & Cheah, I. (2015). Factors affecting consumer attitude and purchase intention of luxury brands. In *2015 global fashion management conference at florence* (pp. 728–733).

Mamat, M. N., Noor, N. M., & Noor, N. M. (2016). Purchase intentions of foreign luxury brand handbags among consumers in Kuala Lumpur, Malaysia. *Procedia Economics and Finance*, *35*, 206–215.

Mathew, J., John, J. P., & Nair, S. (2020). Sense of humor and work culture: A study based in the luxury hotels in Bangalore, India. *Journal of Tourism and Development*, *2020*(34), 99–111. https://doi.org/10.34624/rtd.v0i34.22351

Menezes, K. A., Bhaskaran, S., & Durdyeva, G. (2021). Global high-value luxury brands manufactured domestically: Customer beliefs and attitudes in low-income emerging economies. *International Journal of Business and Globalization*, *28*(3), 262–278. https://doi.org/10.1504/ijbg.2021.115564

Menon, P. B. (2021). Influence of social media marketing efforts on brand equity and consumer response to branded shoes in India. *Indian Journal of Marketing*, *51*(9).

Mishra, S., Jain, S., & Jham, V. (2021). Luxury rental purchase intention among millennials – A cross-national study. *Thunderbird International Business Review*, *63*(4), 503–516. https://doi.org/10.1002/tie.22174

Mohsin, A., Lengler, J., & Aguzzoli, R. (2015). Staff turnover in hotels: Exploring the quadratic and linear relationships. *Tourism Management*, *51*, 35–48. https://doi.org/10.1016/j.tourman.2015.04.005

Mohsin, A., Lengler, J., & Kumar, B. (2013). Exploring the antecedents of intentions to leave the job: The case of luxury hotel staff. *International Journal of Hospitality Management*, *35*, 48–58. https://doi.org/10.1016/j.ijhm.2013.05.002

Mohsin, A., & Lockyer, T. (2010). Customer perceptions of service quality in luxury hotels in New Delhi, India: An exploratory study. *International Journal of Contemporary Hospitality Management*, *22*(2), 160–173. https://doi.org/10.1108/09596111011018160

Nagar, K. (2016). Mediating effect of self-control between life satisfaction and counterfeit consumption among female consumers. *Journal of Global Fashion Marketing*, *7*(4), 278–290. https://doi.org/10.1080/20932685.2016.1208111

Nazir, O., & Islam, J. U. (2020a). Effect of CSR activities on meaningfulness, compassion, and employee engagement: A sense-making theoretical approach. *International Journal of Hospitality Management*, *90*. https://doi.org/10.1016/j.ijhm.2020.102630

Nazir, O., & Islam, J. U. (2020b). Influence of CSR-specific activities on work engagement and employees' innovative work behavior: An empirical investigation. *Current Issues in Tourism*, *23*(24), 3054–3072. https://doi.org/10.1080/13683500.2019.1678573

Nazir, O., Islam, J. U., & Rahman, Z. (2021). Effect of CSR participation on employee sense of purpose and experienced meaningfulness: A self-determination theory perspective. *Journal of Hospitality and Tourism Management*, *46*, 123–133.

Neerattiparambil, N. N., & Belli, S. M. (2020). Why rent a dress?: A study on renting intention for fashion clothing products. *Indian Journal of Marketing*, *50*(2), 20–34. https://doi.org/10.17010/ijom/2020/v50/i2/150439

Özbölük, T. (2021). The pursuit of uniqueness and craving for freedom: The meaning of luxury in the age of access. *Leisure Studies*, *40*(2), 227–242.

Pasricha, D., & Jain, K. (2019). Antecedents affecting purchase of luxury ayurvedic skin care products. *Indian Journal of Marketing*, *49*(9), 7–22.

Pillai, K. G., & Nair, S. R. (2021). The effect of social comparison orientation on luxury purchase intentions. *Journal of Business Research*, *134*, 89–100. https://doi.org/10.1016/j.jbusres.2021.05.033

Pino, G., Amatulli, C., Peluso, A. M., Nataraajan, R., & Guido, G. (2019). Brand prominence and social status in luxury consumption: A comparison of emerging and mature markets. *Journal of Retailing and Consumer Services*, *46*, 163–172. https://doi.org/10.1016/j.jretconser.2017.11.006

Purohit, S., & Radia, K. N. (2022). Conceptualizing masstige buying behavior: A mixed- method approach. *Journal of Business Research*, *142*, 886–898. https://doi.org/10.1016/j.jbusres.2022.01.023

Rehman, A. U., Al Shammari, S., & Al-Mamary, Y. H. (2021). Role of religiosity and the mediating effect of luxury value perception in luxury purchase intention: A cross-cultural examination. *Journal of Islamic Marketing*. https://doi.org/10.1108/JIMA-03-2021-0091

Rodrigues, P., & Borges, A. P. (2021). New luxury vs. Old luxury: What is the definition of luxury brand? In *Building consumer-brand relationship in luxury brand management* (pp. 45–64). IGI Global.

Roig-Tierno, N., Gonzalez-Cruz, T. F., & Llopis-Martinez, J. (2017). An overview of qualitative comparative analysis: A bibliometric analysis. *Journal of Innovation & Knowledge*, *2*(1), 15–23.

Roy, P., Ramaprasad, B. S., Chakraborty, M., Prabhu, N., & Rao, S. (2020). Customer acceptance of use of artificial intelligence in hospitality services: An Indian hospitality sector perspective. *Global Business Review*. https://doi.org/10.1177/0972150920939753

Sanyal, S. N., Mazumder, R., Singh, R., & Sharma, Y. (2021). Uncertainty and affluent teenagers' luxury buying-decision: The role of avoidance-related indecisiveness. *Journal of Retailing and Consumer Services*, *58*. https://doi.org/10.1016/j.jretconser.2020.102305

Sarmah, B., Kamboj, S., & Rahman, Z. (2017). Co-creation in hotel service innovation using smart phone apps: An empirical study. *International Journal of Contemporary Hospitality Management*, *29*(10), 2647–2667. https://doi.org/10.1108/IJCHM-12-2015-0681

Schultz, D., & Jain, V. (2015). Exploring luxury brand country of origin impact on purchasing behaviors in India: A conceptual framework. *Asia-Pacific Journal of Business Administration*, *7*(3), 216–236. https://doi.org/10.1108/APJBA-11-2014-0129

Schultz, D. E., & Jain, V. (2018). Discovering India's three levels of luxury consumption: Exploratory research to find a conceptual framework. *Journal of Marketing Communications*, *24*(3), 250–269. https://doi.org/10.1080/13527266.2014.999250

Senthil Kumaran, P., & Seal, P. P. (2020). *Trends and opportunities: Room linen in hotels*. Manipal Academy of Higher Education.

Shahid, S., Islam, J. U., Farooqi, R., & Thomas, G. (2021). Affordable luxury consumption: An emerging market's perspective. *International Journal of Emerging Markets*. https://doi.org/10.1108/IJOEM-01-2021-0144

Shankar, A., & Jain, S. (2021). Factors affecting luxury consumers' webrooming intention: A moderated-mediation approach. *Journal of Retailing and Consumer Services*, *58*. https://doi.org/10.1016/j.jretconser.2020.102306

Shankari, L., & Suja, S. (2008). Benchmarking on HR Scorecard in the hospitality industry. *Management and Labour Studies*, *33*(1), 80–102.

Sharda, N., & Bhat, A. K. (2018). Austerity to materialism and brand consciousness: Luxury consumption in India. *Journal of Fashion Marketing and Management*, *22*(2), 223–239. https://doi.org/10.1108/JFMM-03-2017-0025

Sharda, N., & Bhat, A. (2019). Role of consumer vanity and the mediating effect of brand consciousness in luxury consumption. *The Journal of Product and Brand Management*, *28*(7), 800–811. https://doi.org/10.1108/JPBM-09-2017-1564

Sharma, S., & Mishra, P. (2019). Hotel employees' perceptions about CSR initiatives and their potential to support the skill India initiative. *Worldwide Hospitality and Tourism Themes*, *11*(1), 78–86. https://doi.org/10.1108/WHATT-10-2018-0064

Shetty, A. S., Anand, K., & A. N, R. (2021). Parle products: The journey of budget brand toward premiumization. *Business Perspectives and Research*, *9*(1), 159–181. https://doi.org/10.1177/2278533720923519

Shukla, P. (2012). The influence of value perceptions on luxury purchase intentions in developed and emerging markets. *International Marketing Review*, *29*(6), 574–596.

Shukla, P., & Purani, K. (2012). Comparing the importance of luxury value perceptions in cross-national contexts. *Journal of Business Research*, *65*(10), 1417–1424.

Shukla, P., & Rosendo-Rios, V. (2021). Intra and inter-country comparative effects of symbolic motivations on luxury purchase intentions in emerging markets. *International Business Review*, *30*(1). https://doi.org/10.1016/j.ibusrev.2020.101768

Singh, J. (2017). *In India skill development is not a luxury, it became necessity*.

Singh, A. (2019). The English language factor as a litmus test for placement with luxury hotel brands in India. *Worldwide Hospitality and Tourism Themes*, *11*(1), 68–77. https://doi.org/10.1108/WHATT-10-2018-0060

Singh, J., Shukla, P., & Schlegelmilch, B. B. (2021). Desire, need, and obligation: Examining commitment to luxury brands in emerging markets. *International Business Review*. https://doi.org/10.1016/j.ibusrev.2021.101947

Sondhi, N., & Basu, R. (2021). Scaling up Sirohi: Can women empowerment and sustainability drive a luxury brand? *Emerald Emerging Markets Case Studies*, *11*(4), 1–42. https://doi.org/10.1108/EEMCS-05-2021-0160

Srivastava, R. K., Bhanot, S., & Srinivasan, R. (2016). Segmenting markets along multiple dimensions of luxury value: The case of India. *Journal of Promotion Management*, *22*(1), 175–193. https://doi.org/10.1080/10496491.2015.1088925

Swaminathan, T. N., & Viswanathan, P. K. (2015). Social marketing – Awareness and satisfaction levels of government aided health insurance project in rural Tamil Nadu. *Indian Journal of Marketing*, *45*(6), 7–20. https://doi.org/10.17010/ijom/2015/v45/i6/79930

Swaminathan, T. N., & Viswanathan, P. K. (2016). Social marketing – Predicting the impact of government aided health insurance project in rural Tamil Nadu. *Indian Journal of Marketing*, *46*(9), 11–23.

Thakur, A., & Kaur, R. (2015). Relationship between self-concept and attitudinal brand loyalty in luxury fashion purchase: A study of selected global brands on the Indian market. *Management (Croatia)*, *20*(2).

Thakur, A., & Kaur, R. (2016). An empirical examination of relationship between emotional attachment and attitudinal brand loyalty towards luxury fashion brands. *DLSU Business and Economics Review*, *26*(1), 70–80.

Thakur, A., Kaur, R., Kohli, S., & Lamba, B. (2015). Attitudinal loyalty &emotional aspects (brand love, self-concept &emotional attachment) in luxury fashion purchase: An empirical study of global brands. *International Journal of Applied Business and Economic Research*, *13*(5), 3159–3182.

Turunen, L. L. M., & Turunen, L. L. M. (2018). Luxury consumption and consumption of luxury goods. In *Interpretations of luxury: Exploring the consumer perspective* (pp. 61–81).

Willis, M. (2006). To adapt or to standardise: Testing Asian views about purchasing Western luxury products in seven Asian locations. *Journal of East-West Business*, *12*(1), 65–94.

Yu, S., & Hudders, L. (2021). Measurement invariance of the modified brand luxury index scale across gender, age and countries. *Journal of Fashion Marketing and Management*. https://doi.org/10.1108/JFMM-10-2020-0235

Printed and bound by CPI Group (UK) Ltd, Croydon, CR0 4YY

29/12/2025

14799345-0001